Writers of Italy Series

General Editor
C. P. Brand
University of
Edinburgh

9

PETRARCH

for Harden Rodgers

© Kenelm Foster 1984
Edinburgh University Press
22 George Square, Edinburgh

Set in Monotype Bembo
by Speedspools, Edinburgh
and printed in Great Britain by
Clark Constable Ltd
Edinburgh

British Library
Cataloguing in Publication Data
Foster, Kenelm
Petrarch.—(Writers of Italy; no. 9)
1. Petrarch, Francesco—
Criticism and interpretation
1. Title   II. Series
851'.1   PQ4505

ISBN 0 85224 485 1

Edinburgh University Press

PETRARCH

Poet and Humanist

KENELM FOSTER

*

Contents

Preface

The subtitle of this book – 'Poet and Humanist' – points to the two-fold source of Petrarch's fame, and at the same time to his bilingualism. For if Petrarch's enduring fame as a poet rests on his lyric verse in Italian, he owes his high place in the history of humanism to the powerful influence, in his own time and through the following century, of his Latin writings in defence and illustration of the classical tradition.[1] Hence in chapter 2 I study Petrarch the poet mainly in and through the *Canzoniere* of Italian lyrics; and Petrarch the humanist in and through the Latin works discussed in chapter 3; where, if the epic *Africa* gets an entire section to itself, this is only inasmuch as it expresses aspects of the poet's thinking about human nature. In a sense, however, the linguistic difference between the texts considered in chapters 2 and 3 is unimportant, and what matters is that in the one they are actual poems but in the other only indications of a line of thought, a theme.

This difference means that the textual material is regarded successively from two quite distinct points of view, literary-critical in chapter 2, broadly biographical in chapter 3; the focus in the former being on a particular sequence of achieved 'artefacts', but in the latter on the mind behind them. It is of course the same mind, but in chapter 3 it is viewed at one remove from the art-objects, the poems that had been the primary consideration in chapter 2. In chapter 3, then, I do not study Petrarch with the concrete particularity appropriate to chapter 2, where (after section 1) attention is given to this or that idea or emotion only as transmuted precisely into this or that poem – where, in short, the focus is on his mind only as productive of certain artistic effects. By contrast, in chapter 3 the only particularisations allowed are those imposed by distinguishing, within the same theme of Petrarch's 'humanism', the various aspects of it studied successively in sections 1–4. In this sense the biographical perspective will be found to widen as we pass from the poet-artist to the humanist – though the fact may be masked to some extent by the necessary, but always here subordinate, consideration of the biographical factors in the *Canzoniere*.

Let me dwell for a moment on this change of perspective. Faced by an actual poem, the critic cannot, of course, afford to ignore history and biography, especially in the case of a poet remote in time; if he does, he is likely to miss seeing what the poem is about. And certainly the question 'what is it about?' is the first that the reader of a poem has to put; but only as preliminary to the more searching, because more properly critical question 'how is it made?'[2] – how does the maker bring about these particular effects? Or again – granted we allow the term beauty into the discussion – what makes this arrangement of words beautiful (or not, as the case may be)? The analysis, that is, has to proceed from effects to causes *within the poem itself*. From this literary-critical point of view questions of biography, once that preliminary question has been sufficiently answered, become for the time being irrelevant. It is true that there is a further stage, once the properly critical task is done, when the critic can allow himself the pleasure of contemplating whatever facet of the poet's personality may have emerged from the foregoing analysis. These stages of the critical process will, it is hoped, be found sufficiently clearly presented (albeit with some overlapping) in the five sections of chapter 2.

To return to the humanist theme. Petrarch's Latin writings are still of great interest in a number of ways, but in none more conspicuously than in the marvellous witness they severally bear to the tensions set up in the mind of the greatest scholar of the late middle ages between a passionate attachment to classical antiquity and a sincere Christian faith. To speak of Petrarch's 'humanism' is, for me, to speak of that tension, and vice versa; and so far I think I need anticipate no disagreement. Where I cannot expect all readers to agree is in the view I take of the abiding positive value – all things considered, and even in the so drastically altered mental climate of today – of the sort of 'Christian humanism' in which Petrarch's mind and heart came eventually to find peace – as much peace, at any rate, as his master Augustine would have said one could reasonably hope for on this side of death (cf. *Confessions* I, I).

The maturest expression of this Petrarchan Christian humanism is the *De Ignorantia*, but the topic itself recurs in all four sections of chapter 3; and with it, never far from the surface, the memory and example of St Augustine. For Petrarch, Augustine was incomparably the greatest of Christian teachers (at any rate since the Apostle Paul) and, what is more to the point, the one nearest his heart. In the story of Augustine's spiritual wanderings in youth, as recorded in the *Confessions*, Petrarch, so he tells us, could almost recognise his own.[3]

Moreover, of all the Christian Fathers, he saw him as the most indebted to the pagan world – severe critic though he had been of it – both intellectually (in relation to Plato) and as a writer (in relation to Cicero). This rapport with Augustine came to completest expression in the *Secretum*, and this is one reason why I have reserved my discussion of that masterly dialogue to the final section of chapter 3.

My other reason for so doing is biographical. Petrarch's humanism, however we define the term, was an idea or set of ideas about Man, expressed in works spread over many years. Inevitably it changed, at least in its mode of expression, with changing occasions and circumstances, or according to the point of view adopted or represented. That represented, for example, through the pagan characters of the *Africa* (1338 – 9 and through the 1340s) is appropriately 'pagan', and Petrarch was careful to exclude, as far as possible, from the narrative itself any Christian overtones; whereas in the *De Ignorantia*, twenty years later, he speaks overtly and passionately as a Christian. There is in fact a good deal of evidence to show that in the intervening period he had been growing into his Christian faith, that by the time he wrote the *De Ignorantia* he had achieved a kind of harmony between these two sides of his mind and nature, the classical-humanist and the Christian. This, at any rate, is the general thesis of my third chapter, becoming most explicit in sections 2 and 3. And with this drawing together of his classical culture and his religious faith I associate the change that I think came over the whole manner and direction of his writing between, roughly, 1346 and the early 1350s. On this change I lay a good deal of emphasis, especially in section 3.

As for the *Secretum*, it plainly had to have a section to itself in chapter 3, being by common consent Petrarch's masterpiece in Latin prose. But which section? My decision to allot to it the concluding section was taken, partly because of the unique importance of St Augustine in Petrarch's intellectual development, and partly because I had become convinced that Francisco Rico was right to shift the date of the *Secretum* from 1342–3 (the commonly accepted dating) to 1347–53. This placed the dialogue firmly within that period in Petrarch's career as a writer, which on other grounds already seemed to me the crucial one. So in my examination of the *Secretum* I have included a statement, as clear and as brief as possible, of the case for that redating. This done, and the *Secretum* section written, the best place for it seemed to be at the end of the chapter, where it would serve to clinch the connection between the thematic and the biographical components: Petrarch's humanism and the actual course of his writing, particularly in the crucial middle years between the mid 1340s and 1350s.

Before taking leave of this book I feel I should offer a belated apology to two very distinguished Petrarchists, Ugo Dotti and A. S. Bernardo, whose work on the poet-humanist – notably Dotti's Introductions to the Letters and to the 'Sine Nomine' collection in particular, and Bernardo's important study, *P., Scipio and the 'Africa': The Birth of Humanism's Dream* – receives, I fear, quite inadequate explicit attention in my pages. A like apology is owed to Marco Santagata for my having totally neglected, while preparing this book, his vigorous pioneering study of the 'pre-history' of the *Canzoniere* form: *Dal Sonetto al Canzoniere: Ricerche sulla preistoria di un genere*. I am the more to blame in this case that until two or three months ago I had not even read Santagata's book, though it was published in 1979; and in its modest way is a landmark in Petrarchan studies.

My warm thanks to the people who have helped me in various ways – with enlightenment or unfailing encouragement, or with both – during the unconscionable time this book has been on the stocks; in particular to Patrick Boyde, Piero Boitani, Uberto Limentani, Roeco Montano, Francisco Rico; to Peter Brand, most patient and considerate and constructively critical of editors; to Jennifer Petrie and Harden Rodgers; finally, to my kind comrades at Blackfriars, Cambridge. For all faults and inadequacies in the work I alone am to blame.

KENELM FOSTER

1. The Life

Childhood and Adolescence, 1304–26

Petrarch always considered himself a Florentine and spoke of his birth at Arezzo as 'in exile' (*Prose*, p.8). In fact his father Ser Petracco (Pietro) di Parenzo, a lawyer from Incisa in the Valdarno, had been banished from Florence nine months after Dante, in October 1302. Both men were of the White Guelf party and had shared in its defeat by the Black faction at the end of 1301. Petracco and his wife, Eletta Canigiani, found a temporary refuge in the still independent city of Arezzo where on 20 July 1304 their first child, our poet, was born. He was christened Francesco. One other child survived infancy, a boy, Gherardo, born in 1307, whose life was to be closely linked with his elder brother's. The family seems to have been happy and united. Petrarch's mother died when he was about fifteen, and he wrote a Latin elegy, his first surviving poem, to celebrate her goodness and piety.

But by this time Petracco had moved to Provence with his family, drawn by the hope of lucrative employment at Avignon, since 1309 the seat of the papacy. They went there in 1312, via Genoa and Marseilles, after a stay at Pisa where Petrarch probably had the sight of Dante which he was to recall, half a century later, in a letter to Boccaccio (*Prose*, p.1004). Once settled in Avignon, Petracco put his sons to school in nearby Carpentras where Francesco had the luck to be taught by a Tuscan grammarian who recognised his promise. The boy took to Latin as a duck to water, loving the sound of the words before he understood their meaning.[1] Meanwhile no doubt he was picking up Provençal, but that was of infinitely less significance than the fact that, with a Tuscan master and a lively Italian colony in Avignon, he was in no danger of forgetting his native tongue.

After four years at Carpentras his father sent him to study law at Montpellier, and thence, in 1320, to Bologna where he followed courses on civil law for three full academic years. A successful legal career lay open to him, but he abandoned all thought of it, he tells us in his 'Letter to Posterity' (1355–61, with later additions; *Prose*, pp.2–18), from a conviction that no honest man could make a success of it. This explanation is suspect, if only because the *Posteritati* letter is plainly an idealised self-portrait. A glimpse of the real reason for Petrarch's decision is given in another allusion to his days at Bologna where he says that he was occupied 'in literarum studiis'. Naturally he did learn some law (as well as some rudimentary Aristotelianism) in that great centre of legal studies, but we can hardly doubt that he was already deep in the more congenial study of the Latin poets and moralists, especially Virgil and Cicero; and that he was already trying his hand at Italian verse, of which there was a lively tradition at Bologna going back through Dante's friend Cino da Pistoia to Guido Guinizzelli.

Young Manhood, 1326–37: Avignon, Laura, Rome

Petrarch definitely left Bologna and returned to Avignon early in 1326, recalled, it seems, by the death of his father. But he had already spent much of 1325 in the papal city, and the fact is worth noting in connection with the first recorded acquisition of books by this life-long bibliophile. At Avignon in February 1325 he acquired through his father an expensive copy of St Augustine's *City of God*; and at about the same time Petracco brought him, from Paris, a copy of Isidore's *Etymologies*, and a little later paid for the famous 'Ambrosian' Virgil, a miscellany of classical texts put together on the spot for Francesco, who, before the end of the year, had acquired yet another, and major, Christian text, the epistles of St Paul. These and other relevant data have been brought to light in recent years, chiefly by G. Billanovich, and they compel us to qualify considerably two hitherto generally accepted notions: that Petracco was stiffly opposed to his son's interest in literature and, more important, that the young Petrarch had little interest in other than pagan authors. The former point need not detain us. It is true that Petracco wanted his son to be a lawyer, but he was not unbending and he had himself a share of the taste for good Latin which was by no means uncommon among lawyers, especially in Italy (*Seniles* XVI, 1). The other matter is more complicated, it raises in fact the chief problem that a biographer of Petrarch must face, that of deciding how far to trust the poet's own accounts of, or allusions to, his mental and spiritual development. Petrarch cultivated self-disclosure to an extraordinary degree, more indeed than any previous human being of whom we have record. On the other hand it has become increasingly clear that in much of this self-portrayal there was a good deal of more or less deliberate impersonation – of the constructing of a public image of himself modelled on certain cherished examples drawn from his reading; notably on that of the Augustine self-depicted in the *Confessions*. And this mimetic tendency affects, of course, the reliability of the various accounts of phases or incidents in his life which Petrarch has left us. I shall return to this point later but it may be said at once that if until fairly recently it was the accepted view that only around his fortieth year did Petrarch begin to take any serious interest in the Bible and the Church Fathers, this was partly due to an uncritical acceptance of his own statements on the matter. For example, in the *Posteritati* letter he remarks that in the course of time he had come to delight in those 'sacred writings' which in youth he had despised (*Prose*, p.6). Now this is almost certainly an echo of *Confessions* III, v, where Augustine recalls how as a young man he had been repelled by the style of the Bible after a first contact with the urbanity and polish of Cicero. And undoubtedly the young Petrarch made the same comparison to the same effect. But it is improbable that he ever despised Augustine: his copy of the *City of God*, acquired when he was twenty-two, shows evidence of early and close study; as does his copy of *De vera religione*, acquired and closely annotated between 1333 and 1335; between which dates he also drew up a list of 'my favourite books' including four works by Augustine; to which he soon added, at Rome in 1337, the enormous *Enarrationes in Psalmos*. It is best then to take 'sacrae litterae' in the *Posteritati* as referring chiefly to the Bible. There is no doubt, however, that Christianity did take a stronger hold on his mind with the passage of time. The great intellectual passion of his youth was for classical antiquity and all his writing down to the early 1340s (apart from the vernacular lyrics) sprang from that enthusiasm. This is the element of truth in the older view of Petrarch's development, the view that is only now being corrected by scholars working directly on the manuscripts of the Christian texts acquired by him between 1325 and 1337.

For a time after his return to Avignon Petrarch did not need to work for a living, and having good health, good looks and a friendly disposition, he slipped into more or less elegant dissipation. But elegance could, and for him did, include the art of writing Italian verse; and more privately he was deepening his knowledge of ancient Rome. Between 1326 and 1329 he critically revised all the then known portions of the text of Livy, a remarkable achievement in itself and the indispensable preparation for much of his subsequent writing in Latin prose and verse (notably the *De viris illustribus* and the *Africa*). In

this connection the importance of Avignon for Petrarch's development must be stressed. His work on Livy could hardly have been done
so well or so rapidly anywhere else. As the new headquarters of the
Church, fourteenth-century Avignon became the meeting-place of
educated men from every corner of Europe; having the added
advantage, for Petrarch, of being roughly equidistant from the
libraries of Paris and Chartres, on the one hand, and those of north
east Italy on the other. Petrarch could not have made his edition of
Livy without two manuscripts, respectively from Chartres and
Verona, to which he had access precisely through his contacts in the
papal city.

   Around 1330, deciding that he must after all do something for a
living, Petrarch took minor orders in the Church (thus renouncing
matrimony) and entered the household of Cardinal Giovanni
Colonna. He was already friendly with another member of that
powerful Roman family, Giacomo, bishop of Lombez, with whom
and some younger friends he passed the summer of 1330 in sight of the
Pyrenees (*Canz.* 10). This connection with Cardinal Colonna and the
Avignon Curia lasted about seventeen years. It brought Petrarch,
with annoyances, many solid advantages; it gave him a livelihood
while leaving him time for study; it brought him opportunities for
travel and some experience of public affairs at a European level.

   Meanwhile, however, the crucial event in his life as artist and poet
had occurred, the encounter with Laura; first seen, and immediately
loved, in the church of St Clare at Avignon on 6 April 1327; he being
nearly twenty three, and she certainly younger. He was to recall that
date, which he identified with Good Friday, in many poems. The
identity of Laura has of course been disputed, but there is no good
reason to doubt her historical existence. From Petrarch's descriptions
and allusions it is clear that she was of the upper class, that she married
and had children, that their love remained 'platonic', that she died of
the plague in 1348. For the rest she lives only as an image in the glitter-
ing mirror of his verse.

   It was in part perhaps to distract his thoughts from Laura that in
1333 Petrarch journeyed into northern Europe, visiting Paris, Ghent,
Liège and Cologne. He must have been curious to see Paris and its
famous university, though the scholastic culture which the latter
pre-eminently represented was already alien to him and would later
become still more so. At Liège he found two lost orations of Cicero,
one of which, the *Pro Archia*, was deeply to influence his own ideal of
humane culture and his conception of the role of the poet in society.

Meanwhile Pope John XXII had died (December 1334) and Petrarch, now back in Avignon, wrote two verse-letters to his successor Benedict XII urging him to bring the papacy back to Rome, the first shot in what was to prove a long campaign. Then early in 1337 he himself made the long-desired journey to Rome, the city of his dreams. He stayed with the Colonna clan and explored the ruins with Giovanni Colonna, a Dominican with scholarly tastes, whom Petrarch had met in Avignon and whose uncle, Landolfo, formerly a canon of Chartres, had helped him with his textual work on Livy.

The Middle Years, 1337–53: Avignon, Vaucluse, Italy

This first visit to Rome was a turning point in Petrarch's gradual development as a writer. To appreciate this, one has only to compare the slenderness of his output before 1337 with the huge body of writing he produced during the next fifteen years. Much later he was to tell Boccaccio that in youth he had aspired, no doubt with Dante in mind, to win fame as a poet in the vernacular (see below, pp.27–32). But he must have soon abandoned this idea; all that remains in Italian from his youth and early manhood are a few score lyrics (most of them eventually included in the *Canzoniere*). He wrote, too, a comedy in Latin, now lost, and a few Latin letters in prose and verse, later carefully revised. That is all. Yet within a year or so after his return from Rome in July 1337 he had set his hand to two major productions, the prose *De viris illustribus* and the epic poem *Africa*. These works will be looked at later. What must be stressed here is the novelty of the effort and aspiration they represented. In a real sense they are Petrarch's *début*, however long delayed. In writing them he drew for the first time on all his learning and artistry to depict, on a large scale, the ancient (Roman) world he so much admired; to turn at last his hard-won 'notitia vetustatis' (knowledge of antiquity) into an imaginative apprehension, both historical and poetic, of pre-Christian western man; to be a new Virgil and a new Livy. It hardly matters that neither work is a masterpiece or that neither was ever finished. Such as they were by, say, the end of 1343, they constituted an implicit point of reference for all Petrarch's subsequent writing (in Latin at least) abundant and varied as this was.

Some time in 1337 his first child was born, a son named Giovanni. Nothing is known of the mother. His other child was a girl, Francesca, born in 1343, again of an unknown woman. Petrarch was a good father to both children, and Francesca and her husband looked after him in his old age.

During the next sixteen years, 1337 to 1351, his life was divided between Avignon, travel in Italy, and a small property he bought at Vaucluse, in the country near the source of the Sorgue. Vaucluse was his refuge from the crowds and noise of Avignon and, as time went by, from the atmosphere of the Curia, which during the 1340s became increasingly irksome to him. At Vaucluse he did most of his writing, when in Provence: his poetry in particular, the Italian lyrics and the Latin hexameters that he wrote with such facility, constantly reflects the sights and sounds of his beloved valley. He went for long walks and was a keen angler and gardener. It was here that on the same day (he tells us) he received invitations from the University of Paris and from the Roman Senate to accept the honour of the laurel crown for poetry. Naturally he preferred the Roman offer, and was duly crowned on the Campidoglio on 8 April 1341, after a visit to Naples to be 'examined' on the poetic art by the learned king Robert whom Petrarch, unlike Dante, greatly esteemed.[2] By this time Boccaccio, who had spent his youth in Naples, was probably back in Florence; but he was already Petrarch's admirer, having heard of him from an Augustinian friar, Dionigi da Borgo San Sepolcro, whom Petrarch had known since the early 1330s; and who had had the happy idea of giving his young friend a book which was to have a great and lasting influence on him, the *Confessions* of St Augustine (*Prose*, p.1133).

Most of the rest of 1341 Petrarch spent near Parma, working on the *Africa*; but he was back in Avignon by the following spring in time for the election, in May 1342, of Clement VI, following the death of Benedict XII.

It should be remembered that Petrarch, while not a priest, was a cleric and drew most of his income from the Church. Thus in 1342 he was given a canonry at Pisa by Clement VI, and later he became archdeacon of Parma and then a canon of Padua – all paid posts and all virtually sinecures. Although, as we shall see, Petrarch was to become a bitter critic of the papal Curia he saw no harm in certain laxities in the Church of his time. He drew the line indeed at accepting a bishopric when one was offered him, nor would he take any benefice that involved the cure of souls; 'I have enough to do', he said, 'looking after my own'. He wanted to be as free as possible, while not avoiding the public business that came his way through his personal prestige and his connections with the European upper class.

In the summer or autumn of 1342 he began to learn Greek, but gave up when his teacher left Avignon (though later he acquired some Greek manuscripts). Early in 1343 King Robert of Naples died, to whom Petrarch had dedicated the *Africa*, the work which he was still hoping would prove his *magnum opus*. But a more important event of this year was his brother Gherardo's decision to become a Carthusian monk, a choice which affected Petrarch deeply, for he was very fond of Gherardo; and it has been the usual view that he himself underwent a religious crisis at this time and that he expressed this, during the winter of 1342–3, in his prose masterpiece the *Secretum*. Personally, however, I am inclined to follow F. Rico in dating this work ten years later, with provisional draftings in 1347 and 1349 (see ch. III). If Rico's dating is accepted there remains no evidence of any grave spiritual crisis undergone by Petrarch in 1342–3.

In the late summer of 1343 he was asked by the Pope to go to Naples on a diplomatic mission connected with the confused situation that had arisen there following the death of King Robert. But Petrarch found the task too much for him and, leaving Naples in December, moved north to Parma where he could be sure of a welcome from its ruler, Azzo da Correggio. However, an invasion by forces from Mantua and Milan drove him to Verona in 1345, and it was there, in the cathedral library, that he found a large part of Cicero's correspondence, a discovery that was to have a decisive effect on his own writing. Petrarch was a born letter-writer – if at times a tediously prolix one – and epistolography exactly suited his taste and talent for mixing moral reflection and biographical anecdote. Moreover he was a man who assiduously cultivated friendship and had friends in many places. But it was the discovery at Verona that led to his composing letters for publication – the hundreds contained in the twenty-four books of the *Familiares* and (as from 1361) the seventeen of the *Seniles*. So it was that the now celebrated humanist found a way of indulging his insatiable but engaging egotism while at the same time leaving us a clear picture of the public he most desired to reach and influence – men who shared, or aspired to share, his literary tastes and ideals, or whose views on politics or religion he thought it might be useful, from time to time, to influence. I shall return to this matter in chapter III, section 3.

Meanwhile the mid-1340s saw Petrarch approaching the height of his powers as a lyric poet in the vernacular. The great patriotic lyric *Italia mia* (*Canz.* 128) was touched off by his experiences at Parma in the winter of 1344–5, and roughly to the same period almost certainly belongs the strikingly original *Di pensier in pensier, di monte in monte* (129). With these two canzoni – and with 126 and 264,

respectively a little earlier and somewhat later – Petrarch rose to the
place hitherto occupied by Dante, of supreme master of what Dante
regarded as the noblest of Italian metres.[3]

From Verona Petrarch returned, unwillingly, to Provence in the
autumn of 1345, following the Adige up to its source and then
turning west. With Parma so disturbed, he had for the time being no
alternative home in Italy; besides, though he felt himself, as he now
said, an 'exile from Italy', and though Avignon was a 'hell on earth',
he still loved the studious quiet of Vaucluse; where indeed he managed
to stay for most of the next two years. But he was now severing his
connection with Avignon and the Curia, though he did not break
with his employer Cardinal Colonna – whom he liked and respected –
until the summer of 1347, by which time he was hoping to get back
to Parma, now temporarily repacified. In the Eclogue 'Divortium'
he took his leave of the Cardinal's service, adducing two main
reasons: his desire to be, at last, his own master, and the call of Italy.
The latter was enough to remove him, in the end, even from
Vaucluse, but he stayed there through most of 1346–7, writing
successively on two chief themes, the one related only indirectly, the
other directly and emphatically, to his growing hostility to Avignon
and the Curia.

The first of these themes or topics was the desirability of a life
detached, as far as possible, from the bustle and distractions of the
world. It is the subject of the two important prose works of this
period, *De vita solitaria* (1346) and the shorter and more conventional
De otio religioso (1347).[4] The latter, a eulogy of monasticism written
after a visit to Gherardo in his abbey at Montrieux, is as insipid as most
such eulogies written by laymen. It is remarkably well-documented –
showing how much biblical and patristic learning Petrarch had
already acquired. But if I call the *De otio* important, that is only
because of the quality it shares with the much more vital and personal
and as literature more accomplished *De vita solitaria* – that of showing
Petrarch entering a new phase in his development as a writer, a phase
involving a radical change in the way he presented himself to readers
present or future. I shall return to this matter in section 3 of chapter
III. Here it will be enough to take note of the essential fact in
the change: that whereas hitherto – in the *De viris illustribus*, the
Africa, the *Rerum memorandarum libri* – Petrarch had made himself
the recorder for his own time of the pagan, principally Roman,
world of the past, its men, events, ideas and emotions, turning
exclusively to that world and the literature of that world for examples

of virtue, wisdom and eloquence; now in *De vita solitaria*, for the first time in a work written for the public, he spoke out explicitly as a Christian, with frequent mention of the 'sacred and glorious name of Christ' (*Prose*, p.528). One can say that from now on his humanism was inseparably linked, as a fact of consciousness, with Christianity, although the integration of the two sets of ideas was usually left implicit. The forthright declarations of Christian faith throughout the *De Ignorantia* (1367) are not characteristic of Petrarch's later work as a whole. Nevertheless the integration was there. One sign of its presence is that pervasive influence of St Augustine which takes concrete, dramatic, quasi-symbolic form in the 'Augustinus' of the *Secretum*. And the fact that 'Augustinus' speaks throughout like a classical scholar imbued with platonised Stoicism is an effect of the same integration seen from the opposite point of view (see ch. III, section 4). To return for a moment to the *De vita solitaria*, the kind of life so warmly recommended by this indubitably Christian work is, in a sense, quite 'this-worldly' – not the life of an earth-spurning hermit, but 'quiet country life, fruitful in its leisure, with or without a companion or two'.[5] In short, another sign of the same effort at integration.

The other theme was occasioned by the brief career of Cola di Rienzo and his dream of a political resurgence of Rome. The rise and fall of Cola concern us, of course, only as they affected Petrarch; but no other events in the political history of his time had a comparable effect on him. When the news reached Avignon of Cola's *coup d'état* on 20 May 1347, Petrarch responded with the utmost enthusiasm. The Roman people under their brilliant new leader had risen against the local aristocracy and proclaimed Rome once more a free republic with Cola as 'tribune' (virtually dictator). Nor could Rome, of course, be a republic like any other; it had to be the ancient one now resurgent, liberated and resolved to reclaim its supreme position in the world ('caput orbis'); with the right to extend Roman citizenship to all Italians and – a far more serious matter in the eyes of the Curia – to grant or withhold the office and title of Emperor. All this was solemnly proclaimed, in the name of the Roman People, on the first of August 1347; and in terms of practical politics it was all a fantastic anachronism. For what could this sovereign 'populus romanus', dreamed of by Cola and Petrarch and some like-minded enthusiasts, what could it, in terms of real politics, effectively do? Had Cola's aim merely been to bring the local nobles to heel, well and good; the Church need have no general objection to that. But the popular government set up in their place could only, in the long run, govern with the consent of the Pope – within whose dominion Rome, after all, unquestionably still remained, at least *de iure* (and Cardinal Albornoz would before long make this true *de facto* as well). Again, what sort of authority could this 'Roman people' effectively exercise over the rest of Italy, divided as the country was into states long established in their own proud independence? Finally, was it likely that the Church would surrender to a few thousand 'popolani' its age-old claim to decide between rival candidates for the Empire?

It was no wonder that Cola threw up the sponge before the year was out, abdicating on 15 December when Petrarch had already left for Italy, apparently intending to join Cola at Rome. Warned, however, of Cola's impending capitulation, Petrarch wrote him a sternly reproachful letter from Genoa on 29 November; and then, changing his mind about the Roman journey, went to Parma instead. The reproaches in that letter (*Fam.* VII, 7, *Prose*, pp.890–4)[6] are somewhat obscure; but later Petrarch clarified them, and it is important that we understand them, not only for the light they throw on Petrarch's 'Idea of Rome', his political ideology, but also because they can help us to understand the subsequent course of his life.

The chief relevant texts, in chronological order, are: four letters to Cola (*Varie* 48; *S.N.* 2 and 3; and the above mentioned *Fam.* VII, 7); a letter to the still uncrowned Emperor Charles IV (*Fam.* X, 1, *Prose*, pp.909–14) written early in 1351; one to Francesco Nelli, of 10 August 1352 (*Fam.* XIII, 6, *Prose*, pp.954–62); one to 'the Roman People', October-November 1352 (*S.N.* 4); and a passage in the anti-Gallic pamphlet, *Invectiva contra eum qui maledixit Italie* (*Prose*, pp.768–802) written as late as 1373. Comparing these texts, the following points emerge quite clearly.

(a) Petrarch never regretted his enthusiastic support for Cola in 1347.[7] (b) What he blamed in Cola was not his *aims* but only his *inconstancy* in prosecuting them. Cola was a man 'more high-spirited than constant' (*Prose*, p.776). His ideal had been splendid, he had only lacked the courage to uphold it to the end, and thus had become 'a traitor to his country', 'proditor patriae' (*Prose*, p.894 – 'patria' here certainly includes all Italy). (c) That ideal, for a time upheld by Cola and maintained to the end – if only intermittently expressed – by Petrarch, may be summed up in three propositions: Rome is the proper seat and centre of the Empire; the Emperor draws his authority, under God, from the Roman People; the Emperor has a special responsibility – left undefined by Petrarch – for the unity and liberty of Italy.[8]

Was then Petrarch an Imperialist? To this question E. H. Wilkins, commenting on the Cola episode, provides an answer on the right lines. 'Of all men then living Cola and Petrarch were doubtless the two who most passionately and intelligently desired...the restoration of Rome to its pristine power and glory. Petrarch to be sure, had supposed hitherto that such...restoration could come only through an emperor; but now that a Roman citizen was actually undertaking the great task...Petrarch was quite ready to transfer his hope to Cola: that Rome restored should be republican rather than imperial was in itself a matter of little consequence.' The truth is that Petrarch's permanent loyalty was primarily to a loved and venerated city and country, not to an institution; to Rome 'mundi caput, urbium regina', 'the world's summit, the queen of cities', and then, by extension, to all Italy, 'domina provinciarum', 'mistress of the provinces [of the Empire]' (S.N. 2; cf. Dante, Purgatorio VI, 78). He began indeed, pace E. H. Wilkins, with a pro-republican bias, and so with an animus against Julius Caesar (see Africa II, 298 ss.) and something of this persisted to the time of the Cola episode, so that he could urge Cola to defend the liberty of Rome as Brutus, Caesar's assassin, had done (Varie 48). But less than four years later came the letter to Charles IV, cited above, a document as imperialistic, in its own way, as anything in Dante. What had happened? The explanation is two-fold, involving on the one hand Petrarch's scholarship, on the other his disappointment with Cola. G. Martellotti has traced the growth, after the 1340s, of Petrarch's esteem for Julius Caesar and a corresponding decline in his fervour for Scipio Africanus, the hero of his earlier 'republican' period.[9] This was in part a consequence of maturer scholarship; but Cola's failure was a factor too. Cola's championing of the Roman idea had been in no sense directly 'imperialist'; nor Petrarch's championing of him. It was in the void caused by Cola's collapse that Petrarch began to turn his hopes towards Charles IV. But this hard-headed Bohemian proved another disappointment. Charles came to Italy in 1354 to be crowned Emperor at Rome. This done (5 April 1355), he returned across the Alps. Henceforth his chief care was the prosperity of Bohemia and it was at Prague that Petrarch met him, for the second time, in 1356, when on an embassy to that city on behalf of the Visconti of Milan; an embassy which represents one of the two kinds of public activity henceforth open to Petrarch; occasional diplomatic tasks for the 'lords' of the cities –

Milan, Venice, Padua – where he spent most of his time after 1353;
and letters written to popes and potentates in order to further causes
dear to himself.

In this respect at least his situation resembled Dante's in exile: both
men had patrons and both served them. In his later years Petrarch
could hardly have afforded to indulge, even had he wished to, in the
anti-aristocratic sentiments discernible in his letters to and about
Cola.

But one strain in those letters persisted to the end: detestation of the
Avignon Curia. This feeling pervades Petrarch's writings to or about
Avignon from the *Sine Nomine* letters (1343–59) down to the
Invectiva of 1373 mentioned above. Common to all is a contrasting
of Avignon with Rome in terms of what the two cities had come to
stand for in Petrarch's mind: Avignon, modern barbarism and
impiety; Rome, the ancient culture as accepted and consecrated by
Catholicism. By the 1370s the quarrel had narrowed down to the
choice between Rome and Avignon as papal cities, with Petrarch, of
course, castigating the impudently 'Gallic' contention that the pope
might just as well remain north of the Alps. In the 1340s and 1350s
that issue was not yet a live one, and Petrarch's attacks bore chiefly
on the personnel of the Curia, both as individuals and collectively –
as in three celebrated sonnets, *Canz.* 136–8. And as these sonnets
inevitably recall Dante at his most 'anticlerical', they offer the occasion for a brief comparison of the two poets as critics of the Church.
Alike in the violence of their language, both men take for granted
(a) the divine origin of the Church, and (b) their perfect right to
denounce the vices and crimes of its rulers. On the other hand, in
Dante's tone and manner there is normally discernible, I think, a
certain independence of the clerical body which it would be un-
realistic to look for in Petrarch who had close ties of familiarity with,
and affection for, individual bishops, priests and friars. But the chief
differences are ideological. Dante possessed, as Petrarch did not, a
clearly worked out theory of Church authority in relation to civil
society; hence his criticism of the Church tends to focus on its
supreme organ of authority, the papacy. By contrast, Petrarch has
virtually nothing to say about the nature or exercise of the papal
office as such. The question of papal jurisdiction never arises for him.
And there is another difference: Petrarch's Catholicism was 'Roman'
in a sense that Dante's was not, in that, intertwined with it was so
intense a devotion to Latin culture, and to the city and region which
most embody this, that his Christian piety may seem at times hardly

separable from his Italian patriotism. This intermingling of motives
comes out most clearly perhaps in his pleas to both Pope and Emperor
to take up their residence in the sacred City (cf. *Prose*, pp.768–70,
780–4, 904–14). Incidentally, it might be argued that, as regards
the Emperor, Petrarch shows less sense of political realities than Dante,
at least in the *Paradiso* (cf. Canto xxx, 137–8).

Petrarch, as we have seen, was back in Italy early in 1348. But the
break with Avignon was not yet complete; and when, after another
three and a half years in Italy, he returned, in June 1351, for the last
time to Provence, he seems to have been hoping for some influential
job in the Curia, and perhaps even for a Cardinal's hat. In the event
he got nothing and found Avignon more repellent than ever. The
fact is that between 1349 and 1352–3 Petrarch was uncertain where
finally to settle down. That it was high time he settled somewhere
was brought home to him, first by the ravages of the Black Death, of
which Laura had died in April 1348, and then a growing estrangement
between him and the bishop of Parma, where he had had his headquarters in Italy since 1341. He stayed at Parma through most of
1348, but during the next two years he spent more and more time at
Padua where he was now a canon of the cathedral. In the autumn of
1350 he made a pilgrimage to Rome, stopping en route at Florence
where he met Boccaccio for the first time. Petrarch's Florentine
admirers had conceived the plan of keeping him at Florence as pro-
fessor in their recently founded university. It was a fond hope but it
led to Boccaccio's staying a week at Padua with the great humanist
in the spring of 1351. Then in May Petrarch began his journey back
to Avignon, picking up his son Giovanni at Parma.

   He had by now begun the series of poems reflecting on the death
of Laura, of which most are found in the second part of the
Canzoniere. Her death had sharpened his sense of the transience of
mortal beauty and, with this, of the problem of the soul's survival.
Here Petrarch's only guide was faith – a faith eked out, as it were, by
'visions' of the beloved in a state of bliss inaccessible to him, yet somehow intimately brought home to him (*Canz.* 277, 282, 302 etc.;
cf. *Eclogue* xi 'Galathea'). Laura's death, in fact, tapped a new vein in
his lyric gift, thus adding a new dimension to European poetry. At
the same time Petrarch as the man of wide experience and much
reading found a congenial vehicle in prose by initiating, in 1350, the
vast series of his letters 'Ad Familiares'. Finally, if Rico's redating of
the *Secretum* is accepted (see chapter iii, section 4), a draft of this work

was ready in 1349 for a final revision, completion and polishing at Vaucluse in 1352-3.

Petrarch arrived at Vaucluse on 27 June 1351 and left it, for the last time, in May/June 1353, having spent in the interval about twice as much time there as at Avignon. It was a period of very intense and varied intellectual activity. Much of this was of his own choosing, but much work also came his way indirectly through the Curia; or at least through letting himself get involved in political affairs of some interest also to the Curia. Thus he intervened strongly, though ineffectively, in a project sponsored by Clement VI for reforming the government at Rome (*Fam.* XI, 16-17, *S.N.* 7); and also in the affairs of Naples (*Fam.* XI, 13, XII, 2), and early in 1352 he addressed another plea to Charles IV, that he should concern himself more deeply with the well-being of Italy (*Fam.* XII, 1); and in November he sent an urgent appeal to the 'Roman People' to intervene on behalf of their ex-tribune Cola di Rienzo, now a prisoner at Avignon on suspicion of heresy. Cola, after his fall, had fled for protection to Charles IV at Prague, who, however, had handed him over to the Pope. This letter, *S.N.* 4, had no practical result but is interesting for two reasons: as a particularly strong assertion of the *de iure* independence and autonomy of the Roman People – an assertion implicitly subversive of the actual papal state; and as including a discussion of a passage in St Augustine (*Sermo* 105) denying the perpetuity of the Roman Empire. But here I must digress briefly on the subject of these *Sine Nomine* letters.

Before returning to Italy in May/June 1353 Petrarch had made a collection of thirteen letters fiercely critical of the Curia, to which he later added six more. These nineteen letters he separated from the *Familiares*, marking the difference by omitting the addressees' names – hence the title *Sine Nomine*, 'nameless' – to protect them from the odium of being associated with such vehemently anti-curial sentiments. Most of the letters attack the morals of the Curia, but nos. 2-4 and 9 are more political, their theme being the shameful subjection of Rome to 'barbarous' Avignon and, in general, the weakness and disunity which left Italy a prey to foreign, especially French, interference.

Anti-curial and anti-gallic, the *Sine Nomine* letters sufficiently explain Petrarch's eagerness in 1352-3 to put the Alps once and for all between Avignon and himself. But where, in Italy, should he now go? The question was only settled *en route*. Passing through Milan in June/July of 1353, and calling on the city's temporary ruler

Archbishop Giovanni Visconti, he was so cordially received by that potentate that he decided there and then to stay. He remained in Milan for the next eight years, in a house near S. Ambrogio where his revered Augustine had received baptism. This decision shocked many of Petrarch's friends and admirers, particularly at Florence where the Visconti were regarded as 'tyrants' and the growing power of Milan was hated and feared. But Petrarch never felt any special loyalty to Florence; and while the Emperor chose to stay beyond the Alps he could think of no protectors in Italy better able than the Visconti to ensure him the security and freedom he needed to get on with his writing.

In old age Petrarch remarked of his own mind that its natural bent had been 'to moral philosophy and poetry' (*Prose*, p.6). Saying this he no doubt recalled his quarrel with one of Clement VI's physicians which led to his *Invective contra medicum* of 1352–3, with its brilliant vindication in Book III of poetry – that is of the classical poets – against the charge of uselessness, mendacity and impiety (*Prose*, pp.648–92). This was Petrarch's major statement on the issue which more than any other divided the new humanist culture of himself and his followers – notably Boccaccio, and in the next generation, Coluccio Salutati – from the reigning scholastic culture of the Universities and of the Friars. The defence of poetry and the study of it is, in fact, one of Petrarch's two chief contributions to humanism as an idea and a moral ideal; the other being his rather later identification of *sapientia* with *pietas*, of wisdom with Christian piety. I shall return to these matters in chapter III. Here it is an autobiographical passage of great interest, in this same Book III of the *Invective*, that calls for attention, a passage that shows us Petrarch consciously drawing away from his own past and entering a new phase – in fact the last one – in his intellectual development. Having repelled one by one the physician's attacks on poetry and poets, Petrarch suddenly observes that in a sense all this is none of his business: *he* does not claim, nor is he even trying, to be a poet; nor have his present studies anything to do with poetry. 'For I don't claim the title of poet... though I won't deny that in my youth I aspired to it'. It is now seven years since he gave up even reading the poets. 'Not that I regret having read them, but to do so now would seem to me a waste of time. I read them at the proper age, and so absorbed them that I couldn't be rid of them now, even if I wanted to be... But to continue into old age the studies of one's adolescence doesn't seem to me at all praiseworthy. As there is a ripeness of fruit and crops, so it is with studies and the mind; the more so in that a raw mind is more useless and more harmful than raw fruit'. This is a characteristic thrust at the scholastics and their obsession with abstract logic, so that 'oblivious of reality, they grow old amongst words' (*Secretum*, in *Prose* p.52). 'But perhaps you will ask', Petrarch continues, 'what I do if I no longer read the poets…I answer that to the limit of my capacity I try to become a better man; and because I know my weakness I beg God to help me, and I find my delight in the Scriptures…You ask me what I do. I strive – and it isn't easy – to correct my past errors.… You ask what I do. I don't read poetry, but I write what men who come after me may read: and content with the applause of a few, I scorn the multitude of fools. And if, with God's help, I succeed in my aim, so much the better; if not, I shall at least have tried. Finally, if nothing else, at least I make maturity my aim…But you, you centenarian whipper snapper, spend your old age still busy with the studies of your boyhood…' (*Prose*, pp.678–80).

When Petrarch wrote this he was nearing fifty, a ripe age in those days. And plainly, he writes both as a scholar preparing for old age by a change in his studies, and as an author preparing his readers for changes in the form and content of his work – changes they might not be disposed to welcome. From this point of view the drubbing he had given the Philistines, in the person of the *medicus*, may seem a sop offered to poetry-lovers before taking his leave of them; or rather, before declaring that he had already done so seven years before. Implicitly, in any case, he was surely telling his admirers, not only that he would probably never finish the *Africa*, but that on the whole he had given up trying to. He had other things to do, better suited to his time of life. He had aspired, unsuccessfully, to be a poet – a clear allusion to the *Africa*; henceforth he will cultivate only that other field of study to which, as we have seen, he felt naturally inclined, namely moral philosophy, but now specifically identified with the quest for a wisdom only accessible through prayer and meditation on the Scriptures. In more philosophical terms, he aspired to a sort of christianised stoicism; in any case, to something *toto coelo* removed from the windy dialectic, as he thought it, of the scholastics. Petrarch, at bottom, had two things against the academic philosophy of his time (which was all 'scholastic' in method and technique): first that its practitioners never grew up, and secondly that it had nothing to do with morals, with conduct, with that caring for the quality of one's soul which Socrates had seen as the ultimate point and purpose of all speculation. And both these defects, for Petrarch, came from one cause, the scholastic obsession with mere logic. Logic by itself is amoral, as is any art or science, as such. To become morally fruitful each art or science has to be integrated into the love of wisdom, *sapientia*, which is inseparable from true piety towards God, *pietas*, which in turn is the crown of moral virtue. Such, in brief, is the mature Petrarch's philosophy, the fruit, in the first place, of his long study of Augustine (for further details see chapter III below).

As for the change in his attitude to poetry, affirmed in the passage quoted above, it has to be remembered that Petrarch normally reserves (in prose) the terms *poesis*, *poetica*, for verse written in the classical metres in Greek or Latin, and that whenever he said (again, in prose) 'poets', *poetae*, without qualification, he meant the classical poets. We need not take too literally the assertion that now, in 1352–1353, it was seven years since he had read 'the poets'; for as Rico says, Petrarch had a free-and-easy way with autobiographical matters; but it is not fair to tax him, as one critic does, with insincerity or inconsistency, because 'in fact he continued to work at poetry to the end of his life' (*Prose*, p.679, n.5); an evident allusion to the *Canzoniere* and *Triumphi*, which of course are in Italian. Petrarch's Latin verse consists of sixty-four verse-letters (*Epist. metriche*), the twelve eclogues of the *Bucolicum Carmen*, the *Africa*, and a few minor pieces. Now, nearly all the verse-letters and all but one of the eclogues were written before 1350; while the *Africa*, Petrarch's greatest effort in poetry as he understood the term, was gradually discontinued after 1345 and virtually abandoned by the mid-1350s. During the last twenty years of his life almost all the poetry, in our sense, that Petrarch wrote was in Italian.

The Later Years, 1354–74

Petrarch spent his last twenty-one years in north Italy, apart from a visit to Prague, to see the Emperor in 1356, one to Paris in 1360–1, and one down to east Tuscany in 1364; the first two of these journeys were made on behalf of the Visconti, the third in order to visit a friend and, en route, to call on the papal legate at Bologna. While in Provence Petrarch had lived much in the country; now he was a city-dweller until his retirement to the Euganean hills near Padua in 1370. And corresponding to this change from a life centred on Avignon to one centred successively on Milan, Venice, Pavia and Padua, went a change in his relations with the ruling powers of the time. After 1353 the only restrictions on his liberty came from the relations he had to maintain – and he did so on the whole willingly – with secular powers, the Visconti at Milan, the Da Carrara at Padua and the government of Venice. These connections all involved him in occasional work of a political nature; and it is worth noting that all through this period his chief patrons, the Visconti, were intermittently at war with the Church and that this situation left Petrarch apparently quite unconcerned; a fact which may be explained, in part, by his steady hostility to Avignon. As a churchman Petrarch's one desire now was that the Holy See should return to Rome, and he worked strenuously to this end after the election of Urban V in September 1362. It was one of his letters to Urban urging this return that led to the most violently anti-gallic of Petrarch's writings, the *Invectiva contra eum qui maledixit Italie* of 1373.

Plague in Milan in 1361 drove Petrarch to Padua, whence in 1362 he moved to Venice where he remained on and off until 1368 when he returned to Padua. Thence in 1370 he moved to a small house he had caused to be built at Arquà in the Euganean hills, where he was fairly soon joined by his daughter Francesca and her husband; and there he died in the night of 18 July 1374.

With three exceptions, Petrarch's literary work after 1353 consisted in revising and completing works already begun (including the first collection of his letters, the *Familiares*). The exceptions are: a bulky moral treatise, the longest of his prose works, *De remediis utriusque fortune* (1354–65); a brilliant defence of his own form of Christian philosophy, *De sui ipsius et multorum ignorantia* (1367); and two other works of aggressive self-defence, the 'Invectives' of 1355 and 1373, the earlier one written to justify his residence at Milan under the wing of the Visconti, the later to justify his urging the pope to leave Avignon and return to Rome. Of these last three works, that on 'ignorance', of 1367, has by far the most general human interest and importance and I shall return to it in chapter III. As for the *De Remediis*, it was intended as a guide to conduct by a critical examination of the four major 'passions', joy and hope, sorrow and fear (cf. *Secretum*, Book I, in *Prose*, pp.64–8; Virgil, *Aeneid* VI, 733). The ground of all four is man's bodily condition. The two 'fortunes' are good luck or prosperity and adversity, respectively the stimulants of the first and second pair of passions, which it is the task of reason to keep in order; this ordering taking the form in the treatise of debates between Reason and one or other of the passions, aimed always at curbing any excess in these. The work was popular through the Renaissance and is still interesting, but whoever today wishes to see a late medieval humanist trying to construct a purely rational ethic would do better to read the *Secretum*.

In his mid-thirties Petrarch had dreamed of being a great poet in Latin, a new Virgil: twenty years later he knew that this could never be. The *Africa* was left unfinished, the metrical epistles ceased, the dull life of the last eclogue – no. XII, on the Hundred Years War – was prolonged just enough to include a reference to the capture of the French king in 1356. Had it not been for the two projects which now begin gradually to be realised, Petrarch would have remained, in his own eyes, on the one hand a Latin poet *manqué*, on the other, on the inferior vernacular level, a piecemeal lyricist, a writer of disjointed poetic 'fragments'. Those two projects were the *Canzoniere*, conceived as an organic whole, and the 'Triumphs'. To the construction of these two poetic unities Petrarch was now quietly to devote what time he could spare from his more publicised writings in Latin prose.

Leaving discussion of the *Canzoniere* to the next chapter, let us pause for a moment on the other vernacular project, as I have called it, of Petrarch's later years. The 'Triumphs' is a long poem in the metre of Dante's *Commedia*, the *terza rima*, representing human life in six phases, each involving a victory and a corresponding defeat: a triumph *for* and a triumph *over*. Triumph I is of Carnal Love (*Cupido*) over the human heart; Triumph II, of Chastity (represented by Laura) over carnality; Triumph III, of Death over Laura; Triumph IV, of Fame (embodied for the most part in the soldiers, rulers, philosophers and orators of Greece and Rome) over Death; Triumph V, of Time over Fame; Triumph VI, of Eternity over Time (and here Laura reappears finally in heaven). Thus it amounts to a poetical treatise on man in terms of three fatalities (Carnal Love, Death, Time) and three correlative liberations (Chastity, Fame, Eternity). From another point of view it represents a systematisation of the various motifs more randomly expressed in the *Canzoniere*. The first two Triumphs may have been written before Laura's death; the last certainly written within a few months of Petrarch's. Most of the work on the rest seems to have been done after c. 1355. Though much in it is beautiful, much is unmistakably a work of old age.

Here I touch only briefly on the other major prose works begun before 1353 and continued through the next two decades: the two collections of letters, the *Familiares* and *Seniles*, and the series of biographies, begun as far back as the 1330s, *De viris illustribus*. To take the letters first, the two collections – the twenty-four books of *Familiares* and the eighteen (if we include the 'To Posterity') of *Seniles* – are the main source of our knowledge of the leading

European intellectual of his time and chief propagator of the new culture, later called humanism, which found its characteristic expression in letters and personal essays rather than in systematic inquiries in the scholastic manner. Literary moralism touched by Christian feeling replaces Aristotelian rationalism, whether as utilised by theology (Thomism, Scotism) or as incipiently 'scientific'. The new mentality was neither theological nor scientific. Petrarch's letters deal with autobiography, politics and literature (including literary scholarship). A few examples will illustrate this statement.

(a) Autobiography. Much of Petrarch's correspondence is a kind of diary open to his friends, but with a wider public also in mind. The focus is usually on his own doings, his own thoughts. But there is much interesting and vivid description too, especially in the earlier *Familiares*, of people and places seen on his travels (*Fam*. I, 4–5, II, 12–15, V, 3–6, VI, 2, VIII, 3). Later, descriptions of actual scenes tend to give place to reminiscence. Memory plays a large and increasing part in the letters (as it does in the poetry), to the joy of course of Petrarch's biographers – who should remember, however, that this charming egotist was something of a *poseur*.[10]

(b) Politics. This matter has been touched on above in connection with Petrarch's reactions to Cola di Rienzo and with his attitude to the Empire. Certain letters referred to there may be called political: *Variae* 48, *S.N.* 2–4, *Fam*. X, I (*Prose*, pp.904–14), all written between 1347 and 1352. Within the same period falls the letter to the Doge of Venice pleading for peace between Venice and Genoa, *Fam*. XI, 8; and compare *Fam*. XVIII, 16, perhaps written at the request of the Visconti, as was certainly XIX, 18, concerning Pavia (*Prose*, pp.980–996). Petrarch continued to urge Charles IV to make Rome the imperial capital (*Fam*. XVIII, I, XIX, 12). And there are the two celebrated letters to Urban V (*Sen*. VII, I and IX, I) pleading for the return of the Holy See to Rome. But on the whole Petrarch was somewhat averse to politics; he was definitely not, as Dante had been, a man of the Communes.

(c) Literature. Study was the breath of life for Petrarch, and writing the natural effect of study; inevitably then his letters contain countless allusions, direct or indirect, to the art of writing. Because of the difficulty of dating any of the *Familiares*, as we have them, earlier than the late 1340s – when Petrarch began to plan that collection – it is best to take all his extant prose letters as products of his maturity; and, for the younger Petrarch's ideas on poetry, to turn to the coronation speech, 'Collatio Laureationis', of 1341.[11] At this early stage Petrarch, already soaked in Virgil and in Horace's Epistles, drew his theory of poetry largely from Cicero's *Pro Archia* which he had found at Liège in 1333. The emphasis was on the nobility of poetry, on the 'glory' the poet can expect from it (cf. *Canz.* 119), and on the defence of its essential 'truthfulness' against its detractors. Conspicuous among the latter were Christian ascetics, so it is natural to find Petrarch sending his Carthusian brother, in 1349, a long defence of poetry on *religious* grounds – the splendid *Fam.* x, 4, itself a commentary on Eclogue I 'Parthenias' where the issue had been very candidly stated.[12] Moreover the art of good writing, in verse or prose, answers to the needs of man considered in himself. The human mind, *animus*, is so related to language, *sermo*, that the cultivation of the one is, or can and should be, the cultivation of the other: eloquence – the ability to render the mind's perceptions clearly, aptly, elegantly – is an essential part of education, along with a directing of the intellect to *veritas*, truth, and of the will to *virtus*, moral goodness. Such is the triple aim of 'studia humanitatis', of which the humanists who came after Petrarch saw him as the great resuscitator, and this especially through his rediscovery of the classics as models of *eloquentia*. His ideal is set out in *Fam.* I, 7–9. And this rediscovery led him to his best achievement in literary criticism, the analysis of 'imitation' as a factor in literary excellence; see *Fam.* I, 8 and XXIII, 19 (1366), *Prose*, pp.1014 ss., where the classical simile of honey-bees is exquisitely developed. Imitation in a bad sense is touched on in the famous letter to Boccaccio about Dante, *Fam.* XXI, 15 (1359), *Prose*, pp.1002 ss.; compare the letter to Homer, *Fam.* XXIV, 12. In a sense that letter about Dante is continued in *Sen.* v, 2 (1364), also to Boccaccio, where Dante is praised as 'ille nostri eloquii dux vulgaris', 'the master-writer in our vernacular', and Petrarch recalls his own ambition, when a young man, to write a 'magnum opus' in Italian – a point I shall return to in chapter II. Details of his lifelong progress as a latinist are given in *Fam.* I, 1 (c. 1350), III, 18, XXIV *passim* and *Sen.* XVI, 1. As to his own artistry in verse or prose, Petrarch says little in his letters or anywhere else about points of technique – another difference between him and Dante – but a small treatise on style might be drawn from such letters as *Fam.* XIII, 6, XXIV, 7, and above all XXIII, 19. The great defence of the *Africa* in *Sen.* II, 1 (1363) (*Prose*, pp.1030 ss.), has to do with content rather than style; its interest is philosophical and religious.

As for *De viris illustribus* – begun c. 1338 as an accompaniment to the *Africa* – Petrarch went on working at it, at intervals, till the end of

his life. The original series of Roman biographies was expanded to
include men from every age. This was from c. 1350. Later, Petrarch's
growing sympathy for Julius Caesar – which went with a marked
loss of interest in his former hero Scipio Africanus – produced his
ripest historical work, *De gestis Caesaris* (see below, pp.155–6,
181–2).

In 1373 the old man amused himself by making a Latin translation
of Boccaccio's tale of Griselda, *Decameron* x, 10.

II. The *Canzoniere*

I. FROM LATIN TO THE VOLGARE

All that remains of Petrarch's writing in Italian, apart from a short letter, is in verse: the 366 poems of the *Canzoniere*; some thirty detached pieces and fragments known as 'Rime disperse'; and the close on 2000 lines, including drafts and revisions, of the *Triumphs*. This is not a great deal compared with Petrarch's huge output in Latin, counting the verse with the prose and not forgetting the innumerable notes and jottings in his books and papers, all of which, even the gardening notes, are in Latin. Presumably he conversed in his native Tuscan with other Italians, and with himself when not thinking in Latin. Anyway, Italian for him had only a limited use, even for practical purposes.[1] As a writer he confined his use of it to certain verse forms – in the *Canzoniere* chiefly the sonnet and the canzone, in the *Triumphs* the Dantean *terza rima*. Not that his interest in the vernacular as a medium of expression remained always on the same level; a certain ebb and flow of such interest is discernible, as we shall see. But from first to last all Petrarch's writing in Italian has something of the nature of an exercise in one of two possible linguistic media; the choice of Italian rather than Latin being determined, in a given case, by *ad hoc* considerations of tone and style rather than by any preference for the vernacular as the more natural medium of expression.

To say this is to bring up the inevitable contrast with Dante. Both men possessed the Florentine idiom as their mother-tongue, but there the likeness virtually ends – the one having been thoroughly formed and penetrated from boyhood by the Tuscan environment, the other brought up in the most cosmopolitan of European cities at that time, papal Avignon. Yet Dante's attachment, as an artist, to the vernacular was, as things turned out, a matter of deliberate choice. But there was this crucial difference between his option for the 'volgare' and Petrarch's occasional choice of it, that whereas Petrarch, inheriting a form of Tuscan as his mother-tongue, saw no reason why, as an artist, he should not be fastidiously reserved in his use of it, it was a main concern of Dante in the *Comedy* to stretch the range of his art to coincide with the utmost potential of the language which, as he said, was by nature 'closest' to him, as having preceded all others in the growth of his mind.[2] Indeed this quality of being the first speech to take shape in a child's mind was for Dante precisely what defined the vernacular ('vulgaris locutio', 'lo volgare') and distinguished it from any and every 'secondary' language such as Latin, which, being 'artificial' and requiring time and study for its acquisition, could be the language only of a few.[3] And it was just this genetic priority of the vernacular, and so its greater 'closeness to nature', that led Dante to his famous assertion of the greater 'nobility' of the mother-tongue: 'And of these two [types of language] the nobler is the vernacular; both because it was the first to be used by human beings, and because it is spoken everywhere, and because it is natural to us, whereas the other, by contrast, is artificial.'[4] Dante here speaks as a scholastic Aristotelian, for whom 'artificial' covers all products of human art or skill – reason applied to appropriate material – which in their turn presuppose that product of divine art called 'nature', including of course the nature of man.[5] From this point of view any given vernacular issues directly from that capacity for articulate speech which God gave to human nature as represented by the first man, Adam[6] – whether or no Adam found himself created with a *particular* language ready-made for him.[7] But it was one thing to talk in *abstracto* about the unique nobility of the 'volgare', it was quite another to champion a particular 'volgare', as a literary medium, in *preference* to so richly developed and long established a medium as Latin. Such a championing had to take poetic form. The *De vulgari eloquentia* (1304–5) drew on contemporary Aristotelianism, but in aim and intention it was not philosophy, but rather what Italians call 'critica militante' – the application of philosophical principles to the promoting of a literary movement or programme. Dante's insight into the special 'nobility' of 'natural' speech – of any and every vernacular – was itself remarkable, but far more momentous in its effects was his application of this insight to literature. In this respect its consequences were nothing less than revolutionary, in principle at least. Reversing the existing, universally accepted scale of values, Dante in effect exalted the young and still largely untested vernacular of Italy over the established linguistic and literary medium of all Western culture. He was announcing, in fact, the coming of age of Italian literature.[8] It is a singular irony of literary history that this announcement went unheeded by the greatest Italian poet of the generation succeeding his own.

While we cannot be sure that Petrarch never read the *De vulgari eloquentia* (would not Boccaccio have at least told him about it?) we know of his disesteem for the scholastic reasoning implicit in the affirmation, in *DVE* I, i, 4, of the special nobility of the vernacular. But that affirmation had been mere prolegomenon to a discussion of one particular vernacular, Italian, and of this precisely as an instrument for poets; which was to draw away from pure philosophy into regions more familiar to Petrarch. And then in turn the *De vulgari* proved to be – it was not planned as such – prolegomena to the *Comedy*; and this Petrarch certainly read, though I fancy with closer attention in his later years than in youth. But there was a leitmotiv in Dante's thinking about Italian – viewed, inevitably, in relation to Latin – of which Petrarch may have been aware but which he never brought up for explicit consideration. I mean Dante's bias, already perceptible (with hindsight) in *Vita Nuova* XXV and XXX, clearly evident, in *Convivio* I, x-xiii, and passim in the *De vulgari*, and of course in the *Comedy*, towards regarding Italian as a language in its own right, quite distinct from Latin; the position he brought at last to the supreme test in the *Comedy*. Now to this there is no exact counterpart in Petrarch. Not that he disprized Italian. He always thought it a marvellous instrument for expressing with delicacy, clarity and sweetness and also, where appropriate, with force and resonance, the sentiments and musings of the heart; in short, for the lyric verse in which he excelled. The *Canzoniere* is proof of that and so, in their way, are the *Triumphs*. And there are indications, as we shall see, that in his later years Petrarch was coming to a deeper appreciation of Italian as a poetic medium. But neither the *Canzoniere* nor the *Triumphs*, nor anything he said in prose, suffice to show that he ever clearly envisaged Italian, Dante-wise, as a language fully fledged and of an expressive capacity potentially equal to that displayed in the past by Latin. As we have seen, he had no philosophy that might have disposed him to take such a view of a mere vernacular. Nor did papal Avignon offer the kind of stimulus to a young writer in the 'volgare' that Dante had found at Florence in the 1280s and 1290s.

And there was another, more positive factor in Petrarch's unwillingness or inability to conceive of Italian in the Dantean manner. This was his life-long habit of representing the Roman civilisation and language as things essentially Italian – what Contini has called Petrarch's 'national interpretation of Roman civilisation'.[9] Petrarch's passionate attachment to Italy – 'the fairest region on earth' – was rooted in his devotion to the Latin culture of which Italy was the homeland and fountainhead. This, it has been already noted, was a recurrent Petrarchan theme, even if never quite distinctly formulated. As regards its linguistic component, it might be expressed as follows: Latin, the language of Rome, became by natural extension the language of the central province of the Empire, the Italian peninsula. Outside were the 'barbari'. These were more or less civilised by Rome and, in the West, by the use of its language. But they shared in this only as in a thing received from the favoured race whose special privilege it was. They were 'latinised' – not intrinsically, authentically, originally 'Latin'. As for the relation between Latin and the Italian vernacular (in its various dialects), Petrarch left this undefined, but it seems plausible to hold, with Contini, that in practice he saw Latin and Italian as two forms or 'levels' of basically the same tongue. The populace of course had only the vernacular form. Educated Italians had both, but it was primarily as Italians, not just as educated Europeans that they spoke or wrote in Latin, among themselves or to foreigners. Consequently Petrarch, a Tuscan by birth, a consummate latinist by education, 'basically never thought of himself as bilingual', in the modern sense of the term: 'radicalmente . . . ignorava dunque di essere bilingue'. Thus Contini,[10] but I do not think that the great critic would say the same of Dante, because Dante, with his conception of a norm, the 'volgare illustre', latent in and in some sense unifying all the dialects of the peninsula, was already possessed of the idea of Italian as, in embryo, a national language in its own right.[11] Such an idea was precluded for Petrarch by his quasi-identification of cultured Italian with Latin. And this would help to explain why he was never troubled by Dante's problem as to the relative 'nobility' of Latin and the vernacular; the comparison would have seemed to him pointless.

His actual use, as a vernacular poet, of his Tuscan idiom is however extremely 'comparative' in the sense of fastidiously selective; reminding one of Dante's 'sieving' of the Italian dialects in the *De vulgari* (cf. I, xi, 6; xii, I); except that Petrarch never stops to explain what he is doing. It was a work of selecting and refining undertaken by an artist who had Latin at his fingertips and at the same time intensely loved his mother-tongue – who could have made Dante's phrase 'questo prezioso volgare', 'this precious vernacular of ours' his own.[12] This love it was, guided by good taste, that kept his lyrics utterly Italian. He was content with traditional Italian metres and, allowing for a discreet use of latinisms, with the resources of pure Tuscan.

What he sought to avoid at all costs, what, in his judgement, Dante had conspicuously failed to avoid, was the 'common touch'. Dante, as Petrarch in a famous letter (*Fam.* XXI, 15) was to try to make Boccaccio admit, was a 'noble poet' who spoiled his work by over-much conforming to popular, that is to uneducated, taste. This, rather than his great predecessor's cult of the vernacular, was what Petrarch blamed in Dante.

Petrarch's earliest surviving poem is a Latin elegy on the death of his mother, written when he was about fifteen and a student at Montpellier. It was presumably during the following years at Bologna that he began to write Italian verse, of which there was a lively tradition in that city. Such early experiments may have left traces in his extant *rime*, but if so they are hardly discernible except as echoes of the 'stilnovisti' – the early Dante, Cino da Pistoia, Cavalcanti. Much later, in *Fam.* I, I (1350), he said he had burned much of his early verse in the vernacular and in fact no Italian poem of his survives that can with certainty be dated before the decisive encounter with Laura on 6 April 1327.

In view of his persistent habit of belittling his Italian lyrics – calling them 'nugae', 'nugellae' (trifles) – it is interesting that in a letter to Boccaccio (*Sen.* V, 2) written not earlier than 1364, Petrarch says that in adolescence he had planned a 'great work' in Italian. It had seemed to him useless to try to add to the massive achievement of the ancients in Latin, whereas Italian was a relatively untried medium (shades of Dante!). We don't know just how long this mood lasted; Petrarch was apt to use terms like 'adolescence' rather vaguely (*Prose*, p.1054); but such a mood was probably already fading when he made the journey to northern Europe in 1333, and had certainly died by the time he returned from Rome in 1337, for within a very short time he was projecting two major works in Latin, the *De viris illustribus* and, more important in this connection, the *Africa*. In any case, that early special interest in the 'volgare' left no discernible trace in the *Canzoniere*. True, there are two early poems in the collection – one perhaps begun as early as 1330, the other of 1333–4, which seem to aim, in their way, at 'greatness': 23, the 'canzone of the transformations', *Nel dolce tempo*, and 28, the Crusade canzone, *O aspectata in ciel*. But it is inconceivable that Petrarch in the mid-1360s should have referred to either composition as a 'magnum opus'. Between 1350 and 1373 all of his explicit allusions to the contents of the *Canzoniere* – all, that is, which imply any comment on them – are more or less disparaging, when not apologetic.[13] Among such 'allusions' I include the title Petrarch finally chose (in 1366–7) for the *Canzoniere*, the relevant words in which are *Rerum vulgarium fragmenta*, which I would render as 'short, occasional pieces in the vernacular'. I shall return to this title in Section 3, but we may note here that that collective term 'fragmenta' can perhaps serve to counterbalance Petrarch's more usual description of his Italian lyrics as 'nugae' or 'nugellae'. While these terms obviously go with a sort of urbanely assumed modesty, 'fragmenta' is, or seems, more objective, as stating simply that the pieces in question are all 'occasional' and all relatively short.

At the same time, however, that title may well be a tacit admission that the work is offered *faute de mieux* – or at least that Petrarch is leaving his readers to take it as such. For in the rest of the title Petrarch did not hide the fact that he was 'poeta laureatus', the poet who had received the high honour of the laurel crown at Rome on 8 April 1341, and received it precisely as the greatest living *Latin* poet. Yet where was the poem on the *expected* completion of which that evaluation had been based? Where was the *Africa*? Alas, by the time the title of the *Canzoniere* was at last decided, the project of that Latin epic had long been virtually abandoned.

Petrarch's enthusiasm for Latin verse had been intense between about 1338 and the mid-1340s, the period of his best work both on the *Africa* and on the Eclogues (*Bucolicum Carmen*). After 1350, however, the greater part of his Latin writing was in prose; to express himself as a poet he turned in fact increasingly to the vernacular, while continuing publicly to disparage it – though this disparagement was, as we shall see, somewhat ambiguous. During the last twenty years of his life he wrote the bulk of the *Triumphs* and carefully constructed the *Canzoniere*, adding new poems to those selected from the 'rime sparse' of his early manhood (see the Prologue-sonnet, *Canz.* 1, 1–8) and ceaselessly revising and polishing each piece in the mosaic. And all this represented, in effect, a rediscovery of his poetic powers precisely through a renewed interest in the 'volgare'. But it was an interest never quite openly declared; hence a certain disparity between Petrarch's private activity and public attitudes. A nice example of this occurs in the famous letter, already mentioned, to Boccaccio about Dante (*Fam.* XXI, 15). Rebutting the charge that he was envious of Dante, Petrarch exclaims, 'I ask you, is it likely that I should envy a man who devoted his whole life to things to which I gave myself only in the first flush of youth; so that what for him was, if not the only, certainly the most important branch of literary art, has for me been only a pastime and relaxation and a first exercise in the rudiments of my craft' (iocus atque solamentum...et ingenii rudimentum) (*Prose*, p.1010). Now this was written in 1359, when Petrarch was already well embarked on the *Triumphs* – no light undertaking – and on the final preparation of the *Canzoniere*. Did it, one wonders, occur to him that these activities hardly tallied with so firm a disclaimer of any serious *continuing* interest in Italian verse? It is hard to acquit Petrarch of a lack of candour here.

But it is more to the purpose to observe that Petrarch's basic argument in this involved and subtle letter is that it was absurd to speak of his envy for Dante, because Dante was in fact unenviable; not in himself indeed, but in his reputation, in his admirers. The whole letter hinges on a distinction between the great poet and the mass of his devotees. The former gets high praise, the latter – Boccaccio excepted, of course – nothing but contempt. The tributes to Dante are fairly warm. A friend of that excellent man Petrarch's father, the great Florentine had been dauntless in adversity, tireless in study. He had possessed a noble mind and also, in its way, a fine literary style; indeed Petrarch does not hesitate to pronounce him easily supreme among writers in the vernacular ('ingenium et stilus in suo genere optimus... ita ut facile sibi vulgaris eloquentie palmam dem', *Prose*, p.1006). In Latin, to be sure, Dante shone less, but who can excel in everything? Having thus neatly 'placed' Dante, Petrarch can easily dispose of the 'odious and ridiculous' rumour that he envied him – was envious, that is, of Dante's enormous fame. For this was the real point at issue, in line with the assumption that where poets are concerned 'Fame is the spur that the clear mind doth raise, / to scorn delights and live laborious days'. And what man of genuine taste and culture could *envy* Dante the sort of fame his poetry had brought him, acclaimed and declaimed as it was by 'ignorant oafs in taverns and market places'? What a warning to young poets attracted to the vernacular! What a warning it had in fact been to Petrarch himself! Certainly, he assures Boccaccio, the experience of hearing Dante's noble lines mangled by his illiterate admirers had been 'not the least of the reasons that led me to abandon the vernacular poetry that I had cultivated in adolescence. I feared that the fate of other men's verses, and of his [Dante's] in particular, would be that of mine also'. In the event, he adds, his fears have been fully justified (*Prose*, p.1008).

Essentially the same story of an early interest in, followed by a revulsion from, the vernacular is told in the other letter to Boccaccio

cited above, written a few years later; but told now in more detail.
The early interest is now recalled as a definite choice of the vernacular,
in preference to Latin, as offering a young poet more scope for
originality. The revulsion, the change of mind – he now explains –
came as he grew more aware of the crass illiteracy of the public for
which, as a poet in the 'volgare', he would inevitably be writing: 'I
realised that I would be building on slime or shifting sand, and be
exposing myself and my work to laceration at the hands of the vulgar
…So I halted in mid course and, changing direction, set out on a
better, as I hope, and nobler path' (*Sen.* v, 2).[14]

This 'better and nobler path' (iterque aliud…rectius atque altius)
was almost certainly, in the first place, that of composition in Latin,
and – seeing that this part of the letter is about Boccaccio's vernacular
poetry – no less certainly in Latin verse. Petrarch would be alluding
to the *Africa*, begun in 1338–9. This is the obvious, immediate sense
of the words. But by 1364, when they were written, Petrarch had
long reached a stage of mental growth beyond that represented by a
mere change from one literary form (verse in Italian) to another
(verse in Latin). This latter change was the 'conversion' that led to the
Africa (and to the Eclogues) and had had its appropriate reward and
stimulus in the Poet Laureate's coronation in Rome in April 1341.
The further stage I refer to, however, was intellectual rather than
literary; the outcome of a gradual shift away from poetry, even in its
nobler Latin medium, to a predominant interest in moral (Christian-
Stoic) philosophy. This was the change alluded to in the 'Letter to
Posterity' (begun, at the earliest, in the late 1350s): 'My intelligence
was well-balanced rather than acute; with an aptitude for every good
and wholesome study, but particularly inclined to moral philosophy
and poetry; which last, however, I abandoned as time went on,
delighting instead in sacred letters [the Bible and the Church Fathers]
…which I had hitherto despised' (*Prose*, p.6). Petrarch never, of
course, simply gave up poetry, but by the age of fifty he was writing
less and less Latin verse, and a general shift of interest, in his middle
age, from imaginative literature to ethics and religion can be amply
documented, as we shall see in more detail presently. And it was
certainly to this change that he *also* alluded in the phrase cited above,
from *Sen.* v, 2, 'a better and nobler path'. For the moment, however,
our concern is still with the early revulsion from vernacular verse in
favour of Latin hexameters – the *Africa*. And here two more points
must be touched on, arising out of this letter.

The topic of vernacular poetry runs through *Sen.* v, 2, but only as a stick with which to beat contemporary illiterates. Casting his net of scorn pretty wide, Petrarch brings together strange bedfellows in that respect; at the start of the letter dealing with the wandering minstrels or reciters of other men's verses, by whom he himself had often been pestered for copies of his Italian poems – which they then mangled in their recitations as they mangled Dante's (who, of course, was both more popular and more defenceless); and concluding with a castigation of that special Petrarchan *bête noire*, the swarm of logic-chopping scholastics of the time who despised not only the entire Latin literary tradition – even Virgil, even Cicero – but also the Church Fathers, and also even St Paul, and even, in their hearts, Christ himself. The portrait of one of these secretly anti-Christian pseudo-intellectuals is the final point and climax of the letter. On the way, however, Boccaccio has been reproved for having burnt his early poems in the vernacular after a first reading of Petrarch's – so much had the contrast depressed him. Petrarch has only recently heard of this and he proceeds to chide his friend for a false humility, a 'proud humility' that really only concealed a reluctance to take the third place in Italian poetry, after Dante and Petrarch, or even the second, if Boccaccio really *does* excel Petrarch – as the latter says he is quite willing to allow; it being understood (Petrarch is prepared, at least, to take this as granted) that Dante is 'ille nostri eloquii dux vulgaris', '*the* master in the art of expression in our vernacular'. This tribute to Dante echoes that in the earlier letter to Boccaccio cited above (*Fam.* XXI, 15). But in the present context – where the Latin/vernacular contrast is less directly involved and where the immediate question is about grades of excellence in *Italian* poetry – the admiration for Dante's peculiar greatness seems to come out more warmly and clearly. And there is this further point – that throughout this discussion, carried on for two pages, about the place due respectively to himself, to Boccaccio and to Dante, as Italian poets, Petrarch seems to assume the value and the dignity of Italian poetry; even if, as is doubtless the case, a certain inferiority to classical Latin verse is still presupposed. This is to be borne in mind in view of Petrarch's disparagements, continued to the end of his life, of his own Italian lyrics.

The other point to be touched on comes at the end of the diatribe against that public which vernacular poets, especially in Italy, had to put up with. It concerns the exact meaning of a hint at some literary decision arrived at by Petrarch. The text is as follows: '...quamvis sparsa illa et brevia iuvenilia atque vulgaria, iam, ut dixi, non mea amplius sed vulgi potius facta essent, *maiora ne lanient providebo*'. The question is whether *maiora* refers to works in the 'volgare' or to works in Latin. If to the former, then Petrarch would presumably be alluding to the *Canzoniere*, which he was certainly preparing when this letter was written (I accept Billanovich's exclusion of any reference to the Triumphs, *Petrarca letterato*, pp.173ff.); but if to the latter – to some work or works in Latin – then the reference would certainly be, in the first place, to the *Africa*, which Petrarch to the end of his life jealously withheld from the public (cf. e.g., *Prose*, pp.1034–42). The point has an obvious bearing on the mature Petrarch's attitude to Italian poetry and the *Canzoniere* in particular. The standard translation of Fracassetti (1869) seems to me to favour taking the adjectival noun *maiora* as standing in direct opposition to the adjectival noun *vulgaria*, rather than to *sparsa, brevia, iuvenilia*, and so as an allusion to *non*-vernacular works; and the same is true of M. Bishop's version: 'My brief works in Italian are now so widely scattered…that I no longer regard them as mine…[but] I shall take care that my major works shall not be similarly lacerated.'[15] Yet Carducci-Ferrari assumed, without argument, that the reference was to the *Canzoniere*: '…the poet told Boccaccio…he was going to see to it that the best of his "rime" should not be mangled by the vulgar' (p.xi); and the same interpretation, slightly qualified, is vehemently urged by V. Branca, and broadly for two reasons: (a) that all of this central part of the letter is marked by an 'enthusiasm' for the 'volgare' and by Petrarch's 'zealous concern' for his own 'rerum vulgarium fragmenta', and (b) that whereas this letter was actually written in 1364, Petrarch's final arrangement of the *Epist. Seniles* makes it appear *as if* written in the summer of 1366, when we know that he was just about to put his copyist to work on the definitive MS of the *Canzoniere*, v.l. 3195 (see below, section 3, p.95). Branca therefore concludes: 'I hold that *maiora* refers to the definitive edition of the *Rerum vulgarium fragmenta*, though without excluding the possibility that other works, in particular the *Africa*, are also alluded to'.[16] Branca's two reasons, the second especially, have a certain weight; yet they seem to me far from decisive. I think it just as likely that Petrarch intended his contrast between *maiora* and *vulgaria* to be understood as between *maiora* and *sparsa illa*….My own tentative conclusion amounts to a reversal of Branca's; that is, I think it probable that *maiora* refers to Latin works, especially to the *Africa*, but without excluding a possible allusion also to the *Canzoniere*.

Petrarch was not a precocious poet in either Latin or Italian. He began the *Africa* in his mid-thirties, and at forty had still written less than half of what was to be the *Canzoniere* (i.e. the greater part of 6–135: 6–52 – minus the second half of 23 – being fairly certainly datable before the summer of 1338, and the remainder between this date and the third return to Provence from Italy late in 1345: for further details see section 2). True, much of the early Italian verse has been lost, much of it perhaps in that bonfire mentioned in *Fam*. I, 1 (see above, p.27). But precocity is not to be measured only in quantities. That Petrarch thought his own development had been slow is suggested by such a typical phrase as that already cited from *Sen*. V, 2: 'those scattered, brief vernacular poems of my youth'. It is true – as I have already suggested and will now show in more detail – that such utterances of the ageing poet were by no means based only on literary considerations; but it seems reasonable to take them as expressing, in part at least, a judgement on the poems qua poems (cf. *Canz*. 293, 1–4). The phrase last cited refers almost certainly to some of the poems Petrarch thought worth including in the final form of the *Canzoniere*; while at the same time regretting their piecemeal discontinuity – the defect which, in the event, he sought to remedy by making a single book of them and of the other poems he went on writing after his youth was past.

For he continued, of course, to cultivate the Italian lyric after that revulsion against the vernacular described in the letters to Boccaccio cited above; indeed some of Petrarch's finest canzoni, 125–9, were written, so far as we can tell, during a period, c. 1340–5, richly productive of work on the *Africa*. This confirms the point made above, in connection with Petrarch's views on Dante, that his revulsion was not against the 'volgare' but, in the first place, against a certain public – that 'vulgus' which so mangled and mispronounced the noble verse of Dante. Now this contempt of Petrarch for the 'vulgus' long preceded, it is safe to say, the disparaging allusions to his own Italian lyrics that occur in letters of his middle and old age. That contempt however, and these disparagements, as the years went by, certainly involved another, ostensibly nobler motive – a disdain that reached through the 'vulgus', the uneducated public, to the subject matter of the sort of verse that held most attraction for it, the emotions and follies of youth in love. The object of *this* disdain was the erotic motif itself in literature – particularly vernacular literature – in regard to which this 'moral' disdain was in turn reinforced by the scholar's tendency to look down on the vernacular as an inferior medium and one only too likely to attract the illiterate. And these two motives, the one moral, the other cultural, combined in the attitude towards his own love-story – that of the *Canzoniere* – which Petrarch tended to take up in the last two decades of his life; that is an attitude of a disparaging detachment, a deliberate distancing of his present self from the passions and illusions of youth, of his own youth (cf. *Canz.* 1.3–4), and so from those 'iuveniles ineptie', 'youthful follies' (*Sen.* XIII, 11), the poems in which so much folly was recorded.

And yet throughout these twenty odd years the formation of the *Canzoniere* proceeded. Perhaps before the death of Laura, perhaps a little later, Petrarch began to make an ordered selection from the lyrics which, as he would from time to time ruefully admit, had brought him fame in youth (presumably at Avignon in the 1330s); in the meantime gradually adding new poems to the old. But for some years he kept the project to himself, only showing the lyrics he was collecting to a few close friends like Boccaccio. The chronology of the whole process will be examined in another section. In the following pages I glance at certain features of the *Canzoniere*, in which its peculiar gestation, as a work conceived and carried on after a strong initial repugnance, and then along with a certain enduring disapproval – sincere or assumed – seems more or less clearly discernible.

The disapproval bore, as I have said, on the erotic theme itself, and consequently appears most distinctly in the penitential frame within which the love-story is set: the Prologue-sonnet *Voi ch'ascoltate* and the concluding canzone to the Virgin Mary, 366, with the sonnets immediately preceding it. Together these poems spell out a condemnation of 'Amor' without making any distinction between love and lust such as Petrarch drew, in self-justification, in the 'Letter to Posterity' and such as he tried to maintain, but unsuccessfully, against the assaults of 'Augustinus' in *Secretum* III ('To Posterity': 'In youth I was tormented by a violent love, but it was pure and it was my only love...I wish I could say that I have been quite free from lust, but if I said that I should be lying' (*Prose*, p.4; cf. *Secretum III*, in *Prose*, pp.132–50; cf. 98–104)). Now in the *Canzoniere* the revulsion from love is expressed rather differently at the beginning and at the end of the book; in the initial sonnet it comes out in terms suggestive of a Stoic-inspired rational ethic, but in the final canzone in explicitly Christian terms. It is sometimes suggested that there is something adventitious about this framework, as though Petrarch devised it only in deference to an ascetic anti-erotic tradition – or rather to two such traditions, the Stoic-Platonist and the Christian – in order to 'get away with' the intervening love story. But in fact the themes and tone of the Christian conclusion are several times anticipated in the body of the work (most distinctly in 62, 81, 142) which in turn contains many echoes of the philosophical anti-eroticism of the Prologue-sonnet (notably in the great *I' vo pensando*, no. 264, which significantly opens Part II of the *Canzoniere*). On the other hand it is evident that the love-story was deliberately set in, and in emphatic contrast with, a framework formed of those two traditions – these being regarded as basically one, in the sense that the Christian ethic is conceived of as resuming, confirming, deepening and clarifying a moral wisdom already adumbrated by the Ancients, in particular by Cicero and Seneca. This blending of pagan and Christian traditions is taken furthest in the most penitential – and the most anti-Laura – of Petrarch's prose works, the *Secretum*; where indeed the terribly austere St Augustine figure, 'Augustinus', is so platonico-stoically 'paganised' as to be almost unrecognisable: his attack on natural instinct and emotion is far more in line with Cicero's *Tusculan Disputations* – especially Books III and IV – than with the New Testament.

Petrarch saw in himself (*Prose*, p.6) a special disposition to moral philosophy – by which he meant philosophical *moralising*, Cicero and Seneca rather than the *Nichomachean Ethics* – and his fairly early reading (c. 1333–9) of Augustine's *Confessions* and *De vera religione* gave that disposition a decidedly Christian orientation, in theory at least. But down to the middle or late 1340s his main ambition was to excel in Latin poetry and Roman history, and be the acknowledged authority on the ancient poets and moralists. The *De vita solitaria* (1346) was the first overtly Christian work that he wrote for the public. By then, however, his chosen guides in 'philosophy', virtually identified with moral reflection, were already Cicero and perhaps still more Seneca. It was as such a philosopher above all that, from about 1350, he chose to present himself to the world, to the point of now publicly insisting on his detachment from his previous enthusiasm for poetry. 'For my part', he wrote in 1353, 'I do not claim to be a poet, though I won't deny that in my youth I aspired to be thought one'; adding, for good measure, that it was more than seven years since he gave up reading the poets (meaning, here, surely the classical Latin poets) – 'not that I regret having read them, but that such reading now would seem to me rather a waste of time (quasi supervacuum videtur). I read them when I was of an age to profit by them. ...And in any case I see nothing in the least praiseworthy about con-

tinuing into old age the studies that occupied one's adolescence. As
with fruit and crops, so with the cultivation of the mind, what
matters is a certain *ripeness*' (*Invective contra medicum*, ed. Ricci, p.74;
Prose, pp.678–80). There is a similar statement in the 'Letter to
Posterity' (*Prose*, p.6). Again, in the letter cited above to Boccaccio
about Dante (1359): 'Today I am far removed from such concerns
[as the desire for fame through poetry]' (*Prose*, p.1006). In the first
two of these texts the poetry in question is Latin; in the third the
immediate reference is to vernacular verse. But all three make the
same point, so characteristic of the later Petrarch's public utterances
(in prose) on poetry – that whereas he *had* been above all else a literary
artist in love with verbal beauty – and so with its supreme model,
classical Latin verse – he is *now* above all a 'philosopher', as befits his
age, a man now fully adult whose concern is with *res* not *verba*, things,
not words (*Prose*, pp.52, 182–4);[17] one for whom verbal beauty is,
at best, only adornment, embellishment – 'poeticis literis non nisi ad
ornatum reservatis' (*Prose*, p.6) – at worst a source of pernicious
illusion, like those 'harlot Muses', 'sweet Sirens', whom Lady Philosophy drove from the sick-bed of Boethius.[18]

And if poetry in general fell out of favour with the 'philosopher' in
the later Petrarch, so *a fortiori* did the vernacular love lyric with its
obsessive harping on unsatisfied desire – the recurrent theme, of
course, of his own 'rime' written in youth and early middle age.
These 'rime', re-read in later years, doubtless gave him pleasure but
also, if we are to believe him, a sense of guilt and shame: '…those
vernacular songs of my youth…of which I am now ashamed and
repent, but which, as we have all seen, are most acceptable to those
affected by the same disease' (*Fam.* VIII, 3–19 May 1349; cf. the
famous letter, of the same period, to Petrarch's brother Gherardo,
now a Carthusian monk, *Fam.* X, 3, *Prose*, pp.922–4). It is significant
that in the final version (*Sen.* XIII, 10) of a letter of 4 January 1373,
accompanying the gift of a copy of the *Canzoniere*, the inevitable
disparagement of the lyrics is focused, not on the language nor on
points of style, but on their amorous subject matter; and that this is
closely associated with the poet's youthfulness when (he says) much
of the work was written. Apologising for these 'trifles in the
vernacular', Petrarch begs his friend to excuse the 'roughness of the
style' – it was to be expected in the work of so young a poet, 'for a
great deal of this…I wrote in adolescence'. And he goes on: 'It is
unwillingly, I confess, that I see these foolish productions of my youth
(iuveniles ineptias) made public, now that I am old; I would rather

they remained unknown – even to myself, were that possible. For…
the subject-matter itself ill befits the dignity of old age (ipsa tamen res
senilem dedecet gravitatem)'. Here the apology for the vernacular
idiom and the 'rough' style is perfectly conventional; indeed, the
deprecatory remark about the style would be ordinary conversational
modesty in any age (a more authentic note is struck in *Canz.* 293.1–8).
But the moral embarrassment? Was this genuine? Who can say?
But certainly one does not answer *that* question merely by referring
to 'the traditional structure of sin, repentance and redemption'.[19]
Anyway, as he expresses it, Petrarch's embarrassment came from his
seeing so clearly the difference between the passion's slave who had
written so many of the 'rime' and the sage imbued with 'senilis
gravitas' that he would like to appear (and also – why not? – to be).
The implication being that an old man should be ashamed not only
of yielding here and now to sexual desire but even of dwelling on it
in memory. Christian moralists called such reminiscence *delectatio
morosa*, and deeply distrusted it,[20] and Petrarch's reading of Augustine's *Confessions* would have inclined him to this view of things. But
so too would his familiarity with Seneca and Cicero, as moralists.
Indeed an attentive reading of the *Tusculan Disputations*, II–IV, is
much to be recommended to those who, doubting the sincerity and
seriousness of the later Petrarch's moral ideal, dismiss as senile fuss all
such statements as those I have quoted from this letter to Pandolfo
Malatesta.

Yet there is something fussy, and oddly so, about the letter; not
exactly as implying a certain ethic (open to question as this is on other
grounds) but simply as being written when it was. By 1373 Petrarch
must, of course, have been aware that the *Canzoniere* was far more
than a record of the ebb and flow of adolescent emotion; that by now
it contained all the moral reflection that any sane judge could require
in a book of its kind – it is enough to say that the concluding penitential poems, 363–6, were transcribed into the final fair copy by
1372,[21] and that both the darkly introspective canzone opening
Part II, *I' vo pensando*, and the Prologue-sonnet *Voi ch'ascoltate*, were
composed, at the very latest, by 1353 (for details, see below section 3).
So much built-in self-criticism – deliberately given prominence by
the placing of the relevant poems – makes the old poet's scruples seem,
to say the least, exaggerated. Of the six poems just mentioned, 363–6
will be discussed together in due course, and room must be found also
for some comment on 264. Here I want to turn to *Voi ch'ascoltate*, as
being, of the six, the poem most directly concerned with the themes

and contrasts evoked by the last sentence cited above from the letter
to Malatesta: youth and maturity, folly and wisdom, passion and
tranquillity. All this the poet has experienced – that is what the
Prologue-sonnet, offered to his readers as a sort of table of contents,
succinctly says:

> Voi ch'ascoltate in rime sparse il suono
> di quei sospiri ond'io nudriva 'l core
> in sul mio primo giovenile errore
> quand'era in parte altr'uom da quel ch'i' sono,
> del vario stile in ch'io piango et ragiono
> fra le vane speranze e 'l van dolore,
> ove sia chi per prova intenda amore,
> spero trovar pietà, non che perdono.
> Ma ben veggio or sí come al popol tutto
> favola fui gran tempo, onde sovente
> di me medesmo meco mi vergogno;
> et del mio vaneggiar vergogna è 'l frutto,
> e 'l pentersi, e 'l conoscer chiaramente
> che quanto piace al mondo è breve sogno.

[You who hear in scattered rhymes the sound of those sighs that
were my heart's food at the time when I first went astray in
youth, when in part I was another man from what I am now:
for the varied style of my weeping and speaking, varying
between vain hopes and vain sorrow, where there is anyone who
knows by experience what love is, I hope to find both pity and
pardon. But now I see how for long I was the talk of the crowd,
so that often I'm filled with shame at myself, which shame is the
fruit of my folly, and repentance, and the clear knowledge that
all that gives pleasure in this world is a brief dream.]

The first thing to note is the detachment of the speaker, the 'I',
from the poet: the *speaker*, addressing the public – 'Voi' –, transmits
the *poet's* 'sighs' to it (lines 1–2). And the detachment is both temporal – the poet (when he wrote) was young, the speaker is not – and
spiritual, because of a further change, alluded to in line 4 and dwelt
on in the lines that follow. The chronological gap is emphasised at
line 4 and again at lines 10–11. But meanwhile a string of verbs in
the present tense identify speaker and poet, while retaining the
spiritual detachment: 'piango/ragiono' (5), 'spero' (8), 'veggio' (9),
'mi vergogno' (11). So bit by bit the sonnet presents itself as a
miniature autobiography in two parts, the division falling at lines 8–9.

Part one declares what the speaker *used* to be, in terms of the states of feeling (2) and intellect (3) which gave rise to the poems now being introduced; and of the emotional ebb and flow that accounts for their futile inconsequent variety (5–6), now offered to the reader for his understanding and sympathy (7–8). Part two (9–14) indicates what the speaker now *is*; and this under two aspects, negative and positive. The negative aspect is shown in lines 9–11 by a return in memory over the shame experienced by the poet as his condition became known, through his poems, to the general public. The positive aspect consists in repentance (13) and clear understanding (13–14). But it is the achievement of this mental lucidity, announced in the sonnet's close – always, in Petrarch's sonnets, the focus of his finest artistry – that takes the chief emphasis. It connects, of course – by contrast – with the initial dark tangle of 'error' recalled at line 3. And these two opposed extremes are each significantly characterised: the 'error', by association with youth – 'giovenile errore'; the lucidity, as a liberation from illusions, as a knowing, at last, 'clearly / that all that gives pleasure in this world is a brief dream' (14) – the bewitching daydream, in fact, which the young, infatuated with transient mortal beauty, mistake for reality. For Petrarch the epitome of such beauty had been Laura; and its removal by her death, the decisive proof of the truth enunciated in line 14. But Laura, of course, is not named;[22] hence that line – and the sonnet which it concludes, and the whole book to which the sonnet is prologue – conveys, intentionally, a universal message. But the ethic implicit in it is more Stoic than Christian. Evil is located in passion itself, or rather in the false, perverse 'opinion' at the root of passion.[23]

While we have this sonnet before us, let us look a little more closely at its construction. The opening address is a pure vocative unsupported by any verb ('ch'ascoltate' is adjectival), but the 'Voi' addressed – who are, in effect, Everyman – reappear, obliquely, in line 7, with its beautifully delayed stress on the sixth syllable, 'pròva'. Meanwhile the poet's initial 'error' and the subsequent swirl of passion have been distinguished (2–5); only to converge, six lines on, in the key-word 'vaneggiar', 'raving' (12). There is a rather similar interlocking arrangement of the shame theme in the sestet. Lines 9–10 recall a *past* shame, which then turns out to be obsessively *present*, in line 11, with its unusually persistent alliteration. This in turn has the effect of carrying the shame theme on into the final tercet, where 'vergogna' now becomes salutary as the first, bitter 'fruit' of all the preceding 'vaneggiar'. The full meaning of that 'fruit' is then shown in the last two lines; summed up in the complementary yet rhythmically so divided and contrasted hemistiches of line 13; the lightness and clarity of the second of which, 'e 'l conoscer chiaramente', both prepares us for line 14 and will be, though more faintly, balanced by its undertone of sadness ('è breve sogno').

Notice that in passing from octet to sestet, Petrarch shifts the focus from the poems themselves, here offered to the public, to the spiritual 'fruit' of the 'raving' which, as a fact now past, gave rise to them: that is, from the poet's work to his soul. The work is over and done. Whatever its intrinsic merits, its effect on him has been salutary, through the shame that its notoriety had made him feel – that popularity of his early lyrics of which we have heard him complaining in the letters cited above.[24] From the precise standpoint of this sonnet the only justification of the lyrics is to win the sympathy of those afflicted by the same sickness which they express (5–8) and to yield, for and in the poet, the far better fruit of repentance and of a mind now clear of illusions (12–14).

Not that Petrarch was really so detached from his poems qua poems or from his 'volgare' as a medium for poetry. This great sonnet alone is proof of an intense appreciation of the expressive resources of Italian. But, along with this, there is genuine detachment here, if not of the artist, of the sage that Petrarch by now quite sincerely, I think, wants not only to appear but to be. And this, in the last resort, was precisely his main problem as a poet – the problem he set out to solve, during the last twenty odd years of his life, by completing the *Canzoniere* – the problem of reconciling the two sides of his nature, the poetic and the ethical. How in fact he tried to do this has still to be shown. Meanwhile these remarks may serve as an occasion for summarising the results, as I see them, of the foregoing analyses of Petrarch's attitude to the vernacular in general and to his own Italian verse in particular. I would set them out as follows.

1) Petrarch never accepted, perhaps never even seriously considered, Dante's view of the vernacular as essentially 'nobler' than Latin, and as capable of rivalling Latin in large-scale poetry at the highest level. For Petrarch the 'volgare', in its Italian form, was a perfect medium for the lyric, and perhaps also for such meditative and not too protracted sequences as the *Triumphs*.

2) For a time he had thought himself capable of epic poetry in Latin on the Virgilian model. This phase may date from his visit to Rome in 1337,[25] though in the 'Letter to Posterity' (*Prose*, p.12) he tells us that the specific subject of the *Africa* first occurred to him after

settling down at Vaucluse (1338–9). Anyway, this Virgilian phase persisted for ten or twelve years. Stimulated though it was by the poetic 'coronation' in Rome, April 1341, by the late 1340s Petrarch was turning increasingly to reflective and descriptive prose; a main factor in this development being his discovery of Cicero's letters at Verona in 1345. By 1353 he was saying that he was not a poet at all. 3) His early interest in Italian verse had declined as his classical culture deepened. He was repelled by the vulgar illiteracy, as he thought it, of Dante's admirers (*Fam.* XXI, 15, *Sen.* V, 2). But he continued to write Italian verse 'on the side', and when in 1349–50 he took stock of his writing to date – with a view to future work – while he spoke in public only of projected work in Latin (*Fam.* I, 1, *Metr.* I, 1), in fact he was already organising and revising the *Canzoniere* and would soon be embarked on the *Triumphs*. As his hopes faded of ever finishing the *Africa*, his surviving poetic energy found outlet in these vernacular works. Traces of some such change of direction are discernible in the *Canzoniere*; hints even of an awareness that the change was not all loss. As such it is still represented in no. 166, *S' i' fussi stato fermo*, but in nos. 186–7 we are told that she of whom Petrarch is now singing in the lowly 'volgare' would have been a fine subject for Homer and Virgil, and that if Ennius sang of Scipio, that 'flower of former times', he, Petrarch, will sing of the 'new flower', Laura (186.9–14). And Scipio, of course, was the hero of the *Africa*.... Nor does the new focus on Laura involve any lowering of the poet's sights, for the greatest poets would be at a loss to describe her beauty and virtue (215.6–8; cf. nos. 307–8).

4) In his Coronation Speech of 1341 Petrarch had come before the educated public as a poet, indeed as *the* poet of his time; a decade later he preferred the role of philosopher. That this was far from being a mere pose is proved, surely, by the transparent sincerity of the *Secretum*, a work he never published (he completed it, I hold, in 1352–3 – but see chapter III, section 4). Now the vital centre of this work is the poet's self-examination in Book III concerning his twofold ideal of 'Amor' and 'Gloria' (*Prose*, pp.131–215). 'Amor' meant Laura, 'Gloria' literary, especially poetic, fame; and with his Stoic-Augustinian conception of philosophy as a way of life, involving the will no less than the intellect, Petrarch was now disposed to consider his option for philosophy as entailing the renunciation of both Laura and poetry. Both renunciations were qualified, in the event; the man's poetic genius was irrepressible. Nevertheless, after writing the *Secretum*, Petrarch could no longer – in theory, at least – regard either

the study or the practice of poetry as worthy of more than passing
attention from one who would live 'ut philosophum decet', 'as befits
a philosopher' (*Prose*, p.210). And while this attitude prescinded from
the differences of language, the near-disdain for poetry that it involved
found its obvious target in the love poets of Provence, France and
Italy – all those predecessors of his whom in *Triumphus Cupidinis* IV
Petrarch sees walking through green meadows 'discoursing of love
in the vernacular'.[26]

Nevertheless the poet had the last word; *and* in the 'volgare' – and
not only in respect of posthumous fame. To see our way clearly
through this rather complicated matter, it is best to start from the
crucial section in *Secretum* where the two partners in the dialogue are
most directly and intensely opposed (*Prose*, pp.132–60). The two
partners are the two Petrarchs: 'Franciscus', the lover and the poet,
and 'Augustinus', the would-be Stoic-Christian philosopher. To
'Franciscus' Laura is an 'image of the beauty of God' and 'the nobler
part, as it were' of his own soul. For 'Augustinus' she is a pseudo-
divinity, an idol. Now both of these attitudes to Laura return in force
in Part Two of the *Canzoniere*; Petrarch's defence of his love for her
as spiritually ennobling pervades, implicitly, most of the poems
between nos. 267 and 362; while 'Augustinus''s finally victorious
attack in the *Secretum* – on that false dream (as he represents it) –
triumphs for the second time in the concluding poems nos. 363 to
366. But what I wish particularly to remark is that that lengthy pro-
Laura sequence in *Canzoniere* II – taken in conjunction with *Tr.
Mortis* II (written after 1349) – stands in close relation, not only to the
conclusion that follows and contradicts it within the *Canzoniere*, but
also to the last poem, as far as we know, that Petrarch ever wrote, the
Tr. Eternitatis (dated, in the autograph MS V.L. 3196, between
January and February 1374). For the apparently total renunciation of
Laura in *Canz.* 366.79–130 is implicitly *withdrawn* in the concluding
lines, 85–145, of this final *Triumph*, which is Petrarch's last word on
the Christian heaven, as the *Paradiso* had been Dante's. It would seem
then that this *Triumph* is a sort of Christian palinode of the equally
Christian but anti-Laura *Vergine bella*, and still more, of the position
taken up twenty years before in *Secretum* III (than which Petrarch
wrote nothing more 'anti-Laura').

And there is a further point. The *Tr. Eternitatis* ends with the poet
rejoicing in the thought of Laura's physical beauty, both in that which
she had possessed on earth, in time, and in that which she will possess,
after the Resurrection of the Flesh, in heaven; it being implied that

the latter will be somehow the same as the former, only transfigured and enhanced: 'se fu beato chi la vide in terra, / or che fia dunque a rivederla in cielo !', 'if he was blest who saw her on earth, / what then will it be to see her again in heaven!' (144–5). The doctrinal basis here is the Christian dogma of the Resurrection, which had come into view at lines 133–4: 'ne l'età più fiorita e verde avranno / con immortal bellezza eterna fama', 'in the flower and freshness of youth, they [the Blessed] will possess / immortal beauty and eternal fame'. But the link between these two phases of Laura's beauty, the temporal and the eternal, is, in the movement of the poem, provided by 'chi la vide in terra', her lover, Petrarch himself; and the argument establishing that connection offers, implicitly, a certain excuse for what was excessive, and therefore sinful, in his past infatuation with her (cf. 248.8). That the argument meant much to Petrarch is shown by his having used it where he did: at the very end of the last of the *Triumphs* and in two of the three structurally most important poems in the *Canzoniere* – in the third stanza (lines 48–54) of no. 264 and in the last stanza (lines 121–3) of no. 366. It is an argument *a fortiori*: if he has found this earthly thing, Laura, so beautiful and desirable, how much *more* beautiful and desirable must heavenly things be (these being left unspecified in no. 264, identified with Mary in 366, and with Laura 'imparadised' – to use the Dantean participle – in the *Tr. Eternitatis*). Notice, however, that while the structure of the argument is the same in all three instances, the moral judgements on Petrarch's love for Laura, that the argument subserves, differ as between the two canzoni, on the one hand, and the *Tr. Eternitatis* on the other. This is because while both canzoni are strongly penitential, this *Triumph* is not. In both of the passages referred to in the former poems – *Canz.* 264 and 366 – the clear implication is that the poet's love for Laura's earthly beauty was excessive; that that beauty, being only 'a little mortal, perishable earth' (366.121), has become, for him who loved it as he did, an 'evil' (264.51). In neither poem does the general context permit of any excuse or justification to be drawn from the argument (save perhaps as a faint suggestion). Nevertheless this *was* a possible implication, as the final *Triumph* quite clearly shows; and it does so by laying the final, decisive stress, not on Petrarch's infatuation, nor on Laura's mortality, but on her future transfiguration in the heavenly glory.

The bulk of the *Canzoniere* is, of course, about Laura. Obvious too is the major change dividing the Laura of all but the first three poems of

Part II from the Laura of Part I – the change that is her death, announced in 267 and emphatically recalled, and its moral significance for her lover expounded, in 363–4. He now finds himself 'in bitter-sweet liberty' (363.8) – that has been the immediate effect of her death. The bitterness should not be glossed over – though, to be sure, it has been more bleakly rendered elsewhere (cf. 292). With Laura gone, the whole world's *intrinsic* desirability has gone too – I mean, according to the dramatic design of the *Canzoniere*. With Laura gone, 'all's but naught', as Cleopatra said of the world bereft of Antony: 'and there is nothing left remarkable / beneath the visiting moon'. There is this difference, of course, that Petrarch's despair, unlike Cleopatra's, leaves him face to face with God – the situation he addresses himself to in 364–5; and then, in a different way, in 366 (the difference being, to put it at its simplest, that the woman lost is replaced by another woman, Laura by Mary, so that the *Canzoniere* may at least end on a Christian note; and how superbly, in fact, it does: 'Raccomandami al tuo figluol, verace / homo et verace Dio, / ch'accolga 'l mïo spirto ultimo in pace' ('commend me to your son, true man and true God, that he may receive my last breath in peace') (366.135–7).

This replacement of Laura by Mary has involved the repudiation, if not of Laura herself (but see 366.92–4, 111), certainly of Petrarch's earthly love for her. Such is the rather abrupt *volte-face* with which the *Canzoniere*, as a love-story, ends. I say 'rather abrupt' because the 97 poems between 267 (the announcement of her death) and 364 are in the main favourable to Laura; indeed they represent, taken as a whole, the strongest vindication of Petrarch's love for her that the *Canzoniere* provides. Some aspects of this vindication will be considered more closely, in relation to the rest of the love-story, in section 2 below. Here a brief general comment on the poems concerned will not be out of place if it draws attention to the intellectual interest of the later 'rime'. Umberto Bosco has said that Petrarch's aim in his Italian verse was to write 'poesia degna della latina con una lingua inferiore', which I would render 'vernacular poetry comparable to that in the nobler (classical) Latin tongue'.[27] That is an acute comment, but whereas Bosco, as the context shows, had style chiefly in mind, I would extend the sense of his words to include what Dante called 'gravitas sententiae', 'depth of thought'.[28] And I have in mind two things. The first is the introspective subtlety so often displayed in this part of the *Canzoniere*.[29] The second is the way Petrarch develops and rings the changes on the theme of his continued contact with Laura after her death. This theme is perhaps the major novelty, the most fertile in poetic results, of the *Canzoniere*. Petrarch must of course have been aware of the parallel with the Dante-Beatrice relationship, as developed in *Inferno* II and in the last cantos of *Purgatorio*; the theme of the loved woman, now 'risen from flesh to spirit' but returning to the world of time to rescue her lover from mortal peril. But there are immense differences, and it would betray gross obtuseness to say that Laura here is simply 'modelled' on Beatrice. Taking broadly the same theme as Dante, Petrarch handles it entirely in his own way.

When Laura revisits her lover on earth she is preceded by no 'Virgil' figure, she comes unattended by allegories, with no pomp and circumstance, no retinue of Virtues, no Chariot, no songs or cries or thunderclaps. She always comes alone; only twice does he see her in company, and then his mind has already been raised to heaven and her companion is Christ himself (345, 362). When she comes she may remain silent (281–2, 336), but more often she comes to converse with him, within his mind (279, 284–5; 302, etc.) or visibly seated by his bed at night (342, 359). Like Cordelia's, her voice is 'ever soft, / gentle and low'. She never lectures or fulminates or rhapsodises. For all her dignity, she is sweetly companionable – even familiar, in the sense of communicative, to a degree hardly imaginable in Beatrice. Alone with her lover, she exchanges memories with him, 'contando i casi de la vita *nostra*' 'recalling the chances and changes of *our* life', 285.12; cf. 305.13, 'il nostro amor', '*our* love', and 343.9–11. She explains and finds excuses for her past severity towards him, 341.12–14; cf. 289–90, and above all *Tr. Mortis* II *passim*. This kind of spiritual intimacy between a man and a woman is something new in Italian literature.

The creation of so original a figure as the Laura of *Canzoniere* II was a remarkable poetic achievement; arguably Petrarch's finest. While hints of it had appeared in relatively early poems like 12 and 123, it was essentially an adult development. By his early forties – say 1345 – Petrarch had given exquisite expression to the fascination of sheer beauty (e.g. 90 or 126) as well as to his extraordinary sensitivity to the ever-changing inner life of imagination and feeling (22, 32, 129, 135). By then too he had written perhaps his most moving directly Christian verse (62, 80–1, 142). His major poetry of argument and reflection came later (264 and 360, probably between 1349 and 1353; 355, almost certainly later). It was an effect of the predominantly ethical and religious direction he gave to his studies from the later 1340s. And this in turn, taking occasion from, and conditioned by, the death of

Laura, prepared the new development in his love poetry that characterises, as we have seen, *Canzoniere* II; the underlying theme of which might be defined as a sublimation of sensual desire, *amor concupiscentiae*, into friendship, *amor amicitiae*. The example of Dante and Beatrice (those of the *Vita Nuova* no less than those of the *Comedy*) no doubt counted for something here, but probably no more than did Cicero's dialogue, *Laelius, de Amicitia*, or certain pages of Augustine, long familiar to Petrarch.[30]

This glance at the contents and manner of the latter part of the *Canzoniere* should put into their proper perspective the disparaging allusions to the book, or to the vernacular tradition which it continued, that Petrarch lets fall from time to time in his letters. Such significance as his expressed indifference or disdain or embarrassment may be allowed to have is partly psychological, partly cultural. These sentiments and attitudes reflect the sense of superiority (I don't mean mere self-esteem) of the consummate Latinist, filtered through an acutely sensitive temperament, which at the same time was impregnated by Stoic moralism and by no means undisturbed by ascetic scruples arising from assiduous study of the Bible and the Christian Fathers, especially Augustine and Jerome. Such scruples, having influenced implicitly the Prologue-sonnet, take control at the book's conclusion. It is in these two places that the poet displays, as it were, his moral credentials, and gives an *imprimatur* to his own work. In that sense their purpose is defensive, a function they share with the other rationally self-critical poems (e.g. 70 and 264) or specifically Christian-penitential poems (e.g. 62, 81) that occur in the work. This is not – most certainly not – to call such poems insincere, but only to point to their structural function in the *Canzoniere*; and incidentally to recognise that there were aspects of the poet's personality which in a sense transcended the limits of his vernacular masterpiece. Only in two places do I personally feel that this inbuilt self-criticism does not perfectly harmonise with the general design; and as to one of them I may well be wrong – namely right at the end, in 364–6, where the anti-Laura mood and theme seem rather too abruptly introduced. As to the other instance however, it is surely evident that the Prologue-sonnet is inadequate as a summary of the book it purports to introduce. Here the poet, proclaiming that he is *now* very different from the man he was *then* (1.4) – when he wrote the lyrics to which the readers' attention is now being invited (1.1–8) – omits to mention that among the poems thus presented with such an air of adult detachment there are many – the bulk of Part II, in fact – that quite evidently express a mature adulthood, and do so, moreover, with no repudiation of Laura – on the contrary. I refer of course to all that poetry of friendship in Part II, on which I have briefly commented.

The *Canzoniere* is both a confession of sin and an assertion of artistic genius. So indeed is the *Divine Comedy*. But in Petrarch's work that assertion is far less explicit. It speaks mostly through the style itself – that of individual poems and also, in a sense, that of the book as a whole, considered less as an artistic unity than as the communication of a certain 'criticism of life', to use Arnold's phrase. Taking style, however, in its more usual limited sense, Bosco's judgement remains true, that it was as a stylist that Petrarch 'entered into conscious competition with the Provençal, French and Italian poets who preceded him, and that he rejoiced to overcome them – the lyric poets in the *Canzoniere*, Dante in the *Triumphs*'.[31] It may be doubted whether Petrarch ever thought he was 'overcoming' Dante in the *Triumphs*; but as regards the *Canzoniere* Bosco is surely right, not only as to the emulation but also as to Petrarch's confidence in his instrument, his style. The evidence is in the work itself, and even more in the actual process of its making; more precisely, in that intense interest (whatever he *said* to the contrary) which held Petrarch for more than twenty years to the task of shaping and organising his 'rime sparse' into the form they finally assumed. It is inconceivable that an artist of his calibre should have spent so much time and trouble on materials he regarded as of only minor or marginal importance. Well acquainted with the vernacular lyric tradition, he knew that in choosing, not only to write in it, but *himself* to edit and publish the results (see section 3) – he knew that in so doing he was inviting comparison with his Italian predecessors and above all with Dante. Evaluative comparison and the emulation that goes with it had always accompanied that tradition, had in Dante indeed become something of an *idée fixe*.[32] Petrarch was far less given to such explicit comparing and emulating; but with his fastidiousness and his rhetorical and historical training, he cannot have differed much inwardly, in this respect, from Dante. And combining in himself, as he did, the old and the new Western literary traditions, it was inevitable that when Petrarch came to assess his predecessors in the vernacular (in particular Dante) he should have been guided by his exceptional familiarity with Roman rhetoric (Cicero, Quintilian) and with those classical Latin writers, in both prose and verse, whom Dante himself had so strongly recommended as models for poets in the 'volgare'; especially in the art of 'constructio', that is, of the composition of complex sentences: *DVE* II, vi, 7. Here the metrical unit that Dante had in mind was the canzone stanza; and it was certainly to his canzoni (not, for example, to his sonnets) – and chiefly, I think, to their 'constructio' – that he was alluding in *Inferno* I, 85–7, when he acknowledged Virgil as the source of 'the beautiful style which has made me famous'. Petrarch's mastery of stanza construction was no less manifest than Dante's; and no less – to say the least – manifestly classical in its origins. Where, in point of 'constructio', he certainly surpassed Dante was in the sonnet.[33] I shall return to this and related matters in sections 4 and 5.

2. THE CONTENTS OF THE CANZONIERE

We owe the *Canzoniere* in all probability to Laura's death in April 1348 – the *Canzoniere*, I mean, not as just a string of poems but as the coherently planned and shaped work to which we give the name. In this, the true sense of the term, there is no evidence that the *Canzoniere* was begun before the news of Laura's death reached Petrarch at Parma on 19 May 1348; such evidence as there is points to the emergence in his mind of the book as we have it – a bipartite miscellany introduced by the Prologue-sonnet, *Voi ch'ascoltate*, and with the canzone 264 opening Part II – at some time between mid-1348 and the end of 1350.[34] So much, I think, was shown in 1976 by Francisco Rico.[35] And Rico's position, as then outlined, will be assumed here as a working hypothesis. This position, it should be noted, entails no opinion as to the precise date of any part of the *Canzoniere* except that it assumes (a) that the Prologue-sonnet and no. 264 took their present form after Laura's death, and (b) that most of Part I was written before her death and most of Part II after it. In particular this Rico-hypothesis, so to call it, makes no assumption as to the date of the poem with which Petrarch chose to conclude his book, *Vergine bella*, 366, nor as to the number of poems he intended it to contain. If in fact we can be fairly certain that 366 dates from the last decade of his life, and that it is no accident that the *Canzoniere* contains no more and no less than 366 poems, our assurance on both points rests mainly on evidence dating from after 1360.[36]

The sonnet announcing the death of Laura, *Oimè il bel viso* (267), may well have been the first poem Petrarch wrote on getting the sad news; but there is no trace of it in his work-sheets v.l. 3196.[37] Contained in this MS, however, are drafts and fragments which show that

between May 1348 and October 1351 he was working on the following poems: the long canzone 23 (the first half of which dates from
c. 1330 – 'it is', he noted, 'one of my earliest productions'); the sonnet
265 (written as if Laura were still alive, but in fact in September 1350);
the ballata 324; the two canzoni 268 and 270; and finally, a short
lament for Laura, not eventually included in the *Canzoniere*.

Of these poems the one that throws most light on Petrarch's ideas
and feelings in the period immediately following Laura's death is the
relatively short canzone 268, *Che debb'io far? che mi consigli, Amore?*
It was worked over with great care, as the MS shows (a first draft on
28 November 1349; retouched twice in May 1350; another revised
draft on 28 December 1351). It is also, as we shall see, of particular
interest as anticipating most of the themes to be developed in the rest
of the 'pro-Laura' part of Part II of the *Canzoniere*, that is down to
and including 362.

To return for a moment to the genesis of the *Canzoniere*. This, as I
have said, I date, following Rico, within the two years or so following
the death of Laura; during which time Petrarch quite certainly
initiated the two collections of his Latin letters, those in prose, the
Familiares, and those in verse, the *Epistolae metricae*.[38] Neither in
Fam. I, I (to Ludwig van Kempen) nor in *Metr.* I, I (to Barbato da
Sulmona) does Petrarch speak of making a corresponding collection
of his vernacular 'rime', though in the former he speaks plainly of
them, and in the latter allusively. But in his work-sheets, V.L. 3196,
there now occurs, and for the first time, a phrase which, to say the
least, indicates that he was now methodically arranging his 'rime' in
an ordered series. On 28 November 1349 Petrarch wrote above the
first draft of 268 the words 'transcriptum non *in ordine*, sed in alia
papiro'; while a note in the same MS tells us that on 3 April 1350 he
decided 'to transcribe *in ordine*' no. 23, after three days spent on this
and other vernacular pieces. In both cases it is reasonable to take 'in
ordine' – 'in a methodically arranged series' – to refer to the same
collection; which would thus have extended from Petrarch's earliest
poems in the 'volgare', represented by 23, to the most recent ones,
represented by 268, and to understand the whole collection as being,
in fact, a substantial part of what became the *Canzoniere*. The dates
of these two notes about transcribing 'in ordine' obviously make the
genesis of the *Canzoniere* – if that, as seems likely, is what they
indicate – contemporary with that of the two Latin collections; and
the two letters which initiate and announce these collections – *Fam.* I,
I and *Metr.* I, I – do in fact throw light, indirectly, on the contents and

arrangement of the *Canzoniere*. The verse letter to Barbato speaks
apologetically of the others in Latin hexameters which will make up
this particular collection, but in terms sharply reminiscent of the way
we have heard Petrarch, in his prose letters, decrying and deploring
his Italian lyrics (see above section 1). 'You will read', he says to
Barbato, 'of my tears and of the wounds I suffered when a boy (!)
from the sharp arrows of the boy-archer. [But] with the passing of
time all things come to an end...Comparing myself with what I was,
I seem to see another person, I neither look the same, nor behave or
think as I did then...Now that a little marble [Laura's tombstone]
covers the fire that for long kept me aflame, I, now cold, feel pity for
those who burn with love, and shame that I too was once as they are...
My mind, now at peace, shrinks with horror from past anguish; and
rereading what I once wrote, it is another's voice that I seem to hear'
(*Metr.* 1, 1, 62–5). In more vivid language this is very like the octet of
Canz. 1, *Voi ch' ascoltate*, especially in its insistence on the gap between
the poet and his own youth. Appropriately, if disingenuously, the
Italian sonnet insists even more on the writer's remoteness from the
love poetry of his youth.

In the first of the *Familiares* (1, 1) the links with the *Canzoniere* are
less obvious; though the general description it gives of the style and
content of those letters does in part fit the vernacular lyrics. But before
we come to that, some remarks dropped in passing here on vernacular
verse are worth a brief attention. Petrarch – so he tells Van Kempen
(his 'Socrates') – has been going through his old papers and sorting
them into three bundles, one of letters in Latin prose (the future
Familiares), one of letters in Latin verse (the future *Epistolae metricae*),
one of vernacular verse. Of this last sort of verse he observes that,
being 'designed to charm the ears of the unlettered' – the 'vulgus' – it
has 'its own rules' (it works, that is, by accentual stress, with or without rhyme, not by quantity). 'Popular among the ancient Greeks and
Latins – if indeed it is true that the common folk at Athens and Rome
were in the habit of using only rhythmic verse (*rithmico tantum
carmine uti solitos*) – it was revived, people say, in Sicily, not so very
long ago, and thence spread through Italy and beyond'.

Here some brief comments seem called for.
1) It is clear that while Petrarch mentions the Greeks (as in a rather
similar way does Dante in *De vulgari eloquentia* 1, i, 3) his interest here
in the historical relation of vernacular verse is focused on that of
Italian to Latin poetry.
2) As was perhaps to be expected, he passes over the purely linguistic

aspect of the matter; while leaving the impression, however, that he thought of Italian and Latin as respectively the 'lower' and 'upper' levels of the same language (see section 1, pp.25–6).

3) Petrarch characterises vernacular verse as the sort written to please the uneducated 'vulgus'; in contrast, of course, with that in classical Latin, like his own *metricae*. Yet it has, he insists, its own rules, 'leges'. These he does not specify, but presumably he had in mind, in the first place, the metrical forms to be analysed in section 4 below.

4) He seems to say that the first of the Romance tongues to be used in verse was Italian; which is odd, since Dante, for example, seems quite clear as to the priority in time of verse in Provençal.[39] And Petrarch was fairly well versed in the Troubadours (cf. *Tr. Cupidinis* IV, 38–57). Is it possible that here he is simply indulging his usual pro-Italian bias?

5) Having mentioned that he had found among his papers many old poems in the 'volgare', and briefly explained what he means by verse of this kind, he says no more about them. So far as the evidence of this letter goes, those old poems of his might have ended in the fire. Yet the mention of them here proves this at least, that by the early months of 1350 Petrarch had assembled materials for an ordered collection of his vernacular lyrics, should he choose to make such a collection. And, as we have seen, we know for a fact (from v.l. 3196) that by early 1350 he *was* arranging specimens of such material 'in ordine'; just as – if more distinctly and in detail – we know from *Fam.* l, 1 that he was busy arranging in ordered series his prose and verse letters in Latin.

And perhaps the reason he gives – still in *Fam.* 1, 1 – for his having decided that the time had come for making the two Latin collections may apply equally well to the *Canzoniere*. The letter opens on a note of crisis. The Plague of 1348, removing so many of his friends, had been a bell that tolled for him too. 'How brief our own expectation of life may be I don't know, I only know it cannot be long'. Like Guido da Montefeltro, he knows that the time has come 'to lower the sails and coil up the ropes'.[40] True, he uses the travel metaphor to point forwards, not backwards, but the sense is the same: 'For my part, like a prospective traveller I am packing my bags and considering what to discard, what to leave to my friends, what to throw in the fire'. It was a question, chiefly, of his accumulated papers, now sorted into bundles, as we have seen. Tempted to burn the lot, he finds the image of the traveller again in his mind; and at once knows what he will do. 'Then, as one thought leads to another, I found myself saying: 'What is to prevent me from recalling [through these old letters] the thoughts and feelings of my youth – as a tired traveller, at the end of a long day's journey, likes to look back from a hill over the way he has come?' So the *Familiares* were conceived; and some such motive, surely, was behind the *Canzoniere* too. Nor is it difficult to assimilate lines 1–8 of *Canz.* I to what he goes on to say about the diversity and seeming incoherence of the contents of the Latin collection – 'so much…inconsistency; with the writer's style and point of view constantly changing as his mind was variously affected by a whole variety of subjects; though for the most part more sadly than happily'. This is almost a paraphrase of the octet of the sonnet. Note that the features common to both collections that Petrarch most stresses are reminiscence and variety. In intention the *Canzoniere* is a man's recall of his past in its mental and emotional diversity. Dante had done something of the kind in the *Vita Nuova*; but on a far smaller and simpler scale.

The *Canzoniere* was the first book of lyrics, selected and edited by the poet himself, that the West had seen since the end of the ancient world. A more obvious, if less remarkable, novelty was Petrarch's break with the practice followed in earlier collections of Italian lyrics of keeping canzoni separate from the slighter metrical forms. The intermingling, in v.l. 3195,[41] of canzoni with sonnets, ballate and madrigals, represented, as Wilkins said, 'a notable poetic innovation'.[42] The purpose no doubt was partly aesthetic, partly auto-biographical – to bring out the poet's artistic and mental development. The various metrical forms will be examined in section 4. Let me remind the reader that the entire book consists of 317 sonnets, 29 canzoni, 9 sestine, 7 ballate and 4 madrigals. A certain concentration of longer poems – canzoni and sestine – is observable in three areas in Part I and two in Part II; that is, at nos. 22–53; 70–80; 119–42; and then again at 264–70; 323–33. Notice, by contrast, how the third group in Part I, with its particularly striking concentration of longer poems – especially between 125 and 135 – is followed by a prolonged sequence of short poems; of the 121 pieces between 142 and 264, 111 are sonnets and there is one short ballata. And along with this tendency to metrical uniformity in the second half of Part I, there is an absence of variety in content. Whereas in the first half – i.e. down to 142 inclusively – there are ten poems that have nothing to do, directly at least, with Laura (7, 27–8, 40, 53, 119, 128, 136–8), the entire series from 143 to 263 is directly concerned with her. Nor does this series show any reaction *against* her, or against the love for her – except, implicitly, no. 189, *Passa la nave mia* – comparable with such overtly penitential poems in the first half as nos. 1, 62, 80–1, 142. From this relative uniformity, formal and thematic, within the second half of Part 1, Wilkins, as we shall see in section 3, drew certain conclusions affecting the chronology of the 'making' of the *Canzoniere*. The fact itself, anyway, is evident, and Petrarch may perhaps have justified it to himself with the kind of 'proviso' he used in *Fam.* 1, 1, anticipating such critics of the *Familiares* as might find the middle books of the collection maudlin and tedious: it doesn't matter if a book is rather weak in the middle, provided the beginning and end are 'robust and virile' (*Fam.* 1, 1, 46).

The order of the poems is roughly chronological, beginning with Petrarch's falling in love with Laura – the 'innamoramento' – on 6 April 1327 and ending in his old age with death in sight (366.131; 365.12). Note that this precise dating of the 'innamoramento' *belongs to the love story as we are told it*; whether it tallied with the facts is another matter. Emerging in the *Canzoniere* at 211.12–14, it re-appears (but only as to the month and day of the month) in *Tr. Mortis* I, 133–4 (mid-1350s?) and in the obituary of Laura that Petrarch wrote on the fly-leaf of his Virgil and which, following Martinelli,[43] I am inclined to date 1352–3. Now this Virgil note declares a coincidence obviously intended as significant: 'Laura... first appeared to my eyes...in the year of our Lord 1327, *on the sixth day of April*, in the church of St Clare at Avignon; and in the same city, *also on the sixth day of April*,...but in the year 1348, the light of her life was withdrawn'.[44] The coincidence raises a problem the adequate treatment of which would require more discussion than I have space for here. I will only indicate what seems to me the more probable solution. The problem is posed by the fact that Petrarch, besides, as we have seen, dating the 'innamoramento' on 6 April 1327, also, in *Canz.* 3 and 62, identifies that day with Good Friday; whereas in fact Good Friday in 1327 fell on April the 10th. Was Petrarch himself aware of this inconsistency? In what follows I shall assume that he was; and that he must therefore have had some reason for treating it as relatively unimportant; in other words, that he attached a special meaning to the sixth day of April – or simply to the *sixth* day – which inclined him to associate it with his 'innamoramento' at the cost of chronological exactitude.

But to pursue the argument we need to be clearer on two points with regard to the 'innamoramento' as the crucial moment in the poet's self-told love story – that is on its connection with Good Friday and with the date of Laura's death. As to the first point, of the two poems, *Canz*. 3 and 62, identifying the day of the 'innamoramento' with Good Friday, the penitential sonnet 62, *Padre del ciel*, is probably the earlier. Critical opinion favours 1348–9 as the probable date of no. 3, whereas 62 is self-dated as written on the eleventh Good Friday since the poet came under love's 'merciless yoke', that is to say Good Friday 1338. Nothing is said, either here or in 3, about 'April the sixth'. Elsewhere in the *Canzoniere* the closest association of the Laura theme with Good Friday comes in the penitential sestina 142, lines 37–9, where Laura's tree, the laurel, is set in opposition to the Cross of Christ. On the second point, the phrase 'April the sixth' occurs twice in the *Canzoniere*: once at 211.12–13, as specifying the date of the 'innamoramento', and once at 336.12–13, as specifying that of Laura's death (and the two time-references are implicitly brought together as 'one and the same moment' in 275.13). The date of 211 is uncertain. We know that it was transcribed into the final fair copy of the *Canzoniere* in June 1369, from a copy written 'many years' before.[45] It is just possible that these 'many years' stretched back to some time *before* Good Friday 1338, the date of 62, *Padre del ciel*; but that seems unlikely if only because 211 is placed so much later in the *Canzoniere*. So it seems more likely than not that the 'innamoramento' was *first* associated with Good Friday and only later with the sixth day motif. What, then, gave rise to this motif? What else but Laura's death itself which, as we have seen, Petrarch, in the Virgil obituary note, dated the 6th of April 1348? This was a private note, written for his eyes alone, with no intention therefore to deceive. The date, moreover, is circumstantially plausible; given the distance between Avignon and Parma where Petrarch tells us he received the news of Laura's death on 19 May.[46]

As to the 'innamoramento' therefore I am suggesting two things: first, that it either really did take place on the Good Friday of 1327 (a 10th of April) or that Petrarch fairly early – at the latest by 1338 – chose to associate it, paradoxically, with that sacred day; second, that after Laura's death, but before writing the Virgil note, he decided to link *this* fatal event with the previous one, the 'innamoramento', by adapting the date of the latter to the date of the former, as regards the day of the month – that is by changing April 10th to April 6th; and that he did this because of the sacred associations, in Christian liturgy and numerology, of the number six, in particular of the sixth day of the week, which from early Christian times had been closely associ-

ated with the Crucifixion; Jesus having died on the Jewish 'day of
Preparation' for the sabbath (Mark 15.42, John 19.31). This in the
Roman liturgy became 'feria sexta in Parasceve', 'the day of Preparation, the sixth of the week'. Consequently a Christian significance
came to be attached to the number itself. Adam, whose sin Christ had
redeemed, was created on the sixth day, and on the same day was
widely believed to have sinned; Christ, who was crucified at the sixth
hour, initiated the 'sixth Age' of the world.[47] It was certainly into
this tradition that Petrarch chose to insert his love-story.[48] But the
occasion of his doing so would seem to have been, not the fatal
encounter in 1327, but Laura's death in 1348, if we can believe the
Virgil note that she died on 6 April; which, be it noted, coincided
that year with the fifth Sunday of Lent, traditionally called Passion
Sunday, as initiating the liturgical celebrations of 'the Lord's Passion'
which reached its climax, of course, on Good Friday. For it was *this*
Friday, the sixth day of Holy Week, that the poet had had in mind
ever since he had chosen to link it with the 'innamoramento'; not so
much the sixth day of the *month*, therefore, as the sixth of the *week* was
what interested him. As to just *when* he decided to date the 'innamoramento' on the 6th instead of on the 10th of April, a difficulty is
admittedly raised by lines 12–13 of *Canz.* 211: 'In 1327…at the first
hour of the sixth day of April, I entered the labyrinth…'; for it
cannot be proved that the earliest known draft of this sonnet, which
survives in v.L. 3196, f.5, dates from *after* Laura's death. But this
perhaps is a minor detail.

The general result, at any rate, of the above analysis is surely to
reveal a strong Christian strain in the *Canzoniere*; always bearing in
mind that while more than half of the book was written when Laura
was alive, the crucial period of its shaping and organising was the
decade following her death.

One result of that organisation was the series of 'anniversary'
poems. Eleven in Part I and one in Part II present themselves as
written this or that number of years since the 'innamoramento' on
Good Friday 1327; they are nos. 30, 50, 62, 79, 101, 107, 118, 122,
145, 212, 221, 266. One poem, *Ne l'età sua* (278), relates in the same
way to Laura's death on 6 April 1348; and one, 364, the sonnet
Tennemi Amor, to *both* fatal events and dates. It is self-dated as if
written on or soon after 6 April 1358: 'Love held me for twenty-one
years, happy in the fire, hopeful in my pain, and then, since my
Beloved, and my heart with her, rose to Heaven, for *ten* more years
weeping. Now I'm weary and, blaming myself for a life so mis-

directed,...to you, Most High God, I give back, devoutly, all that
remains of me and to me' (lines 1–8). Here, suitably so near the end
of the book, the double dating serves to draw together and recapitulate the entire *Canzoniere* as a love story unfolded through
time. Thus it terminates all the previous self-datings. And the whole
series serves, obviously, to maintain a generally ongoing time-
sequence throughout the whole book; while at the same time it
allows a good deal of freedom in the placing of particular poems; so
that one cannot assume in every case that a given poem or group of
poems was written as early or as late as its position in the series may
at first sight suggest. Thus, as already noted, most critics are now
inclined to date nos. 2–5 after Laura's death; and 265, which purports
to be written during her lifetime, was in fact composed in September
1350.[49]

Some of the poems are not concerned with Laura at all: some that are,
are not amorous. In those I call penitential the poet renounces or
struggles against his attachment to Laura as a hindrance to the love he
should have for God, as for example in the sonnet *Padre del ciel* (62;
see also 80–1, 142, 264, 364–6). No. 264, *I' vo pensando* may also be
linked with the long canzone 360 in that each represents a major
pause for moral reflection; essentially they are debate-canzoni, with
the crucial difference that whereas 264, though not an explicitly
Christian poem, is intensely 'penitential', 360 is neutral; the long
debate here, for and against Laura, ends, one may say, in a draw. The
judge, who is Reason, 'the queen enthroned in the diviner part of our
nature', refuses in the end to pass judgement; and does so, rather
strangely, with a smile (lines 155–7). This smile of Reason, coming
so near the end of the whole book, is curious. What, one is compelled
to ask, is the relation between this smiling Queen Reason and that
Queen of Heaven who will receive, only six poems further on, the
poet's final, tearful repentance?

   But let us turn to the poems that are simply not concerned with
Laura. The ethical sonnet *La gola e 'l sonno* (7) derives from Cicero's
'Tusculan Disputations', III, i, and has its exact parallel in the preface
to Petrarch's own *De viris illustribus* (*Prose*, p.218). The moral norm
is the 'kindly divine light' (Cicero's *igniculi*, 'sparks') gleaming in the
depths of human nature but all too easily smothered by vicious habits
and the false values of the world (lines 1–6, 10–11)). Though an
early poem, Petrarch wrote no more elegant *résumé* of his ethical
humanism. The next non-Laura poem is the Crusade canzone 28,

with its introductory sonnet; an oration in the grand manner, of classical-humanist inspiration. The wars on behalf of 'the Son of Mary' against Islam are viewed as somehow continuous with the Greek victories at Marathon and Salamis and the wars of the Roman republic. This too is an early piece (1333–4) and Petrarch would later modify his admiration for republican as distinct from imperial Rome. Four or five years later probably, after his first visit to Rome in 1337, he then wrote, again in the grand manner, the 'Roman' canzone, no. 53 (this is now the prevailing opinion as to the date of *Spirto gentil*, against the older view that it was occasioned by Cola di Rienzo's seizure of power at Rome in 1347). This poem is Petrarch's most eloquent celebration of Rome, republican and imperial, pagan and Christian; in the Latin tradition 'the City' *par excellence* – the theme touched on in chapter 1, in connection with Petrarch's 'imperialism' as compared with Dante's, and his relations with Cola di Rienzo. Contini here discovers a Dantean influence, especially in the second stanza. Certainly the two poets shared a veneration for 'il nostro capo Roma', 'Rome our head' (in the double sense of source of political authority and of civilization), line 20; compare the whole of this stanze 3 with what is said in *Convivio* IV, v, 20 about the reverence due to the very stones of 'the holy city'. But in all this they had behind them a long and strong medieval tradition; which in turn suggests a comparison with Petrarch's other great 'political' canzone, *Italia mia*, 128. That tradition being European rather than narrowly Italian, *Spirto gentil* has always appealed less directly than *Italia mia* to Italian patriotism; even though in Petrarch this was virtually one thing with his 'romanità' (which in part no doubt accounts for the warm admiration for *Spirto gentil* of such nineteenth-century patriots as Leopardi and Carducci – though, to be sure, the no less patriotic De Sanctis found it 'cold and laboured').[50]

The same 'romanità', is latent in *Fiamma del ciel* and the following poems (136–8), though the immediate inspiration of these ferocious sonnets against the papal Curia at Avignon is the old 'evangelical' longing, so vehemently expressed in Dante's *Comedy*, for a return to the poverty and simplicity of the early Church (136.12–14; 138.9–14). U. Dotti has rightly drawn attention also to the humanist and laicist strain in Petrarch's anti-Curial polemics; but the links between these sonnets and, on the one hand, the poet's support for Cola di Rienzo, on the other, his campaign to get the papacy back to Rome, must be sought outside the *Canzoniere*.[51]

The most celebrated of Petrarch's non-amorous poems is the

beautiful *Italia mia*, 128, written at Parma in 1344–5. This and Dante's
lament over divided Italy in *Purgatorio* VI, 76–151 are the loftiest
expressions of Italian patriotism, and the central aspiration in both is
the same, that the whole peninsula should live at peace with itself. Yet
how they differ in tone and feeling. The difference is apparent in the
opening words of each, in the contrast between Petrarch's tender 'My
Italy' and Dante's harshly admonitory 'Ah, servile Italy...' Petrarch's
canzone is subjective and lyrical throughout, whereas in *Purgatorio* VI
the feeling for Italy takes the form of serried, cut-and-thrust ratiocination, except in the final address to Florence where the poet's civic
patriotism finds its only possible expression in a sarcasm very close
to tears. Petrarch's love for his country is the more directly expressed;
two aspects nevertheless may be distinguished in its object. His
attachment in the first place is to Italy as a concrete physical reality;
and this is less for its beauty as such – but see lines 3, 18, 56 – than
because it is, quite simply, *his* land: 'Is not this the ground I first
touched?...the nest, where I was so sweetly nursed?' (81–3). Next,
there is the sentiment superbly expressed in stanza 7 – a love that is not
patriotism in the ordinary, limiting sense of the term, but rather the
love of life itself as an infinitely precious and at the same time
desperately transient gift, a gift all the more, therefore, to be used
worthily while it lasts; a gift moreover – and this is deeply Petrarchan
– for every moment of which we have each to render strict account
after death:

> Signor', mirate come 'l tempo vola,
> et sí come la vita
> fugge, et la morte n'è sovra le spalle.
> Voi siete or qui; pensate a la partita:
> ché l'alma ignuda et sola
> conven ch'arrive a quel dubbioso calle.
> Al passar questa valle
> piacciavi porre giú l'odio et lo sdegno...
> et quel che'n altrui pena
> tempo si spende, in qualche acto piú degno
> o di mano o d'ingegno,
> in qualche bella lode,
> in qualche honesto studio si converta:
> cosí qua giú si gode,
> et la strada del ciel si trova aperta.
> (128.97–112)

[Lords: see how time flies, how life flies, and how Death is at

our backs. You are here now; think of your departure; for to
that perilous passage the soul will come, naked and alone. As
you pass through this valley put away, I beg you, hatred and
scorn…and let the time now spent in causing pain be turned to
some worthier action of hand or mind, to some fair work of
praise or noble study; and so find both happiness here below
and the way open to Heaven.]

Upwards of a dozen non-amorous poems have to do with poetry
itself under various aspects. All are sonnets except the allegorical
canzone 119, *Una donna più bella*, occasioned by Petrarch's coronation
at Rome as poet-laureate in 1341. The 'donna' is Fame or Glory. Here
it is she who crowns him with the laurel, after showing him the
splendid figure of her immortal sister Virtue. Both sisters are immortal, both of that same 'divine' world represented by Love and
the 'three Women' in Dante's allegory of Justice, *Tre donne* (CIV),
to which Petrarch is here clearly much indebted. His intention,
evidently, was to enhance his coronation by associating literary fame
with that 'virtus' – intrinsic human nobility – of which Cicero had
said that glory was its 'shadow'.[52] But here there is an ambiguity in
the very notion of fame; and within a few months, probably, of
writing this canzone Petrarch was to begin, in *Fam.* v, 17, a critical
re-examination of the concept; which, continued in *Secretum* III
and in the *De Remediis* (*Prose*, pp.632–6), was to lead to a thorough
devaluation of all worldly glory such as the Roman coronation had
brought him.[53] On the part of the most famous writer of his age, such
reasoned critique of fame, sustained through thirty years, shows
remarkable detachment. In the light of it *Canz.* 119 cannot but seem a
trifle showy. It certainly shows a poet conscious of his powers, and
in this, and in the linking of poetry with undying fame, it had been
anticipated by the correspondence sonnet no. 104. The fame in
question, of course, was that which Petrarch still sought as a poet in
Latin, above all through the *Africa* (and we have seen in section 1 of
this chapter what he thought of Dante's reputation with the unlettered
vulgar); so that the bleak confession of poetic sterility that he makes
in 166, *S'i fussi stato* (of the late 1340s?), is the more affecting, for it is
exclusively to verse in Latin that its lines 1–4 allude: 'Had I kept to
that cavern [on Mount Parnasus] where Apollo became a prophet,
Florence would today, perhaps, have her poet – not only Verona
[with Catullus] and Mantua [with Virgil] and Arunca [Juvenal?].'
Alas, his own field, he goes on, now yields only thistles and thorns;

his olive tree withers, the waters from Parnasus that once nourished it 'are turned elsewhere'. That olive tree was doubtless his languishing Latin epic; but the modern reader will be more struck by the deliberate disregard of Dante in the phrase implying that Florence did not yet have a 'poet'. Here the term 'poet' 'poeta' is used with the linguistic restriction – as suited only to writers in Latin or Greek – from which Dante had begun to break free already in the *Vita Nuova* (xxv, 3–4) and from which the Laura theme will eventually liberate Petrarch himself, as we shall see (215.8; 263.2). With the *Africa* again is often identified the 'new cloth' referred to, hopefully this time, in the obscure sonnet 40; but the identification is implausible.[54] If *S' i' fussi stato* (166) implied a disparagement of the 'volgare' and even of the Laura theme associated with it, an interesting reaction on both counts appears in 186 and 187, and again, after Laura's death, in 293, 304, 307–9. A subtle contrast with this is perhaps discernible in the slight piece on the death of Cino da Pistoia *Piangete, donne* (late 1336, no. 92); the 'volgare', the language of the dead *love* poet – this qualification is stressed – is given its due, no more. The same close association of the vernacular with love poetry returns, more imaginatively, in the lament for Sennuccio del Bene, 287 (1349). Both of these laments seem to go in the same direction as the young Dante's assertion in *Vita Nuova* xxv, 6, restricting vernacular verse to 'amorous matter'. Suitably, then Laura is remembered in *Sennuccio mio* (287). Sennuccio will meet her in heaven (lines 12–14) and since he is going to 'the third sphere', the Venus heaven of lovers and love poets (Dante, *Paradiso* viii–ix), this would seem to be her heavenly mansion too (and cf. 302.3–6).[55] In a way the allusion to Laura in 287 removes this sonnet from the 'non-amorous' group we have been considering; to which, finally, may be added a few correspondence sonnets like 139 – probably addressed to the Carthusians at Montrieux after Petrarch's visit there, early in 1347, to see his brother Gherardo – and, much later in Part II, no. 322.

Our general survey of the contents of the *Canzoniere* has so far distinguished three types of poems: (1) those – far the greater number – expressing this or that aspect of the poet's love for Laura; (2) penitential, and in this sense 'anti-Laura' poems; (3) the poems simply not concerned with Laura. Let us designate the first type as *L*, the second as *AL*, the third as *NL*. The neutral debate-canzoni, 360, can be left to stand on its own. Note that I count as penitential poems, besides the seven listed above – 62, 81, 142, 264, 364–6 – nos. 1, 80, 189 and 355.

This study is chiefly concerned with types *L* and *AL*; but to get a clear view of the *Canzoniere* as a whole we need to see, in general, how the thirty or so poems that stand outside the prevalent type *L* – whether in opposition to it (type *AL*) or as ignoring it (type *NL*) – fit into the overall structure of the book. As to the penitential type *AL*, then, four things may at once be noted. First: this type fixes the *design* of the *Canzoniere* as a whole, in that the entire collection opens and closes with an *AL* poem (1 and 366), and that one of the same type, 264, opens Part II. Second: poems of this type predominate towards the end of the book, between 355 and 366. Third: in Part I their incidence is strongest between the self-dated sonnet 62 (1338) and the sestina 142 (1345–7?). Fourth: metrically this type is represented by two canzoni, 264 and 366, two sestine, 80 and 142, and seven sonnets; giving *AL* a relatively high proportion of longer poems. As to the *NL* type, its occurrence is almost confined to Part I; the only unquestionably *NL* poem in Part II is the drastically post-dated 322. Metrically, this type is represented by four canzoni (28, 53, 119, 128) and a dozen sonnets. Understandably, there is no *NL* sestina. Thus while the non-amorous poems are almost confined to Part I, the penitential theme is marked out from the start, by the Prologue-sonnet 1, for a major role in the book as a whole. In Part I, after *Padre del ciel*, 62 (self-dated, as we have seen, as of 1338), 80, 81 and 142, this theme comes to a kind of quiet climax with 189, *Passa la nave mia*, dated by Wilkins 1342–3. It then disappears from Part I, but is powerfully reasserted by the sombre canzone that opens Part II, no. 264 – in effect a moral stock-taking by the poet on his entry into late middle age and at the prospect of approaching death, the prospect brought home to him by the plague of 1348. Then the penitential mood recedes – so far, at any rate, as it had entailed a repudiation of Laura – before the resurgence of Laura in her new *post mortem* role of heavenly visitant, consoler and counsellor; the role and theme that come to final expression in the delicate canzone 359, the effect of which, however, is at once strikingly counter-balanced by the long, inconclusive debate of 360. There follow three sonnets which, while acknowledging Laura's heavenly state (especially 362) amount in effect to a farewell, which is also, so far as the *Canzoniere* is concerned, a final detachment from her – or better, from her beauty, of which his folly had made a spell-binding 'Medusa' (366.111–12); thus clearing the ground for the final repudiation – in the sense indicated – and repentance of 364–6.

As for the *NL* type, it had involved, as we have seen, four principal interconnected themes: the cult of Rome; detestation of the Avignon Curia; Italian patriotism; literary fame; of which themes the major expressions in the *Canzoniere* are, respectively, nos. 53, 136–8, 128 and 119.

As will be shown in section 3, the general design of the *Canzoniere*, its bipartite division and interweaving of themes, is already clear in the earliest extant MS of the book while still in process of formation, the so-called Chigi MS, now in the Vatican Library, which contains the *Canzoniere* in the form it had acquired by 1362. In this form, Part I, containing 174 poems, ended with no. 189, *Passa la nave mia*; while Part II ran from 264 to 304. Already included, then, were virtually all the poems of the *NL* type, and, of the *AL* type, all those in Part I, plus no. 264. This means that by the early 1360s Petrarch had little to add, thematically, to his collection apart from (a) some enrichment of his portrait of Laura in Part I; (b) the section containing premonitions of her death, nos. 248–63; (c) the completion of his image of Laura in her Part II *post mortem* role; (d) the debate-canzone 360; (e) the penitential conclusion, 355, 364–6.

Of course, just what he was repenting of has yet to be defined. The crucial question may be put thus: is there anything in Petrarch's attachment to Laura that is *not* repudiated in the final canzone, *Vergine bella*, 366 – in particular, in the two lines (111–12) most antagonistic to Laura: 'Medusa e l'error mio m'an fatto un sasso / d'umor vano stillante' (Medusa and my error have made me a stone dripping with vain moisture [tears])? 'Medusa' is of course Laura in some sense, or something closely connected with her. But precisely in what sense? Or what precisely is that 'something'? This is surely the fundamental question to which the entire *Canzoniere* has been leading. Nor is it an unanswerable question, provided we view it in the context of the poet's love story as a whole. So let us examine this story stage by stage; on the assumption that, as set out in the *Canzoniere*, it was intended to make coherent sense – to reveal, on examination, some pattern of succession and development. The alternative to such an assumption would be a purely 'aesthetic' reading of the book; and to that I would rather not simply resign myself. And that some such pattern was in fact intended by the poet is suggested, to say the least, by the series of self-dated poems success-ively recalling, as we have seen, the first encounter with Laura on Good Friday 1327; and then again by the Prologue-sonnet and by the bipartite division of the book. But Petrarch leaves it to the reader to discern more deeply. As a first step then to such a discernment, I

divide the material as follows (with, as will appear, some slight overlapping of the second division by the first, and of the third by the
second): nos. 1–142; 143–263; 264–366.

The First Section: Canzoniere 1–142

A little chronology is indispensable here, and so some repetition of
things said in chapter 1, and anticipation of section 3 of the present
chapter. First then, as to the poems themselves. While a few in this
series may have been drafted before 1330, the first poem datable with
certainty is no. 10, written in the spring/summer of that year. The
date of 2 is doubtful; 3–4 and perhaps 5 were almost certainly added
much later. The self-dated poems in this series are the sestina 30
(1334), the canzone 50 (1337), the sonnets 62 (1338), 79 (1340), 101
(1341), 107 (1342), 118 (1343), 122 (1344). This suggests a date in
the mid or later forties for no. 142, the sestina *A la dolce ombra de le
belle frondi*; it is written, at any rate, as from the standpoint of one who
feels his youth to be long past: line 27, 'many years'. Next, as to the
circumstances of Petrarch's life. We should take account of his fairly
prolonged absences from Avignon and Provence, Laura's city and
country, between 1327 and 1347: the journey to northern Europe in
1333; to Rome between late in 1336 and the summer of 1337; to
Rome again, followed by the stay in or near Parma, from early 1341
to the spring of 1342; the journey to Naples late in 1343, followed by
nearly two years in North Italy – in all six years out of twenty spent
away from Provence. Some of these journeys, or events connected
with them – the Roman coronation, for example, in the spring of
1341 – are obviously reflected in poems of this period. It is less obvious,
but seems to me very probable, to say the least, that certain facts and
experiences in Petrarch's private life are reflected in such more or less
overtly religious poems as the madrigal 54, the sonnets 62 and 81,
the sestine 80 and 142, the canzone 70. I refer in particular to the
poet's friendship, dating from the early 1330s, with Dionigi da Borgo
S. Sepolcro, the Augustinian friar who introduced him to St
Augustine's *Confessions* (*Prose*, pp.1132–4) and is the 'father'
addressed in the famous Mt Ventoux letter, *Fam.* IV, 1; to Petrarch's
close study in the mid-1330s of Augustine's *De vera religione*;[56] to the
birth of his two children, Giovanni in 1336 and Francesca in 1342–3;
and to the retirement into a monastery, in 1343, of his much loved
brother Gherardo. These facts help us to understand Petrarch's
poetry of the 1330s and 1340s in so far as it expresses a heart divided
against itself – the tension and spiritual conflict that comes most

clearly to the surface in poems like *Padre del ciel* (62 – see also 80, 81
and 142). Such poems are not to be accounted for merely by
Petrarch's having been a cleric and Laura another man's wife. A
crucial factor surely was his freely chosen theological formation,
however limited this so far was; in particular the already strong
influence on his mind of certain writings of Augustine. I shall return
to this point presently. Meanwhile there is another factor also to be
kept in mind, I mean that quality of reserve in Laura to which the
Canzoniere incessantly bears witness, whether fretfully or with
admiration; though in this earlier part of the book it is fretfulness,
not to say exasperation, that easily predominates; Laura's reserve
being represented in poem after poem as coldness, hardness, indifference, implacable aloofness. The nobler term chastity, 'castità',
incidentally makes its first appearance as late as the last line of the
last poem in Part 1: 263.14; nor is 'casta' said of Laura before 228.10.
The general tone, in this respect, of the earlier poems is set by the
'attack' of the second sestina, *Giovene donna*:

> Giovene donna sotto un verde lauro
> vidi piú biancha et piú fredda che neve
> non percossa dal sol molti et molt'anni...
>
> [A young woman under a green laurel I saw, whiter and colder
> than snow untouched by the sun for many, many years...].

That Petrarch carnally desired Laura is proved by the last stanza of
the first sestina (22.31–3):

> Con lei foss'io da che si parte il sole,
> et non ci vedess'altri che le stelle,
> sol una nocte, et mai non fosse l'alba!...[57]
>
> [Would that I could be with her from when the sun goes down,
> with no other witness than the stars, and might the dawn never
> come!...]

But normally this craving is masked or sublimated, either in terms of
the Apollo/Daphne myth and the cult of the laurel – which Petrarch
made very much his own (nos. 5–6, the long autobiographical
canzone 23, and nos. 30, 34, 60, etc.) – or in the more conventional
manner labelled *stilnovismo* of seeing the woman as supernaturally
'radiant' (*Prose*, p.136), the radiance showing especially in the eyes
but also in the 'divine bearing' (126.57) of the whole person – face,
smile, speech, flowing hair, breasts, arms, hands and feet (37; 71–3;
90; 126 and 127); all of which has become a sign, a pointer to heaven
(13; 72.2–3; 73.67ss.). And involved in both sublimations, but
breaking through time and again with expressions of weariness or

disgust (6; 32; 60; 93) is a steady current of restless desire (6.1–8; 16; 50, etc.). Restlessness is of course a *leitmotiv* of the *Canzoniere*, but more especially of Part I, where the poet is more at grips with his 'fierce desire' (62.3), now struggling against it, now acquiescing, now wavering between surrender and resistance. Indeed, the variation of mood from poem to poem is so marked as strongly to suggest that Petrarch intended it as his way of witnessing to the truth of the great affirmation at the beginning of his master Augustine's *Confessions*, 'Thou hast made us for Thyself, Lord, and our heart is restless until it rests in Thee'. Much then of the *Canzoniere* is dominated by dissatisfaction – with Laura, with the poet himself, with the human condition as such. Moreover, it was a dissatisfaction consciously fostered and cherished, as we are told in *Secretum* II, with 'gloomy pleasure' (*Prose*, p.106). And as pleasure in sorrow gives sorrow permanence, so Petrarch's propensity to 'feed on tears' (ibid. pp.106–128; *Canz.* 93.14; 229.14) becomes an element in that fixity in restlessness of some of his most characteristic poetry (22; 50; 129; 135).

That is a very rough thematic outline of *Canz.* 2–142, so far as these poems bear on Laura. Now, in all this varied material is any *story* discernible? Any interior development such as the series of self-dated poems that punctuate the decade 1334–44 might lead one, after all, to expect? *Pace* U. Bosco with his influential *dictum* that the Petrarch we know in his works is static, unchanging, 'senza storia',[58] I think it possible to trace in the *Canzoniere* the outlines of a moral autobiography, however faint and uncertain as to details and dates.

All or nearly all of *Canz.* 6–53 had been written when Petrarch got back from Rome in the summer of 1337; and most of these poems have to do with Laura. Now while they express a variety of moods and feelings – a sense of frustration predominating – not one, with the possible exception of *Io temo sì* (39), expresses or implies repentance, in the sense of renunciation, on moral or religious grounds, of something desired. Yet we know that from 1333, if not earlier, Petrarch had been familiar with that great classic of repentance Augustine's *Confessions*; and that c. 1335 (as noted above) he had studied and applied to his own case (as the notes in his copy of the work show) the same saint's *De vera religione*. Again, the *Confessions* play a central part in the account Petrarch gives of his own young manhood, through the decade 1326–36, in the great Mt Ventoux letter (*Prose*, pp.830–844), self-dated 26 April 1336 but certainly written, in its present form, a good deal later.[59] But more to our immediate purpose than

the letter's exact date are three outstanding and obvious features of
its content. First, this is thoroughly penitential in the sense defined;
and the thing most repented of is precisely the attachment to Laura
(*Prose*, p.838: 'Nondum michi...') – the mother or mothers of his
natural children being left in decent obscurity. Next, there are the
two events that stand out in the account of the ascent of the mountain:
Petrarch's being easily outstripped by his younger brother Gherardo,
and the marvellous view they both obtained from the summit, which
led in turn to Petrarch's opening at random his copy of the *Confessions* (x, 8), and finding himself reading, with amazement, 'And
men go afar to marvel at the height of mountains, at the mighty
waves of the sea, at the long course of great rivers, at the vast ocean
and the circling stars – and leave themselves unnoticed!' But the
prolonged description of his own laboured, faltering ascent, as compared with Gherardo's rush to the summit (*Prose*, pp.834–6), has
already made it clear, in view of Gherardo's choice of the monastic
life, that the brothers' actual climb of Mt Ventoux – granted that it
really took place – has become in the letter the symbol of a spiritual
ascent.[60] Now Gherardo became a Carthusian in April 1343; so that
if, as can hardly be doubted, the letter is in part an allegory of that
event, it must of course have been written later. And Billanovich has
shown a number of reasons, too complicated to be gone into here, for
pushing the date still closer to the early 1350s;[61] in other words, to the
crucial period 1348–52, during which Petrarch first gave organic
form and shape to the *Canzoniere*, fixing the bipartite division and
arranging in ordered sequence a substantial portion of Part I –
reaching perhaps as far as no. 142 – together with the first 30 or so
poems in Part II.[62] And critical opinion has in the main followed
Billanovich, at least as regards his shifting the probable date of *Fam.*
IV, I to c. 1350;[63] which is tantamount to regarding it as at least
probable that the penitential reflections on the decade 1326–36,
contained in the Mt Ventoux letter were roughly contemporary
with the choice and arrangement of the poems we are now concerned
with, *Canz.* 1–142. The relevant passage is as follows (Petrarch has
just described the view from the mountain's summit):

> I began to say to myself: Today completes the tenth year since
> you left Bologna [April, 1326]... How many and profound have
> been the changes in you since then!...The day will perhaps
> come when I shall tell the whole story in a clear and orderly way;
> with those words of your Augustine [he is writing to the
> Augustinian friar, Dionigi da Borgo S. Sepolcro]: 'I wish to

recall my past foulness and the carnal corruption of my soul, not
for love of such things, but that I may love you, my God.' In my
case, to be sure, much remains still uncertain, still troublesome.
What I once loved, I no longer love. Not true! I do love it, but less
than I did. Wrong again: I love it, but with more shame and
more distress. Now I have told the truth; that is how it is: I love,
but it is a love of what I would rather not love, would rather
hate. I love indeed, but unwillingly and under constraint,
grieving and lamenting; experiencing in my misery the truth
of that famous line: 'I'll hate if I can; if not, I'll love unwillingly'.[64]

Such was the position, then, in the spring of 1336, Petrarch being
nearly thirty-two; it being now nine years since the 'innamoramento'.
He then says when the change for the better began in him; it was less
than three years previously – let us say, in mid-1333. And then,
looking forward, he reckons that he can hope to be pretty well rid of
his infatuation – indeed of all lust – by about his fortieth year, that is
eight years hence, in about 1344 (*Prose*, pp.838–40). This prediction,
according to the later Letter to Posterity, turned out to be correct
(*Prose*, p.4); but there are reasons for doubting whether it was so in
fact.[65] Note that the distinction I have implied here between Petrarch's
infatuation (with Laura) and his 'lust(s)' is not drawn in the Ventoux
letter itself. It corresponds to that between 'amor' and 'luxuria' in
the *Secretum*, and between 'amor honestus', 'chaste love', and 'libido',
'lust' in the *Posteritati* (*Prose*, pp.132–88, 98–106, 4). In the *Canzoniere*, since all the love poetry has Laura ostensibly for its object,
and since the penitential poems make no such discrimination, but
condemn the Laura-love *en bloc*, the distinction is hardly needed;
though of course the critic is free to distinguish, among the love
poems, between the more 'carnal' (e.g. 22) and the more 'spiritual'
(e.g., 263, 309, 359).

Let us see now, briefly, what light the passage cited from the
Ventoux letter can throw on *Canz.* 1–142, on the presumption that
the *Canzoniere* is in substance autobiographical, and that the Prologue-
sonnet *Voi ch'ascoltate* was almost certainly written no *later* than the
Ventoux letter. From the hostile standpoint, then, of this letter
Petrarch's love story would fall into two stages: 1327–33, a total
infatuation with Laura; 1333–6, a gradual liberation from her. Now,
of *Canz.* 1–142 the poems which most closely and clearly seem to
correspond to the second stage are 1, 39, 54, 62, 79–81, 142. To the
first stage would answer 8–9, 11–26, 29–31, 33–8; above all the

exceptionally long canzone 23, *Nel dolce tempo*, the first half of which (down to line 89) can be dated as early c. 1330; and which is all a sustained application of the Ovidian 'metamorphosis' (transformation) motif to Petrarch's case; in terms mostly of woe and dismay but with no hint of repentance, rather with a solemn renewal, in the long *congedo*, of total commitment to the Laura-laurel. As already remarked, this Daphnean motif is recurrent in Petrarch's earlier love poetry (see especially 30 and 34). Another, incidental early feature is the half-profane playing with religious themes and imagery of 12.9–11, 16, 25, 26, 31, 208.12–14 – though the placing of this last sonnet, *Rapido fiume*, could indicate a later date (1345?). Certainly of the first Avignon period, 1333–7, however, are such brilliant compositions as *A qualunque animale* (22), and *Verdi panni* (29), and the two 'travel-canzoni' 37 (1333?) and 50 (1337). I pass over 1–5 which, as a group, are probably of the late 1340s; and 6 and the exquisite 32, which, though certainly early poems, might be called, in their very different ways, incipiently 'penitential'.

A 'first leap' away from 'the fair eyes where Love and my death dwell', is alluded to in the letter-sonnet *Io temo sì* (39). It was made 'a long time since' (line 4) and this and the apology in lines 12–14 for delay in returning to Avignon suggest that Petrarch was writing from Vaucluse after his return from Rome in the summer of 1337, and to his employer Cardinal Colonna; and that the 'leap' had been the journey into N. Europe in 1333. This would perfectly tally with the important *Epist. metrica* I, 6 (1338?) with its long account of Petrarch's efforts – ending with the retirement to Vaucluse in 1337 – to shake off the obsession with Laura (*Rime*, pp.726–34). Against this background the intensely penitential *Padre del ciel* (62) comes as no surprise; self-dated as it is on Good Friday 1338. But already Petrarch may have written the allegorical madrigal *Perch'al viso d'amor* (54), so remarkable for its echoes both of Augustine's *Confessions* and, I think, also of the *Inferno*.[66] Yet with the next poem, *Quel foco*, set in deliberate contrast with 54, we hear of a grave relapse, a second and worse 'error' (55.6, cf. Matthew 12.45), a surrender, apparently, to the 'blind desire' of 56.1; and cf. 57.9–11. Laura's painful aloofness, implied in these last two sonnets, might seem sufficiently explained by the revulsion from her influence evinced in 39, 54, and 62; but there was another factor to trouble their relationship in 1337: the unknown woman who presented Petrarch with his first child, apparently on his return from Rome in that year.[67] Yet in the previous year, before leaving for Rome in December, and apparently at peace with Laura, he had written the two sonnets relating to the portrait of her by Simone Martini, 77 and 78.

To the same period may belong the celebrated 'canzoni of the eyes', 71–3, which take sublimation to an extreme point through a sustained transposition to the experience of mortal beauty of the language of religious ardour and ecstasy. Anyone with any reading in the theology of Grace, or simply any knowledge of the Christian liturgy and the biblical texts it draws upon, will recognise the kind of language Petrarch is using when, for example, addressing Laura's eyes he declares:

> Fugge al vostro apparire angoscia et noia,
> et nel vostro partir tornano insieme...
> Onde s'alcun bel frutto
> nasce di me, da voi vien prima il seme:
> io per me son quasi un terreno asciutto,
> còlto da voi, e 'l pregio è vostro in tutto.
>   (71.97–105)

[At your appearance all anguish and distress flee, and at your departure they return together... Thus if any good fruit is born in me, from you first comes the seed: in myself I'm like a parched soil that you till, and the praise is all yours.]

Or again, with the emphasis on the joy enkindled by those eyes:

> Vaghe faville, angeliche, beatrici
> de la mia vita, ove 'l piacer s'accende
> che dolcemente mi consuma et strugge:
> come sparisce et fugge
> ogni altro lume dove 'l vostro splende,
> cosí de lo mio core,
> quando tanta dolcezza in lui discende,
> ogni altra cosa, ogni penser va fore,
> et solo ivi con voi rimanse Amore.
>   (72.37–45)

[Lovely angelic sparks that make blessed my life, where the joy is kindled that sweetly consumes and destroys me: just as every other light vanishes and flees when yours shines out, so from my heart, when such sweetness descends into it, every other thing, every thought, departs, and alone there with you remains Love.]

Or again, describing the effect on him of Laura's smile, with a phrase that at once calls to mind the Pauline 'peace of God' (Philippians 4.7, cf. Colossians 3.15, Romans 15.33, etc.):

> Pace tranquilla senza alcuno affanno,

> simile a quella ch'è nel ciel eterna,
> move da lor inamorato riso...
>   (73.67–9)

[Tranquil peace, utterly untroubled, like the eternal peace of
Heaven, proceeds from their smile of love.]

It was with such texts in mind that 'Augustinus' in the *Secretum*
taunts 'Franciscus': 'Praise the little woman as much as you like; *I*
won't object! Call her a queen, a saint, a goddess...' (*Prose*, p.142).
Or, more seriously, when he charges his pupil with worshipping
Laura in place of God (ibid. pp.146, 160). But perhaps already in the
Canzoniere, with the rational detached self-criticism of *Lasso me* (70,
to which I shall return later) and with *S'al principio* (79, self-dated
1340) we are at the start of a new upsurge of repentance which comes
to splendid expression in 80 and 81. What is remarkable about the
sestina 80, *Chi è fermato*, is first, the entire absence of any asperity
towards Laura herself – its tone in her regard is quite different from
that of the Ventoso letter, for example – and secondly, the consciousness of maturity, in both years and experience, that it evinces. The
poet's youth, and Laura with it, have been left far far behind and he is
out in mid sea, his eyes held by certain far-off signals, 'insegne', of
'that *other* life' such as, using the *same* metaphor, he had once fancied
he saw shining in the eyes of Laura (lines 19–24, cf. 73.45–51). In
the sonnet *Io son sì stanco* (81) the metaphor of the sea voyage is
replaced by the ancient Platonic and biblical image of the wings of the
soul (*Phaedrus*, 246; Psalm 55.6). This religious aspiration then drops
out of sight during the next 60 poems (if we except stanza 7 of *Italia
mia*, 128), only to reappear – under another metaphor, that of the two
contrasted trees, the laurel and the Cross – in the next sestina, 142,
A la dolce ombra. During this period, with Laura back at the centre of
attention, there are two principal themes: reminiscence, and then,
emerging within it and from it, bewilderment and dismay. The first
theme is developed in various ways, for example, in *Erano i capei d'oro*
(90, and also in 125–6, 127); the second appears most notably in *Di
pensier in pensier* (129) and *Qual più diversa* (135). The reminiscence
may bear particularly on *changes* in Laura since the original 'innamoramento' (90) or simply on her beauty as such with relatively little
attention to moments in, or the passage of, time (127), or it may
focus, ecstatically, on some privileged moment in the past (126).
Presupposed to both thematic developments is the enchanting
experience evoked in *Chiare fresche e dolci acque* (126.40–65; cf. 90.1–
13; 127.80–4; 129.34–9, 60–1); the enduring effect of which, how-

ever, is present distress and confusion (90.13–14; 129 and 135 passim).

The Second Section: Canzoniere 135–263

The penitential poetry in Part 1 reaches its climax with 142. In other respects however Part 1 can be more appropriately divided, as we shall see, somewhere between 129 and 135.[68]

Petrarch was back in Provence by the late autumn of 1345, and returned to Italy in November 1347. Much of these two years he passed at Vaucluse writing the *De vita solitaria* and, with his brother's example in mind, the *De otio religioso*, in praise of monasticism. He was now increasingly detached from the Avignon Curia. To this period belong most of the poems between 130 and 263. No less than 110 are sonnets, with 62 at a stretch, apart from a ballata, between 143 and 205. Grouping by themes is inconspicuous – except for the last 18 of the series – and chronologically several poems are clearly out of place. To some extent this rather random arrangement may be due to the fact that when in April 1367 Petrarch's copyist Malpaghini ceased work on the fair copy he went on with the job himself, but did so intermittently, as the fancy took him (*Sen.* XIII, 11).

What novelty, if any, is discernible in the style or the content, or both, of this second half of *Canzoniere* 1? As to novelty in style the poem, surely, that will first draw the perceptive reader's attention is the brilliant canzone, 135, *Qual piú diversa e nova*. True, there is much in the manner of this piece that recalls that of earlier poems – notably 29 – but here it is intensified to match a new, or relatively new, theme. The style itself with its close-knit intertwining of difficult rhymes, its intricate syntax and pictorial brilliance, Petrarch certainly derived in part from Dante's 'petrose' (*Rime* C–CIII), and through them from Arnaut Daniel with his 'dir strano e bello', 'the strange beauty of his verse' (*Tr. Cupidinis* IV, 42), and in part of course from the classics, notably Horace in his *Odes*. And the term 'strano', 'strange', applied to Arnaut's style, is plainly suited to Petrarch's in *Qual più diversa* (135), and even more aptly to the subject-matter to express which this style was purposely chosen, that is, the *strangeness* of the lover's condition – the theme virtually proposed by the five preceding sonnets after its first magnificent elaboration in canzone 129, *Di pensier in pensier, di monte in monte.*

This then is the initial theme of the second half of *Canzoniere* 1; from which, as from a background, particular aspects of that 'strangeness' successively detach themselves. To some of these we are already accustomed, so that our attention is held only by some special felicity of style or diction. So it is in 141, treating of the conflict between reason and desire; or in 161, 178, 214, where the irrational factor stressed is illusion; or in 164, 180, 211, dwelling, respectively, on the opposition of joy and grief, soul and body, hope and despair. A shade of novelty appears when the emphasis shifts from the divided self to the occasion of its divisions and confusions, the 'overwhelming beauty' of Laura (143.12–14; compare 165, 173, 196–7); or where the inner conflict reaches an extremity of disintegration and confusion (152, 195, 198, 211). But the love-induced 'strangeness' most characteristic of this part of the *Canzoniere* is the lover's being content to suffer in his love, even to die of it: 'Ché bel fin fa chi ben amando more', 'for his end is fine who dies loving well' (140.14). On this paradox conclude epigrammatically a number of poems (140–141, 163, 209, 217, 229; and cf. 167.8). And with one or other aspect of this strangeness there enters from time to time, as we shall see, a sharp sense of spiritual danger.

The greater part of this second half of *Canzoniere* I – to within less than 20 poems from the end at 263 – represents Petrarch's final celebration of Laura in her lifetime.[69] This has suggested to R. Amaturo a parallel with Dante's 'praise-poetry' in the *Vita Nuova*.[70] But Amaturo himself points out a capital difference – that whereas for Dante the essential precondition of his writing 'pure praise' of Beatrice was a renunciation of all self-concern, a pure contemplation of the Beatricean 'miracle' (*V.N.* XVIII–XIX, XXVI), in Petrarch's case a torment of self-concern continually dogs and frets the worship of Laura. Only in the last few poems of the present section is he free from it; and that may well be because when he wrote those last poems, or most of them, Laura had long been dead (see note 34). Even the 'strange' happiness he claimed to find – in the poems cited above – in the sufferings that love brought him would have been regarded by Dante as no fit theme for 'praise-poetry'.[71]

But it is time we looked more closely at the Laura shown us between, say, 143 and the 'presentiment' series that begins at 246. The first thing to note is that while the nostalgic recall of Laura as she was in youth, at the time of the 'innamoramento', so vivid in *Erano i capei d'oro* (90) or *Chiare fresche e dolci acque* (126), has not quite disappeared, it is no longer much in evidence (cf. 143.9–11; 156, 175, 190;207.53–5). Certainly Petrarch is ageing (175.11; 195; 212; 221), but Laura herself, in these poems, is curiously timeless; unaffected in general by the chances and changes of life, including relations with her lover. As such, and as an object contemplated and celebrated, she is a nucleus of certain qualities which may be described as follows (I give references for the reader with leisure to pursue the matter in detail for himself):

1) She is the epitome of all created beauty (159.1–4; 160;[72] 165; 173.4; 185; 188.3–4; 193.12–14) and of natural perfection in general (215.1–6; 246–8, with this last sonnet recapitulating the entire theme).

2) She is a trace of the Divine Beauty (144.7–8; 159–60; 167.14), so that the sight of her can be compared to the vision of God (151.5–6; 156; 191–2; 193.1–4. Theologically, these last three poems verge on idolatry, and if reminiscent of the *Paradiso*, are not so in this respect, Dante being always careful to keep Beatrice in her creaturely place).

3) She is a trace and token of other divine perfections: luminosity[73] (163.9–11; 204); joy (173.4); sublime goodness (215; 228.9–14; 247.12–13).

4) Finally, she surpasses in virtue or beauty, or both, all the heroes and heroines sung of by the greatest poets (186–7; recapitulated in 260); indeed human speech is quite inadequate to her beauty (198.12–14) and other perfections (215.1–8; 247).[74]

To go carefully through these texts is to see that while Laura is praised for both beauty and virtue, the chief emphasis is on her beauty; and naturally so, in this part of the *Canzoniere* (in Part II – indeed already by the end of Part I – the emphasis is reversed). Now, Petrarch's response here to that beauty is manifold but through it all runs a subtly modulated sense of danger. For all her virtue, her 'innocence' (*Prose*, p.146, and cf. no. 207, 80–4), Laura alive in the body is in effect a temptress. Such is the conclusion of the famous debate in *Secretum* III; such the *general* drift of the *Canzoniere*; such in particular is the implication of much of the 'praise-poetry' of the second half of Part I, and especially of the poems referred to under heads 2 and 3 of the foregoing analysis.

The sense of danger is clear, of course, in the two most overtly 'penitential' poems in the present series, the sonnet *Passa la nave mia* (189) and the sestina *Anzi tre dì* (214). While the motif of the former is the usual one of restless, futile desire (rendered particularly memorable here by the first line), that of the latter is the loss of spiritual freedom. Entering a wood in springtime, the poet finds himself caught in a dark tangle of thorn and briar from which only God can deliver him (lines 28–36; cf. *Prose*, p.58). The lament for lost liberty, never far from the surface in Petrarch's chafings against love, is here unusually explicit. As to the other motif, that of restless desire, I would draw attention not only to *Passa la nave mia* but also to *Voglia mi sprona* (211), chiefly because of the incisive clarity of the second quatrain. (Note how 'vago' here anticipates 214.31, and how the rare word 'laberinto', line 14, anticipates the tangle-wood imagery of the sestina, rather as the ship-adrift imagery of 80 had anticipated, from a greater distance, that of 189):

> regnano i sensi, et la ragion è morta;
> de l'un vago desio l'altro risorge.
> [the senses reign and reason is dead; one yearning desire gives birth to another.]

Still more interesting are the danger-signals given out by the 'praise-poems' themselves. The first principle of Christian morals is 'Thou shalt love the Lord thy God with all thy heart…all thy soul… all thy mind…all thy strength' (Mark 12.30). Petrarch had not only been brought up on this principle, he had studied its careful elucidation by the Christian Fathers, Augustine in particular. When, then, he came to write of Laura's beauty 'I care for no other good, I desire no other food' (165.8), he must have been aware of the latent impiety. In *Secretum* III he admitted as much, where the whole point of the debate consists in his admitting finally that, 'stupefied' by that beauty, he had risked substituting Laura for God as the final term of desire (*Prose*, pp.144–52). In Augustinian terms he had turned a 'utendum' into a 'fruendum', for 'frui…est amore alicui inhaerere propter seipsam', 'to enjoy is to cleave lovingly to something simply in and for itself' – the very definition of sin when the 'something' is less than God.[75]

What I am suggesting then is that the function in the *Canzoniere* of such poems as *Come 'l candido piè* (165), and others I shall cite, is to witness to sins and errors from which the book as a whole records the poet's conversion. They flash out danger signals intended to alert the reader not to be wholly taken in by their celebrations, however splendid, of Laura's beauty:

> Per divina bellezza indarno mira
> chi gli occhi de costei già mai non vide

'He looks in vain for divine beauty / who never saw her eyes' (159.9–10) may seem a harmless hyperbole; and perhaps that is all it originally was. It is the recurrence of such 'divinisations' of Laura, within the penitential framework of the *Canzoniere* as a whole (and in the light also of *Secretum III*) that renders them suspect; that and certain suggestions latent, as I think, in terms and images employed in her

representation. The assimilation of the sight of her to a 'divine' vision
(159.9–10, already discernible at 123.5–8 and 126.53–63) comes out
most clearly in the sonnet 191, *Sì come eterna vita è veder Dio*; though
qualified here in terms of duration, the vision of God being 'life
eternal', that of Laura transient. But this is the latter's *only* defect:

> Et se non fusse il suo fuggir sì ratto,
> più non demanderei...

['if its flight were not so swift, *I would ask for nothing more*']; for the
present, at any rate, it is all he desires or hopes for (lines 1, 9–10, 1–8).
The same theme returns in *Pasco la mente* (193), and again with a
qualification; this time the implication, lines 12–14, that Laura
belongs to the sublunary created world, epitomising as she does all
that is best in it. Where then is the danger-signal? Surely, in lines 3–4:

> ché, sol mirando, oblio ne l'alma piove
> d'ogni altro dolce, et Lethe al fondo bibo
> [simply gazing at her, oblivion rains into my heart of all other
> sweetness, and I drink Lethe to the dregs.]

This last phrase, continuing the other classical allusion, to the food
and drink of the gods (line 2), points to the quatrain's latent meaning –
that the earthly delight offered by Laura quite puts out of mind the
heavenly sort enjoyed by the gods (note '*every* other', line 4), so that
Petrarch can feel no envy even of 'Giove' (God), nor, by implication,
any desire for whatever share in heavenly joy which God may in fact
be offering. All of which, if read in the light of *Secretum III* (*Prose*,
pp.152–4), points to that 'God-forgetfulness' which is the gravest
charge that 'Augustinus' brings against the poet in this work. Again,
in the magnificent quatrains of *Mirando 'l sol* (173), which is all a
study of fascination in the old, strong sense of coming under a spell,
the same two objects of desire, earthly and heavenly, human and
divine, are opposed; and this time more poignantly. Looking into
Laura's eyes, Petrarch is drawn, as in ecstasy, into his '*earthly* paradise';
only to find it no less bitter than sweet; so that in it he sees, as in
miniature, the *illusory* beatitude which is the best that all this world
can offer (lines 1–8; cf. the Prologue-sonnet, 13–14). In two other
sonnets the danger-signal is held in reserve till the last line. In *Quando
Amor i belli occhi* the sweetness of Laura's singing is suddenly likened
to that of the Sirens: 'questa sola fra noi del ciel sirena' (167.14).
True, she is a 'heavenly siren', but the epithet is touched, surely, with
irony.[76] And in *Grazie ch'a pochi* (213), after a conventional enumera-
tion of Laura's charms, both moral and physical, these are all in the
end reduced to 'magi', 'wizards', 'magicians'. The shadow of witch-

craft falls more darkly still over 179 and 197, with that image of
Medusa which will epitomise the 'anti-Laura' position in 366.111–112:

> L'aura celeste…
>
> pò quello in me, che nel gran vecchio mauro
> Medusa quando in selce transformollo.
>
>   (197.1, 5–6)

[The heavenly breeze…has the power over me that Medusa
had over the old Moorish giant, when she turned him to
flint.][77]

But, leaving this 'witch' aspect of Laura, I turn to a subtle linking,
in 188, *Almo sol*, of her beauty with the Genesis story of the Fall. This
sonnet, a relatively late variation on the Apollo–Daphne theme,
begins with an address to the sun (Apollo) about a laurel (Daphne-
Laura) planted by Petrarch in his garden:

> Almo Sol, quella fronde ch'io sola amo,
> tu prima amasti, or sola al bel soggiorno
> verdeggia, et senza par poi che l'addorno
> suo male et nostro vide in prima Adamo.

[Life-giving Sun, you first loved that tree which alone I love;
now she alone [as an evergreen in this winter season] flourishes
green-leaved in this fair place, unequalled [in beauty] since
Adam first saw his fair bane and ours.]

Note the 'logic' of this extraordinary quatrain. As the evergreen
laurel is uniquely beautiful in the wintry scene, so Laura is unique
among all women present or past, Eve alone excepted; Eve, that is, as
Adam first saw her, newly created and unfallen; who nevertheless –
indeed in a sense just because of this fresh perfection of hers – was the
occasion of Adam's fall from Grace ('l'addorno suo *male*'), and so of
all the sins of us, Adam's progeny. Much further on, at 354.12–14,
the same comparison of Laura to the unfallen Eve will be made, but
applied differently. There the sense will be: in Laura alive I saw all
womanly perfection, as Adam saw it in Eve; she being now dead,
there is nothing left on earth to hinder me from turning wholly to
God. But in *Almo Sol*, Laura is still of course alive, so that she, or what
she represents, is a present danger. The moral point is all in the
oxymoron 'addorno male', 'fair evil', as extended by the two
possessive pronouns, 'suo…e nostro' (3–4) to take in and poetically
account for the entire history of mankind in its fallen state – the evergreen tree, and so the woman whose emblem it is, becoming a symbol
of the whole created world in its beauty as a good set over against,
and in rivalry with, the one transcendent and properly Divine Good

(cf. 1.14; 366.85–6; Dante, *Purgatorio* XVII, 133, XXXI 34–5). This moral point once made, the sonnet proceeds on a different tack.

Such a Laura-figure would of course be an allegory of evil; and if I am right, the construction of such an allegory was what Petrarch in fact intended in the present poetic series. Observe that 'evil' here means self-deception, error, illusion. All the fault was on Petrarch's side (cf. *Prose*, pp.144–6). The real Laura was innocent, *his* 'Laura' only a projection of self-delusion. This he had already clearly seen and stated in *Lasso me* (70), a poem whose deeper import has often been overlooked[78] and the last two stanzas of which, recanting the first three, I render, rather freely, as follows: 'What am I saying? Where am I? What is deceiving me / except myself and immoderate desire? / If I were to pass through the heavens one by one, / no planet would compel me to weep. / If a mortal veil [my body] dulls my sight, / what fault is that of the stars, / or other lovely things? / Close by me is my daily and nightly tormentor / … All things that make the world lovely / came out good from the hands of the Eternal Artist, / but I, short-sighted as I am, / am dazzled by the beauty manifest around me; / and if ever I do return to a sight of the true splendour, / my eye cannot stay fixed on it, / weakened as it is / through my own fault…' (lines 31–48).

The argument is Augustinian; Petrarch had found it, probably in 1335, in *De vera religione* XX–XXIII, where Augustine finds the root of evil in illusion. In themselves all things are good, in their degree and kind. The material world in all its beauty is simply an unfolding through time of the timeless beauty of the Divine Mind. To see it thus is to see it aright; and this the rational creature would do with ease and joy were he not caught and held by sensible appearances. As it is, he succumbs to illusion, mistaking the lesser for the greater, means for ends, effects for their Cause: he seeks perfect joy where it cannot be found, and so passes, inevitably, from illusion to dis-illusion, and thence to the false judgement which condemns the whole world with Solomon's 'all is vanity' (Ecclesiastes 1.2); whereas the only 'vanity' really involved is in the minds of those who place their *summum bonum* in material things which are good indeed, but only as traces of the Divine Good. Augustine will have no truck with any blaming of the material world for human ills (the line taken by Leopardi, for example). At their root is misdirected desire, which in the last analysis is culpable. Pessimism and determinism are closely interrelated errors. This teaching Petrarch tries to apply to himself in the *Secretum*: in the matter of determinism in Book I, in that of pessimism in Book II (*Prose*, pp.28–46, 106–28). He had the sense never to try to tackle either issue philosophically, to speak only as a moralist. But even so he is very seldom found, in the *Canzoniere*, relating moral judgements to a vision of the cosmos as a whole; as he does in *Lasso me* (70), and again in the sonnet 355, *O tempo, o ciel*. This is the importance of *Lasso me* in particular. Statements made elsewhere, as expressions of passing mood or feeling (or what may appear such) can be brought to it as to a touchstone, for correction or elucidation: for correction as with 22.24, with its astral determinism ('lo mio fermo desir vien da le stelle', 'my unwavering desire is from the stars'); for elucidation as – to take one of many possible examples – the choice of the adjective 'soverchio', 'excessive', 'immoderate' in *Quando io v'odo* (143) and *Chi vuol veder* (248); in the former sonnet to describe Petrarch's pleasure in the beauty of Laura, in the latter the mind-dazzling light she irradiates: 'Ma 'l soverchio piacer, che s'atraversa / a la mia lingua' ('But the overwhelming delight that keeps me from speaking' 143.12); 'l'ingegno offeso dal soverchio lume' ('...my wits overcome by excess of light' 248.13). Both *loci* gain in depth by reference to *Lasso me* (lines 31–2, 44–5). A similar use of the latter poem might be made in respect of two other import-ant words in Petrarchan moral vocabulary: 'vano' (with 'vaneggi-are') and 'errore' (with 'errare') (the former e.g. at 1.6 and 12; 54.2; 62.2; 244.4; 366.112: and the latter at 1.3; 132.12; 224.4; 359.58; 366.111). 'Errore', 'errare' usually retain in Petrarch (as in Dante) some thing of their original Latin sense of wandering, going astray. They are his favourite terms for self-delusion and it is no accident that 'errore' appears in the first and the last poems of the *Canzoniere* (as indeed does 'vano/vaneggiare'). The whole book is penetrated by the vigilant lucidity that Petrarch's use of these terms implies. Even where this vigilance may seem to be relaxed, the very placing of the poems concerned is often enough to show that it is not. Thus 62, *Padre del ciel*, is the corrective to 61, *Benedetto sia 'l giorno*, and the three 'canzoni of the eyes', 71–3, serve as magnificent examples to confirm the lesson contained in *Lasso me*, especially in lines 41–44:

> Tutte le cose di che 'l mondo è adorno
> uscir buone de man del mastro eterno;
> ma me, che cosí adentro non discerno,
> abbaglia il bel che mi si mostra intorno...
> [All things that make the world lovely came out good from the hands of the Eternal Artist, but I, short-sighted, as I am, am dazzled by the beauty manifest around me....]

In such cases it is left to the reader to discern the poet's intentions, comparing poem with poem. Elsewhere, as we have seen in the case of *Lasso me*, one part of a poem explicitly corrects another. A good example of this, again, is in *Ben mi credea*, where having blamed Amor and Laura for his misery, he comes to his senses with a decisive No, it is I who am at fault – 'who ought to have turned away / from that blinding light, and against the sound of the sirens / have stopped my ears...' (207.81–3).

Our survey of the second section of the *Canzoniere* (135–247) – nearly a third of the book – may now be summarised as follows:

1) The centre of interest is Laura's beauty as physically and visibly present. This theme comes to a climax here, especially between 144 and 198, before the premonitions of her death begin with the great sonnet *Chi vuol veder* (248 – for a *post mortem* recapitulation, in memory only, on Laura's body, see 292). Her beauty is celebrated less in itself than in its effects, whether fearful (as e.g. in 152) or beatifying (as in 159, 191, 193, etc.).

2) At least until 228 *Amor co la man*, Laura is presented less as a person than as an object. Very occasionally (as at 193.9–11) she speaks, but we are never told what she says. She scarcely *does* anything – the exquisite close of 160 is an exception proving the rule. All this is in obvious contrast with the disembodied Laura of Part II; to become a person, she had first to die.

3) With Laura's general impersonality goes an abstraction from time and change. This in part is due to two factors – first, that the series of self-dated poems is interrupted between 122 and 212, secondly that the motif of 'sweet memory', which had its perfect expression in the canzone 126 (of which 143, 144 and 207.85–6 serve as reminders) is here much less in evidence.

4) In line with its main theme this series is rich in visual imagery, most of it drawn from the natural world, as is usual in Petrarch whose poetic imagination was that of a countryman steeped in Virgil and Horace. Skyscape or landscape offer comparisons with or settings for Laura's beauty, or for Petrarch's frustration. When she blushes he is reminded at once of sunrise on a cloudless morning and of the rainbow after a shower (144). Elsewhere we see her seated on the grass 'like a flower', then going through the fields 'alone with her thoughts' (160). In the sonnet on the laurel in Petrarch's garden (188), the tercets turn us away from that emblem to watch the shadows falling from the hills at Vaucluse on a winter's evening. In 164 night is 'wheeling her starry chariot' overhead while Petrarch lies sleepless.

In a happier mood there is the splendidly complex image that fills
180, of the two-way contrary movement of river-flow and bird-
flight between opposite ends of earth and sky. But more characteristic of this series are the 'close-ups' – of Laura's eyes (173) or hair
(198; 227) or of her face in which 'in less than a hand's breadth visibly
appears' all imaginable perfection (193.12–14). A 'close-up' is also
the gorgeous Laura-Phoenix figure of 185; a purely descriptive,
amoral piece, as also are 180 and 192. In the extremely sophisticated
L'aura soave (198) the moral point is left implicit in the description of
stupefied bedazzlement (with its marked Dantean echo at lines 5–6);
as it is, more or less, in the description in 152 of the poet's agony and
dread.[79]

5) A number of the more remarkable poems between, say, 156 and
214 seem to give substance to the grave charge of 'God-oblivion'
brought by Petrarch against himself in *Secretum* III (*Prose*, pp.154,
160).

6) Finally, there is the praise of Laura's virtue along with her beauty,
expressed 'stilnovistically' in 154.12–14, and with more originality
in 186 – balancing Laura, as this sonnet does, against Scipio, the hero
of the *Africa*, and by the same token putting the *Canzoniere*, considered at least in its subject-matter, on a level with the Latin epic.
This moral praise of Laura comes into view again in 204, 215, 228,
and above all in 247, preparatory to its triumphant *finale* in 260–3.

The Third Section: Canzoniere 264–366

Of the 103 poems in Part II, 92 are sonnets; there are nine canzoni,
one sestina and one ballata. The canzoni are grouped towards the
beginning and the end (264, 268, 270 and 359, 360, 366) with two
pairs of them in between to break the long sequence of sonnets
(323, 325 and 331, 332).

The canzoni at each end, *I' vo pensando* (264) and *Vergine bella*
(366), are severely self-critical – far more so than the Prologue-
sonnet, 1, which was more a statement of disillusion than a confession
of sin and was not explicitly religious at all; whereas the moral issue,
the choice between good and evil, absolutely dominates *I' vo
pensando*; and *Vergine bella*, is from first to last a prayer.

The bulk of the thematic material in between can be grouped under
four heads: Lament; Apparitions (of Laura); Spiritual Liberation;
Poetry. All four themes are anticipated in the canzone *Che debb'io
far? che mi consigli, Amore?*, 268, Petrarch's major piece in the *genre*
'planctus' already cultivated by Dante and Cino. Petrarch's 'planctus'

is clearly reminiscent of Dante's *Li occhi dolenti* (*Vita Nuova* xxxi) while unmistakably Petrarchan in its tone and rhythm and apparently effortless simplicity.[80] What is noteworthy about its content is, first, the large role played by 'Amor' as the poet's consoler and counsellor, and then the implicit promise, conveyed by Amor from Laura now in heaven, of future communications with her (lines 70–7). This promise, it is hinted, is all that restrains the poet from suicide (lines 67–9; cf. nos. 331–2). It also prepares for the actual apparitions of Laura, which begin in 281; and which, taken together, are the second of the two decisive factors in what I call Petrarch's liberation; the first being the removal of Laura's real body by death (announced in 267). Between that death and the final group of poems, 363–6, the liberation or purification proceeds, under Laura's influence, exerted through the apparitions, in three stages. Petrarch is first freed from despair, then from the carnal desire of Laura, finally from identifying his *summum bonum* with Laura whether carnally or spiritually considered. This is the logical order of the process, but in fact the stages overlap. Even as late as 359, the last and most circumstantially detailed of the apparitions (as distinct from 'visions' – I shall come to this difference presently), Petrarch has to be weaned from sensuality in her regard (lines 56–66); and even the suicidal death-wish returns as late as 331 and 332. But of these three liberations, that from carnal desire is the most subtly represented, as we shall see.

Once Laura's body was removed by death, the dramatic action of the *Canzoniere* required (a) that Petrarch should not forget that lost loveliness, and (b) that, continuing to remember it, he should be divided between, on the one hand, hopeless nostalgia, on the other, the hope of recovering the sight of it eventually in heaven. The former was the pagan alternative, the latter the Christian one based on the doctrine of the Resurrection of the Flesh. The tension between them is proper to Part II. At the same time the persistent memory of Laura as she *had* been involves a continuance of the old conflict between Petrarch's sensuality and the ideal represented by Laura's chastity, the conflict seemingly resolved by the sublimation achieved in the last three sonnets of Part I which had celebrated at once her beauty and her chastity. I say 'seemingly resolved', because through much of Part II the character who says 'I' notably fails to maintain that sublimation in himself. It persists steadily only in the figure of Laura; for certainly the woman of the apparitions is the same woman celebrated in 261–3. This continuity was obviously intended; the three sonnets serving as the prelude to Part II in as much as the whole

of this Part down to 361 (if we omit the debate-canzone 360) shows
Petrarch responding or failing to respond to the example depicted
in those last sonnets in Part I. An essential part of her incomparable
distinction – the physical part, her beauty – could not, of course, be
imitated. As she had not acquired it 'by art', she could not impart it
by teaching. It was her 'luck' to be lovely; the result, then, could only
be contemplated (261.12–14). But the other, deeper element in it,
her virtue – this indeed was an example to learn from (ibid. 5–11). So
we are shown it at work in *Cara la vita* (262), where Laura refutes the
worldly wisdom of an older woman who said that life was more
precious than chastity; for, as Petrarch will say to Laura, concluding
Part I

> L'alta beltà ch'al mondo non à pare
> noia t'è, se non quanto il bel thesoro
> di castità par ch'ella adorni et fregi.
>   (263.12–14)

[Your peerless beauty is irksome to you, save as it adorns and
sets off the fair treasure of your chastity.]

Nevertheless, though her body is now dead and buried, the memory
of it could still inspire a sonnet like 292: 'The eyes I wrote of so
fervently, and the arms and the hands and the feet and the face…the
waving locks of pure, shining gold, and the flash of that angelic smile
…all are a little dust that feels nothing. / And I, I live on…' (lines
1–9).

I have already dwelt a little, in section I of this chapter on the
apparitions of Laura, drawing attention to her human womanly
qualities as a *revenant*; and consequently to the interest attaching to
Canzoniere II as a delineation of spiritual intimacy between a man and
a woman. Here I am more concerned – still confining myself to bare
essentials – with the apparitions as moments in a narrative. As we
have seen, their eventuality was already hinted at in *Che debb'io far*
(268, stanza 7). The first mention of them as actually occurring is in
the two singularly beautiful sonnets *Quante fiate* and *Alma felice* (281–
282); where they are described indeed as already of frequent occurrence; the place being apparently Vaucluse. They are then recalled
in *Discolorato ài, Morte* (283.9–14), with a stress on Laura's purpose
in thus perceptibly 'returning' to her lover; which is, quite simply, to
console him (cf. 282.1–2). There is so far no hint of chiding or
warning. Admonition only begins – introduced with great delicacy –
at the end of 285 ('*praying* that I delay not to raise my soul towards
God', line 13). Meanwhile the scene has changed. Instead of the rural

setting of 281–2, with Laura in it as an object visibly external to the poet, she is now *within* him, 'at the door of the soul' (284.7–8). And with this interiorisation of her presence to him comes the great change in Laura herself, the principal change that she undergoes throughout the entire *Canzoniere*, the change transforming her from the 'Laura-*object*' of Part I (and especially, as we have seen, of its second half) to the 'Laura-*subject*' of Part II (and incidentally of *Tr. Mortis* II). This change is achieved, without the slightest fuss or strain, in the marvellous tercets of *Nè mai pietosa madre* (285). She is revealed as a person in her own right, and at the same time, in all her womanliness (lines 8–10), intimately self-communicating. Nor ever again in the *Canzoniere* – not even in 341.12–14 – does she so merge her life in Petrarch's as in the untranslatable line 12: 'contando i casi de la vita nostra' ('telling over the events of our life'[81] – the best commentary on which is *Tr. Mortis* II, 88–9, 127–53).

After the group 281–5 there is a long gap before the apparitions are resumed at 341. I do not count the superb *Levommi il mio penser* (302) as strictly an apparition-poem – nor yet 362, *Volo con l'ali*. These two sonnets are better called 'visions'; the experiences they describe are the effect, not of a 'downward' movement of Laura from heaven, visiting her lover on earth, but of an 'upward' movement of Petrarch's own spirit to the sight of her in heaven. There is a parallel difference in Dante between the apparition of Beatrice recounted in *Vita Nuova* XXXIX, and the heavenly vision of her described two chapters later in the sonnet *Oltre la spera* – the probable model, incidentally, for *Volo con l'ali*. To the latter poem I shall return apropos of Petrarch's final (in the *Canzoniere*) 'liberation' from Laura. Meanwhile we may note that he prepares us for the vision of *Levommi il mio penser* (302) in 277.9–11 and 287, and for that of *Volo con l'ali* (362) in 346 and, by already closely associating Laura with Christ, in 349.14 and in 357.

Returning to the ten apparition poems – 281–5, then 341–3, which group is rounded off by 356, and above all by 359 – their function is to show Laura as lifting Petrarch out of his dejection and as purifying his love for her from every residue of carnality. The former, consolatory purpose predominates in the first group, as we have seen; to the point that the consolation is a fully reciprocated love, she both consoling him like a mother and returning his love like an 'amante', a 'lover' (285.9); though an 'amante' who 'burns with chaste fire' (9–10), the oxymoron resuming and condensing the suggestion, in line 2, of passionate *conjugal* love: 'né donna accesa al suo sposo dilecto' (nor a loving wife to her loved husband). Here Petrarch, let

me repeat, reaches the limit of what he ever dared write concerning
Laura's feeling for him (even in *Tr. Mortis* II, where the most that he
makes her say – echoing Dante's Francesca, *Inferno* V, 135 – is 'never
was my heart divided from you'). In the next, later group, 341–3,
356, 359, the emphasis shifts to the cathartic and disciplinary side of
the matter. But before we come to that something must be said of the
non-apparition poems between the two groups.

The apparitions, in the sense I give the term, are concentrated near
the beginning and near the end of Part II, there being none between
nos. 285 and 341. Nor indeed are there any 'visions' – again, as I use
this term – between 302 and 362 (for the latter is only prepared for by
346). This means that as an account of Laura's relations with Petrarch
after her death, *Canzoniere* II goes through three phases: a phase of
nearness to and communication with him is followed by a prolonged
'absence', after which communication is resumed and brought to a
twofold climax – on the one hand by the chief apparition poem, the
canzone *Quando il soave mio fido conforto* (359), on the other, by the
last and boldest of the heavenly vision poems, *Volo con l'ali* (362).
The audacity, which is in the tercets, is theological, Laura presents her
poet to Christ, who then assures him of his eternal salvation.

It is in keeping with this pattern that the middle phase shows
Petrarch's dejection at its intensest; see nos. 310–17, and again 320–
321, and the sad conclusion of *Al cader d'una pianta* (318 – after a
nostalgic memory of the Laura-Laurel as the one-time inspirer of his
poetry) and the harsh realism of *I dí miei più leggier* (319.8, 12–14 – this
second tercet sharply contrasting with the assertion of Laura's
heavenly state in the first one):

> tal ch'è già terra, et non giunge osso a nervo.
> …
>
> et vo, sol in pensar, cangiando il pelo,
> qual ella è oggi, e 'n qual parte dimora,
> qual a vedere il suo leggiadro velo.
>
> [she who is now earth, every bone and muscle dissevered…and
> I go my way, my hair turning white, thinking of what and
> where she is now, and of the sight that her lovely veil [her body]
> now presents.]

Sonnets 318 and 319 form, in fact, a pair, each focusing on a principal
element in Petrarch's dejection: 318 on his loneliness (line 14), 319
on his horror of physical death. A similar complementary pattern
is found in 335–6. No. 336, *Tornami a mente* – which in its structure

resembles the strophes of the canzone 323, to be glanced at presently –
begins by evoking the beauty of Laura as she was in youth, a beauty
both physical (lines 1–4) and spiritual (5–6), an evocation so effectively brilliant that the poet, imagining he sees her alive, begs her to
speak (6–8). But he is deluded, as the tercets, spelling out the date
of her death, coldly state; and is left in his solitude. In 335 the contrast
is not, as in 336, between Laura alive and Laura dead, but rather
between her soul as a 'heavenly spirit', which it was even before it
left the body (lines 1–6) and the *therefore* ghastly degradation of
physical death (there is a rather similar line of thought in Leopardi's
Sopra il ritratto di una bella donna). This sonnet has interesting links also
with 307, *I' pensava assai destro esser su l'ale*, of which it seems at first
to be resuming the theme of the poet's incapacity to render in words
the marvel of Laura. The wing imagery supplies the obvious link.
But in 335, *Vidi fra mille donne*, Laura's swift vanishing upwards out
of sight (cf. 323.55) turns out to be due not to her intrinsic sublimity
as in 307, but to the brute fact of Death entering by the 'windows'
of her eyes.[82]

The subtitle of F. Chiapelli's fine study of 323, *Standomi un giorno*[83]
is 'the canzone of the visions', in line with the description in the
poem's *congedo*, 'these six visions'. But the objects seen by the poet
through his interior 'window' are not heavenly, but six symbolic
enactments of the same tragic theme: the marvel of Laura alive, the
eclipsing disaster of her death. A late and very mature poem (1365–
1368?), *Standomi un giorno* gives definitive, distilled expression to
Petrarch's spontaneous horror of death (a different thing from his
Christian fear of it, as expressed, for example, in 128.97–102;
366.131–7); and it does so by showing, six times over, the transient
brevity of the Laura-miracle. Six of the more recurrent emblems of
that marvel are turn by turn blotted out by death; each strophe
ending with the poet-watcher's horrified dismay, and the whole with
his own longing for death (line 75). It is an epitome of the *Canzoniere*,
minus the Christian component.

Despite my remark above that 359, *Quando il soave mio*, and 362,
Volo con l'ali, together represent the point of maximum nearness of
Laura to Petrarch in *Canzoniere* II, I in part also agree with Amaturo
who finds an increased 'distance' in Laura as the book draws to its
close.[84] Certainly, from, say, 326 to 362 (the poem which concludes
the whole account of the Laura/Petrarch relationship as *mutual*) the
stress is increasingly on her heavenly state; nor, certainly, does the
almost passionate tenderness on her side, recorded in 285, *Né mai*

pietosa madre, recur in the later apparitions. In these she consoles much
less than she warns and spiritually guides. But this, in its way, brings
her closer than ever. She remains full of affection (341.12), she wipes
away his tears (342.10), she listens to his long tale of woe (343.10–
11), but when he persists in complaints, she tells him sharply not to
be a fool (359.56–9); immediately, however, softening the rebuke
with words that sum up once and for all her final role in his regard.
Here is the crucial passage, rather freely rendered:

> 'Spirito ignudo sono, e 'n ciel mi godo:
> quel che tu cerchi è terra, già molt'anni,
> ma per trarti d'affanni
> m'è dato a parer tale; et anchor quella
> sarò, piú che mai bella,
> a te piú cara, sí selvaggia et pia
> salvando inseme tua salute et mia'.
>
> (359.60–6)

> ['I am a bodiless spirit, rejoicing in Heaven; what you seek has
> been earth long since; it is only to console you that I am allowed
> to appear in bodily form. And yet I shall once more be that
> woman who once, for your good and my own, was so cruel
> and so kind to you; only I shall then be lovelier than ever, and
> more than ever dear to you'.]

The last two phrases anticipate the conclusion of the *Tr. Eternitatis*,
already touched on in section I of this chapter (above pp.42–3).
We need not delay here on Laura's memories of the days when she
used to school and train her lover with 'sweet variety' of mood and
attitude (351.13–14, cf. *Tr. Mortis* II, 85ss.), 'turning my course', as
he says, 'towards the better shore', and doing so not only with snubs
and scoldings (341.13) but also 'lusingando', with a sort of 'entice-
ment' (290.13–14) which it is left to us to imagine, but on which
Petrarch insists enough to show that the general effect of Laura's
defence of her chastity was to sublimate, not extinguish, his desires
(see especially 290.9–11; 270.99–101; 289.5–11; 352.11). Loving
him, she had had to resist him, for his good. And it is essentially the
same chastening process that she continues after death by the expedi-
ent of the apparitions, above all that of *Quando il soave mio*, and the
successful outcome of which is revealed to Petrarch in *Volo con l'ali*,
where Laura is quite simply his introducer to Christ; as Beatrice had
been Dante's in the *Paradiso* taken as a whole, but especially in canto
XXIII. In this sense, 362 is a *Paradiso* in miniature. In this sense too the
later poetry of *Canzoniere* II, down to 362 inclusively, may be said to

reverse the anti-Laura drift of *Secretum* III (*Prose*, pp.132–88). Only the four following poems, 363–6, leave a quite different impression.

It is true that that reversal only developed and expanded two points in Laura's favour already conceded in the *Secretum*: that she 'did what she could' to prevent Petrarch's moral decline and that anyway she herself was 'innocent' (*Prose*, pp.154, 146). The former point is developed by the sequence of apparition-poems. The latter, the affirmation of Laura's innocence (of unchastity), can and, for its full understanding, needs to be set in the light of the basic distinction already noted (pp.77–8 above) apropos of the last two stanzas of no. 70 – the distinction between the inbuilt objective order of Nature constituting all things, however slight and transient in themselves, as signs of God (cf. 360.138–9) and, on the other hand, fallen man's culpably blurred vision of that order. The objective 'thing' in question being of course, in the first instance, Laura's body. The distinction is implied at the opening of *Canzoniere* II, in 264.48–54; it reappears near its close, and more clearly and powerfully, in one of Petrarch's greatest sonnets, *O tempo, o ciel* (355); and then, less explicitly set out, in the last 4 stanzas of 366. In the light of it Laura's physical beauty is seen as what it became for Petrarch, an occasion of sin. This is that 'error' referred to in 364.6 and 366.111, which had made of the 'innocent' Laura a 'Medusa' and which stemmed in the last resort from the poet's obsession with 'mortal beauty': 'Mortal bellezza, atti et parole m'ànno / tutta ingombrata l'alma' ('Mortal beauty, acts and words have altogether entrammelled my soul', 366.85–6. See also 70.32 and 44 and 365.2). And it is of course on this aspect of the Laura-cult that the *Canzoniere* lays the final stress. And it is true that such a conclusion, so far as it is a judgement on Petrarch, besides being perfectly logical, has been prepared, from near at hand, by 355, and from a distance by 264, not to speak of the penitential poems in Part I (in particular by 62, 81, 142). Nevertheless, so far as it appears also to judge Laura, it cannot but strike us as both harsh and abrupt. Laura who, in the last poem showing Petrarch and her together, 362, has told him that she loves him and has then led him 'to her Lord', whereupon he has asked to be allowed to stay there in heaven, 'to contemplate both faces', Christ's *and* Laura's (lines 7–11) – this same Laura is in the next four poems dismissed as the unworthy object of an infatuation from which only her death has delivered him, and the evil effects of which only God, operating through the Virgin, can repair (363 passim; 364.9–11; 365.1–8; 366.92–137).

Appropriately, *Vergine bella* (366), sums up the 'case' against

Laura, and in this way reconnects the *Canzoniere* with *Secretum* III.
It does so both positively and negatively: positively in stanza 9,
where Laura is in *some* sense identified with the witch Medusa and
made to share the blame with Petrarch's folly, 'l'error mio', for his
being turned into a stone 'dripping with vain tears' (111–12), and
negatively in stanza 8 – but here we must pause a moment, for the
line in question, 94, 'et de mille miei mali un non sapea', has been
understood differently by two such authorities as Leopardi and
Carducci. Leopardi took it as an assertion of Laura's almost total
ignorance of the various ills and afflictions – these being left unspecified – that Petrarch had suffered on her account – 'she didn't
know a thousandth part of all I suffered because of her'. Carducci
however, more subtly, and giving 'mali' a specifically *moral* sense,
understood Petrarch to be pointing to one evil in particular that his
love had involved him in, namely the desire to possess Laura carnally,
expressed unequivocally only twice in the *Canzoniere*, at 22.31 and
237.31; and of this lust of his, he would be saying, Laura knew
absolutely nothing. It must be admitted that this reading gives a sharp
point to the three following lines, 95–7, if in the light of it we paraphrase them thus: 'and if she *had* known, it would have made no
difference, for had she taken any other course [i.e. other than resist
my lust] I'd have been in mortal sin, and she disgraced [neither of
which eventualities was she prepared to face]'. But – granted that
the whole passage is full of hyperbole – is it likely that Petrarch would
have made Laura out quite so ingenuous? It is not thus that he represents her in *Tr. Mortis* II, 88ss. Moreover, Leopardi's interpretation,
it seems to me, ties in better both with the first two lines of the
stanza (92–3) and with the praise of Mary that concludes it (100–4).
Lines 92–3 I would render thus: 'Virgin, a woman is now dust,
leaving me grieving, who while she lived kept me continually in
tears [in pianto]'. And lines 100–4: 'But you...wise Virgin, *you* see
all, and what another [Laura] could not do is nothing to your great
power – that is, to put an end to my sorrow [por fine al mio dolore]'.
Now, it is surely evident that 'in pianto' in line 93 – the 'tears' Laura
continually caused him to shed while she lived – refers quite generally
to Petrarch's sufferings as a lover, the theme explicitly introduced
into this canzone by the preceding stanza 7: 'Virgin, how many tears
I have shed...Since my birth on the banks of the Arno, my life has
been nothing but distress. Mortal beauty...has completely entrammelled my soul' (79–86); words that in a real sense recapitulate
the entire *Canzoniere*, here in its concluding poem; and are precisely

those presupposed, surely, by the 'pianto' of line 93 and the 'mio dolore' of line 103. It is all this, surely, that Mary is said to 'see', all this that the poet begs her 'to put an end to' (100–3). The range of her compassion, extolled here, must surely include – when viewed in the context of the *Canzoniere* as a whole – far more than that sting of lust which in the entire book is only twice distinctly alluded to.

For these reasons I prefer Leopardi's interpretation of 366.94, which incidentally is the more usual one. And yet the line, so understood, is strangely insulting – and, what is perhaps more to the point, strangely abrupt. There is no more glaring contradiction in the whole Laura-saga than thus so bluntly to deny her any such knowledge of her lover's heart as had been so repeatedly asserted or implied throughout the previous 80 poems (to say nothing of *Tr. Mortis* 11). Indeed, the *Vergine bella* repudiation of Laura seems so decided that it is super-ficially tempting to say that the *Canzoniere* ends on a note of revulsion from Laura herself, or at least from her as assumed into the Medusa-symbol of quasi-petrifying carnality.[85] But Laura was only a 'Medusa' because Petrarch's 'error' – 366.112 – made her so; in *Tr. Pudicitiae* she is expressly Medusa's adversary, as bearing the shield of Perseus, so fatal to that Gorgon (Ovid, *Met.* IV, 769ss.). Only in this indirect sense – as the innocent occasion of Petrarch's moral decline[86] – is Laura ever repudiated. Nevertheless the abruptness of Petrarch's refusing her, at 366.94, any intimate knowledge of him certainly jars with most of *Canzoniere* 11. It is hardly offset by the hint at the ulti-mate function, in his salvation, of her beauty (final stanza, lines 121–3) – for all the pathos of these lines and for all their anticipating the *amende honorable* at the end of the *Tr. Eternitatis*. The truth seems to be that Petrarch, having chosen to end the *Canzoniere* with Mary replacing Laura, sacrificed one side of his artist's nature to another, his instinct for unity and continuity to the claims of dramatic con-trast. To enhance Mary's compassionate wisdom, Laura's had to be depreciated. Similarly, it was to be expected that in a poem like *Vergine bella*, Mary should be appealed to as 'beatrice', 'bringer of happiness' (line 52), but the addition of 'vera', 'true', in a stressed position in the line – '*vera* beatrice' – this, in the context, was unquestionably intended to mark a contrast with Laura; who, earlier in the *Canzoniere*, had twice been called 'beatrice' (72.37; 191.7).

In stanza 7 of 268 Petrarch, we have seen, had implied that he would continue to write verse in praise of Laura, now dead; and in 276 he added the conventional reason that this would bring him relief in his sorrow. So began an interesting series of poems, worth a more detailed study than I have space for here, having his own love poetry as their common theme. Something of the kind, he may have felt, was called for at this stage in his career; that having by now – the early 1350s – virtually dropped the *Africa*, he had to justify, to himself and to posterity (which he had much in mind), the alternative course he was by now consciously adopting, that of expressing his deeper thoughts and feelings in the lowly vernacular. To be sure, he would keep this undertaking – hardly one to be expected of the Poet Laureate in Latin – concealed behind a screen of Latin prose, epistolary and polemical; but at heart, as he well knew, he was first and foremost a poet. Perhaps, too, the example of Dante's incessant self-commentary, in verse as well as in prose, counted for something in the little series I now glance at.

It consists of some 20 poems or parts of poems, in some of which the focus is mainly on the poet himself, in others on Laura. Of the first group, some focus almost entirely on Petrarch's loss of his erst-while inspiration, Laura's physical beauty, as in the bitter close of sonnet 292. 'No more love songs for me: the vein is dry…and my lute turned to mourning' (cf. Job, 30.31). The same tone echoes throughout the sestina 322. Meanwhile, however, in 293, *S'io avesse pensato*, and 304, *Mentre che 'l cor*, this lament at the loss to his poetry caused by Laura's death is complicated, not only by considerations as to Petrarch's motives, past and present, for writing about her (293.9–12; 304.5–6), but, in the first quatrain of 293, by the craftsman's regret that while he had the chance he had not taken her more seriously as a poetic subject; he should have written more about her and in a more studied, a choicer style. But in those days, he goes on, he wrote *this* sort of poetry only to relieve his feelings, not to win fame. *Now* he would like to win fame, *and as her poet*; but, alas, it is too late. In other words, as I interpret this, Petrarch is regretting hav-ing set his heart in early manhood on winning fame through the *Africa*. He would have done better to have written more, and better, on Laura and in the 'volgare'. Taken in this sense, 293 – and also, I would say, the more richly metaphorical 304 (especially in lines 9–14) – would go far beyond such a poem as 166, *S'i' fussi stato*, which implicitly showed Petrarch conscious of being a poet *manqué* in Latin. They would belong rather with 186 and 187, wherein Laura, as a subject for poetry, is raised above the heroes sung of by Homer and Virgil, and declared at least the equal, in this respect, of

Scipio, the hero of the *Africa*. But they would go beyond these two earlier sonnets inasmuch as what they are exalting is not only the subject but implicitly also the *language* of his love poetry, the lowly 'volgare'. This is the nearest that Petrarch ever came to Dante's position on the dignity of vernacular poetry.

The poems of this series that focus chiefly on Laura, do so in respect of two topics, her fame and her ineffability. In 268.73–7 Laura, through Amor, has acknowledged the fame already won for her by Petrarch's verse, and begged him to continue to promote it. This, then, is the motive presupposed by all the love poetry of *Canzoniere* II; as the following sonnets more or less explicitly declare: 295.12–14; 297.14; 327.12–14; 333; 354. The last of these poems, being addressed to Amor, the speaker in 268.67–77, returns this series to its beginning in that canzone. As for Laura's 'ineffability', this motif, adumbrated as far back as the 'canzoni of the eyes', 71–3, and more distinctly in 247.12–14, is here resumed in 307–9 and brought to a climax in 339 *Conobbi, quanto il ciel*. Note, in this development, the conceptual framework and the metaphors employed. As to the former, Petrarch, unlike Dante never sets out a theory of the 'humanly inexpressible'.[87] For him the superiority of Laura's intrinsic qualities to his own powers of expression rested on a simple distinction between her body, as the work of Nature, and her soul, conceived as 'the divine part' in her, the direct work of God (308.12). In his poetry he has indeed been able to 'ombreggiare', indicate faintly (ibid. 11) her physical beauty, Nature's handiwork; for the rest, she was simply beyond his expressive capacities, whether in words or even in thought (307.9–14; 308.5–14). Hence, in the end he can only contemplate her in silence and 'sigh' (309.12–14). This 'sigh' inevitably recalls the close of two famous sonnets in *Vita Nuova* XXVI. Less obvious, and possibly unconscious, is the Dantean echo in the beautifully handled 'weight' metaphor in 307.5–8:

> Trovaimi a l'opra via piú lento et frale
> d'un picciol ramo cui gran fascio piega,
> et dissi: 'A cader va chi troppo sale,
> né si fa ben per huom quel che 'l ciel nega'.
> [I found myself far more yielding and weak in the work than a little branch bent by a great burden, and I said: 'He flies to fall who mounts too high, nor can a man do well what the heavens deny him'.][88]

And the same might perhaps be said of the 'stars' metaphor in 308.10.[89] What Petrarch certainly didn't owe to Dante was the expression 'breve stilla d'infiniti abissi' at 339.11 – that all he had ever said or written of Laura was 'a drop in the ocean'.

3. THE MAKING OF THE CANZONIERE

The indispensable guide into this topic is E. H. Wilkins' study of the MS data in chapters IV–IX of *The Making of the Canzoniere*. Those data span nearly forty years, from the later 1330s to 1374, during which the *Canzoniere* was being composed and put together. Wilkins' detailed reconstruction of this process, though in part conjectural, is fairly generally accepted as regards both the earlier stages, down to *c.* 1346, and those subsequent to the mid-1350s. As regards however the stage in between, centred on the death of Laura in 1348, Wilkins' views have met with serious criticism in recent years. I myself have reserves also concerning the pre-1346 stage. In what follows I shall first summarise the American scholar's reconstruction, and then touch on the doubtful points referred to, particularly those involving the crucial middle period, 1346–1352/3.

The two chief MSS in question are in the Vatican Library: V.L. 3195 and 3196. V.L. 3195 contains the *Canzoniere* as Petrarch left it at his death in July 1374, and is about one third autograph. Known to Cardinal Bembo and others in the sixteenth century, it passed to the Vatican Library in 1600, where it lay unnoticed until its rediscovery by Pierre De Nolhac in 1886. Only less precious is V.L. 3196. Entirely autograph, it consists of work-sheets used by Petrarch in the composition or fair-copying of his verse in Italian. The earliest datable entries were made in 1336–8, the latest, the entire *Tr. Eternitatis*, within months of his death. Along with fragments of poems and many annotations in Latin, V.L. 3196 contains upwards of 60 complete poems, most of which found their way, often after much revision, into V.L. 3195.[90]

Close study of these two MSS, and of all other available sources, led Wilkins to identify nine successive 'forms of the *Canzoniere*'. Besides these he identified and dated four other groups of poems in V.L. 3196, which he called, however, mere 'reference collections', as apparently lacking 'any principle of arrangement' (p.87); and of which the most interesting is the earliest, made in 1337–8, containing 17 sonnets destined eventually for the *Canzoniere* and lines 1–89 of the canzone *Nel dolce tempo*, no. 23 (pp.81–92). But it is Wilkins' nine 'forms of the *Canzoniere*' that most concern us. They fall into three groups: 'forms' 1–4; 5, 6 and 9; 7–8. Now as regards the second and the third group, everyone, I think, would agree that they clearly do represent stages on the way to the final form of Petrarch's book (this will be shown briefly later on). But Wilkins' identification of each of the 'forms' 1-3 is on his own admission at best only 'probable' (pp.94-102; 145-58). The one quite certain 'form' in this first group is the fourth, the so-called Chigi form of the *Canzoniere*, put together in 1359-62 and preserved in another Vatican Library MS, Chigi L.V. 176. It contains 215 of the 366 poems of the *Canzoniere* (p.160). As to the other three 'forms' of that first group, they would represent successive approximations to the Chigi form - approximations in the form of three collections of his poems made by Petrarch between about 1340 and 1358, of which the second would have both included and added to the first, and the third have both included and added to the second; this third one constituting the 'form' immediately preceding the Chigi form. Such, broadly, is Wilkins' reconstruction of the making of the *Canzoniere* down to c. 1358. On what does he base it?

The evidence he gives is of two kinds: first, certain discontinuities in the arrangement of the poems in the *final* 'form' of the *Canzoniere* as contained in v.L. 3195; second, certain annotations and cancellation marks in v.L. 3196. As to the former, Wilkins argues that both in Part I (nos. 1-263) and Part II (264-366) of the final form a series of carefully ordered poems is followed by one much less carefully arranged; the division between the two series occurring, in Part I, at or shortly after no. 142 (the penitential sestina *A la dolce ombra de le belle fronde*) and, in Part II, at or shortly after the bitterly nostalgic sonnet *Gli occhi di ch'io parlai*, no. 292. Each series *before* the division, that is nos. 1-142 and 264-92, Wilkins calls 'an *original* group... followed [after 142 and 292] by an *addendum* of poems much less carefully ordered' (p.94, my italics). The 'ordering' in question is based by Wilkins on three principles: chronological sequence (roughly observed in both of the groups indicated); variety of metrical form (i.e. a fair frequency, among the more usual sonnets, of canzoni etc.); and variety of content (i.e. a fair admixture, among the love poems, of poems on other themes). The third of these principles has been considered in section 2 above; the second will be discussed in section 4. Meanwhile, as regards this part of Wilkins' analysis, three points may at once be conceded: (1) the *Canzoniere* does alternate between series more and less carefully arranged; (2) these series do coincide fairly well with those specified by Wilkins, the divisions in both Part I and Part II of the book falling more or less where he says they do, that is at or a little after, nos. 142 and 292 respectively; (3) it does seem that Petrarch, in constructing his book, became, as time went by, less careful about arranging its contents (though, as we shall see, this does not apply to the last 31 poems).

However, if we ask just when the phase, or phases, of more careful arranging came to an end, we are brought up against the fact that the *first* 'form' of the *Canzoniere* to exhibit any difference between two more and two less careful arrangements of poems is that contained in the Chigi MS, which is the earliest extant form of the *Canzoniere* and represents the results of Petrarch's work on the book down to about 1362 (pp.160–3). Not one of the earlier 'forms' distinguished by Wilkins exists in fact, as a distinct and self-contained series, in any extant MS. All the evidence for such 'Pre-Chigi forms' as Wilkins speaks of is contained in Petrarch's work-sheets – in the notes and signs, referred to above, that punctuate the random collection of poems in V.L. 3196.

Certainly, as Wilkins shows, these notes (which are dated) and these signs do prove something. They prove that at three periods before 1358 Petrarch was making selections of his poems, arranged in a definite order. On 21 August 1342 he chose no. 34, *Apollo, s'anchor vive*, as the first of an ordered series which included 13 other sonnets from 3196, and probably others from work-sheets now lost. This for Wilkins constituted 'the first form of the *Canzoniere*' (pp.99, 140–50). In 1348–51 the MSS show us the poet at work again, selecting, revising and arranging. This time the poems he was working on included four from Part II of the *Canzoniere*: 265, 268, 270, 324. As we shall see, he had very probably by this time decided on the bipartite division of his book; but the MSS do not yet show the starting point of either Part (pp.150–3). Finally, we see Petrarch at work again in 1356–8, preparing a selection of his poems for his friend Azzo da Correggio, the collection Wilkins calls 'the third or Pre-Chigi or Correggio form of the *Canzoniere*'; it, in his view, must have included all the carefully arranged poems in the Chigi form, minus its not so carefully arranged addenda (pp.153–8). But as already stated, no such Pre-Chigi 'form' is extant in MS.

So far we have been looking at the first, and more obscure, of the two main phases in the shaping of the *Canzoniere*: that which – so far as the MS evidence goes – began in 1342 and ended twenty years later with the Chigi form and its 215 poems, divided into 174 in Part I and 41 in Part II, and bearing the title *Francisci Petrarche de Florentia Rome nuper laureati fragmentorum liber* (the Book of short pieces by

Francis Petrarch of Florence, lately [or 'once'] crowned with the Laurel at Rome).

The second main phase began in late 1366, when Petrarch set his copyist Giovanni Malpaghini to work transcribing poems into V.L. 3195. Reduced to essentials the making of this last, definitive text went in turn through two phases. Between late 1366 and 21 April 1367, when he refused to continue the work, Malpaghini transcribed nos. 1–190 (minus 179) of *Canz.* I, and 264–315 of *Canz.* II – in all 244 poems. Then, after Malpaghini's departure, Petrarch continued the job himself, working intermittently until its completion within the last months of his life (pp.165–86, 194). He had already, before Malpaghini left him, chosen a new title for his book, at once more concise, precise and modest than that used for the Chigi form: *Francisci Petrarche laureati poete Rerum vulgarium fragmenta* (Short Pieces in the Vernacular by Francis Petrarch Poet Laureate) (*The Making*, p.167). The following details are also important:

1) The four sonnets concluding Part I, nos. 260–3, were the *last* poems that Petrarch transcribed into 3195 (p.186).

2) After 263 there are seven blank pages in the MS, and the initial letter of 264 is elaborately foliated, as is that of no. 1. At least this latter fact proves that the bipartite division of the *Canzoniere*, already apparent in the Chigi form, was maintained to the end (pp.190–1).

3) By 1370–1 Petrarch had already decided to terminate the book with 366, *Vergine bella*.

4) In 1373–4, having decided to re-order the last 31 poems of Part II, Petrarch put arabic numerals 1 to 31 in the margin beside the poems concerned, indicating the position he wished each one finally to occupy. The principal effect of this was to stress the religious and penitential character of the *Canzoniere*'s conclusion, and so of the book as a whole. Thus the nos. 363, 364, 365 of our printed editions – which of course conform to Petrarch's final re-ordering – have changed places with 352, 354 and 353 respectively, which are notably non-penitential and indeed relatively non-religious; whereas, by contrast, nos. 363–5 form a perfect prelude to the final canzone to the Virgin (pp.77, 187).

As already stated, it is clear that Petrarch intended the bipartite division of his book, and intended that Part I should begin with no. 1, Part II with 264, and the whole conclude with 366. But the series of blank pages after 263 has seemed pointless to some critics, and notably to Wilkins (pp.186–7) unless we suppose that it was Petrarch's intention to go on adding poems to Part I. And *prima facie* this might seem a reasonable inference. Nevertheless two considerations tell against it. No. 263 is manifestly a splendid conclusion to Part I (especially in view of the run-up to it through the four preceding sonnets, which surely resembles the run-up to 366 through nos. 362–5). Secondly, Wilkins ignores the symbolic significance that Petrarch could well have seen in the number 366. With the actual total of 366 poems corresponding, minus the Prologue-sonnet *Canz.* I, to the number of days in the year, the poet could very well have intended his book to represent his entire life as symbolically reduced to one 'year'. This would be analogous to the symbolic reduction, fairly common in the Middle ages, of all mortal life to a single 'day'; a piece of symbolism of which, as it happens, Petrarch was particularly fond, as he makes 'Augustinus' say in *Secretum* III, *Prose* p.210.[91]

The above outline of the making of the *Canzoniere* is, I hope, clear as far as it goes. Some doubtful points remain for further discussion; but many details given by Wilkins have had to be simply omitted. And, as I have said, Wilkins' reconstruction of the story is often conjectural, as based on scanty MS evidence – a fact he sometimes, not always, admits. For the transcriptions into V.L. 3195 there is indeed no important lack of evidence; once Petrarch had set Malpaghini to work, late in 1366, all becomes clear enough. And by 1362 the Chigi MS, which is extant, had been completed (Wilkins, pp.160–3). It is the dozen preceding years that raise difficulties; most teasingly the crucial four years from early 1348 to early 1352, during which, however, it is certain that Petrarch was at least beginning to put the *Canzoniere* as we have it together. Wilkins went further, as we have seen, making this the period of 'the second form of the *Canzoniere*'; but that, in my view, was a misnomer – I shall say why in a moment. In any case, as I said at the outset, it is against his reconstruction of this period that the weightiest objections have been urged. The critic I have chiefly in mind is Francisco Rico with his brilliant study of the Prologue-sonnet,[92] *Voi ch'ascoltate*. But before we turn to that article I want to digress briefly on a recurrent slight flaw, as I see it, in Wilkins' nevertheless fundamental work on our topic.

Superb scholar though he was, Wilkins had the weakness of one of his most conspicuous qualities, a meticulous mental tidiness. This, I think it fair to say, made him rather inclined to turn conjectures into certainties, and so to jump to conclusions. An example meets us early in the long chapter IX from which *The Making of the Canzoniere* got its title. Examining certain annotations and markings, datable as

from 21 August 1342, inserted by Petrarch against 14 sonnets in
v.l. 3196, Wilkins showed that they prove that at that time Petrarch
was collecting and arranging in ordered series some of his early lyrics,
with *Canz.* 34, *Apollo s'anchor vive*, occupying the important first
position in the series. So far, so good. But he went on: 'this collection
is therefore properly to be considered as...the first form of the
Canzoniere'. To which one may as properly reply: that depends on
what you mean by the *Canzoniere*. Granted that Petrarch in the later
months of 1342 *was* making a collection of some of his poems, and
that this may well 'have contained other poems' – other than those
14 sonnets – 'drawn from sheets now lost' (p.148); and granted, what
is true, that these 14 sonnets reappear in the final form of the *Canzoniere* as it began to emerge in the 1360s and remained when Petrarch
died; – what does this prove? It is one thing to recognise that the 1342
collection is contained in the final one; it is another thing to identify
the former with one of the 'forms' of the latter. A work of art – and
the *Canzoniere* is certainly that – is not defined by its content alone;
still less by one particular element or aspect of its content, such as
those 14 sonnets represent, broadly speaking, in respect of the *Canzoniere* as a whole. Let us consider them. Of the fourteen, five refer
to Apollo, and, of these, three refer to the god's love for Daphne (the
Laurel), nos. 34, 41, 60; and of these, one, 34, was deliberately chosen
(as the MS shows) to open the little series. From which choice it is a
reasonable inference, as Wilkins himself implies (pp.147–8, n.5), that
in Petrarch's mind the whole of this 1342 collection stood in significant relation to the Apollo-Daphne-Laurel theme; that in some sense
this theme determined the choice of poems for this series. Whence
one might go on to argue, though one cannot prove, that Petrarch
already intended to fit, eventually, this brief 1342 series into a longer
poetic sequence that would have taken its general character from what
an Italian critic has called the 'Apollinean inspiration' – perhaps by
leading off with, at any rate by including, the very long and elaborate
canzone 23, *Nel dolce tempo de la prima etade*, the first half of which had
been finished well before 1342. Indeed, given the importance of the
Laura/Laurel motif in the *Canzoniere*, especially in Part I, it is hard to
put a limit within Part I to the expansion that Petrarch conceivably
might have planned of that original 14-sonnet nucleus contained in
v.l. 3196.

   To say this is to say that the 1342 collection was admirably suited for
its eventual inclusion in the *Canzoniere*. But it does not follow that in
1342 Petrarch already had the *Canzoniere*, as we know it, in mind –

that is, as a work with a certain definite outline and structure and a coherent thematic drift. To assume the contrary is to beg the question whether the *Canzoniere* can be adequately described as the successive accumulation of a certain number of poems – those eventually copied into v.l. 3195; a poor description indeed. To be more precise, it is surely arguable, to say the least, that it is of the essence of Petrarch's vernacular masterpiece to be (a) divided into two Parts, and (b) to be expressive in general of a moral, indeed a religious tension, amounting at times to positive conflict, between flesh and spirit, the pull of this world and the pull of God (see section 2). And both of these features – if more obviously of course the first one – are lacking from the little sonnet-sequence of 1342. True, the religious conflict had already found expression in no. 62 (self-dated Good Friday 1338) and also probably in 54 and 70, and perhaps 81. But there is no evidence that any of these was to be included in the 1342 collection; nor in the poems certainly included in it is there the least trace of any such conflict.

The next period for which there is MS evidence (again in 3196) of Petrarch's collecting and arranging poems eventually included in the *Canzoniere*, runs from 17 May 1348 to 28 December 1351; the poems concerned being a ballata (324), a sonnet (265) and three canzoni (23, 268, 270). Through all but the last six months of this period Petrarch was in Italy, and through most of 1348–9 in Parma; and it was here, on 19 May 1348, that he heard of the death of Laura, an event of obviously decisive importance in the shaping of the *Canzoniere*, dominating as it does Part II, and plainly prepared for in the last 18 poems of Part I. But with this mention of Laura's death in connection with the structure of the *Canzoniere*, we are brought back to Rico's critique of Wilkins in the article referred to above.

In fact that critique takes up only a few pages (101–16) in the part of Rico's article directly concerned with dating *Voi ch'ascoltate* and, concomitantly, with the bipartite division of the *Canzoniere*. When this important article was written (1976) Wilkins' dating held the field, as it largely still does. According to Wilkins the probable date both of the Prologue-sonnet and of the bipartite division was 1347 – in any case *before* Petrarch heard, on 19 May 1348, of the death of Laura (*The Making*, pp.151–3, 190–3). Rico dated them later, in 1349–50; and this on the basis of a 'new approach' (art. cit. p.107) to the whole matter of the *Canzoniere*'s 'making' during the crucial period 1348–52. In fact the novelty of this approach was two-fold. Firstly it viewed the *Canzoniere*, and in particular the Prologue-

sonnet, in close relation to the other major – and better-attested –
literary activities of Petrarch during this period, the planning and
inception of the two great series of letters, those in prose, the
Familiares, and those in Latin verse, the *Metricae* (pp.108–16).
Secondly it showed certain important connections between the
Prologue-sonnet and the title which Petrarch eventually, in 1366–7,
chose for his *Canzoniere* (see above, p.95), and in particular how
'rerum vulgarium fragmenta' in that title repeats *in nuce* certain key
words and phrases used in the first two quatrains of the sonnet, which
in turn, on close examination, reveal essentially the same moral and
mental attitude as that deliberately adopted by Petrarch in the 'introductions' to the *Familiares* and to the *Metricae* – respectively *Fam.* I, 1
to Ludwig van Kempen and *Metr.* I, 1 to Barbato da Sulmona – both
of which are firmly datable within 1350 (pp.117–37). One may say
that of these two parts of the 'new approach', the first has to do more
directly with chronology – the dating of *Canz.* 1, and by implication
of the bipartite division – and the second with the *meaning* of that
division, and this not only as a major factor in the structure of the
Canzoniere but also as indicative of a major turning point in Petrarch's
life, a turning point much influenced, of course, by the death of
Laura, but not to be explained by it alone. So much, then, for the
principal topics treated by Rico in this article. The principal text all
through is *Voi ch'ascoltate*, viewed in relation, successively, chiefly to
Fam. I, 1, to *Metr.* I, 1 and to the title chosen by Petrarch for his
vernacular *chef-d'oeuvre*.   *225376*

Speaking for myself, the effect of careful study of Rico's closely
reasoned and richly documented article is to make Wilkins' treatment of the problems concerned seem curiously superficial. The one
chronological point here on which the two scholars agree is that
Petrarch wrote *Canz.* 1 and decided on the bipartite division at about
the same time. But Wilkins, as I have said, insisted that this must have
been before Laura's death. Why so? For two reasons: that *Voi ch'*
ascoltate, though a poem of great disillusion, does not refer to Laura's
death; and that Part II of the *Canzoniere* only presupposes her death
as from the fourth poem in it, 267, *Oimè il bel viso*. It is true that 265
'was not written until 1350' (*The Making*, p.192 – and cf. Carducci-
Ferrari, p.364), but '266, self-dated as of 1345, is glaringly *in vita*'
(*The Making*, p.193); and as for 264, with which Part II begins,
Wilkins, after inclining to date it in 1347 (p.191) ended by pushing
it back to c. 1344, chiefly because it 'is the poetic equivalent' of
Secretum III, and the *Secretum* was written in 1342–3.[93]

Clearly, the first of these reasons proves nothing: it isn't obvious
that line 14 of *Canz.* 1 – 'che quanto piace al mondo è breve sogno',
'all that gives pleasure in this world is a brief dream' – does *not* imply
an allusion to Laura and her death. There is, however, this to be said
for Wilkins' position, that at least it raises the question whether more
than the death of Laura may not be involved in the disillusion expressed in *Voi ch'ascoltate*; so that if on *other* grounds one is persuaded
that this sonnet was written after Petrarch knew of her death, and
also that it was closely connected with the division of the *Canzoniere*,
then one is the better prepared to associate both the sonnet and the
division with the *general* theme of mental and moral self-reform,
accompanied by detachment from 'youthful follies', which predominates in the twin introductory Latin epistles – both certainly of
1350 – one in prose and one in verse, the *Familiares* I, 1 and the
Metricae I, 1.[94] Moreover, if Rico's dating of the *Secretum* is correct
(as I think it is, but see chapter III, section 4) it was during this period
1349–51/2 when Petrarch was organising, more or less simultaneously, the *Familiares*, the *Metricae* and the *Canzoniere*, that he was
also preparing the final redaction of the *Secretum*; the intimate connections of which with that general theme of self-reform are obvious.

Wilkins' second reason for dating the Prologue-sonnet before
Laura's death is *prima facie* more cogent: assuming that this poem was
roughly contemporary with the bipartite division, how can you say
that Petrarch wrote it after he knew of Laura's death when part of
Canzoniere II clearly assumes her to be still alive? But the argument
is specious. The part in question consists of three poems: the great
moral canzone *I' vo pensando*, 264; a sonnet about Laura's 'harshness',
Aspro core, 265; and a sonnet addressed to Petrarch's patron Cardinal
Giovanni Colonna, linking the poet's 15 years' devotion to him with
his 18 years' devotion to Laura, *Signor mio caro*, 266. As to 264, all we
know for certain of its date on external evidence is that it was written
by the time the Chigi MS was put together, c. 1360, while the only
clue offered by the poem itself is the sense it conveys of being written
after long experience of life and with death already in sight (lines
109–21, 130–4); which clearly favours, if anything, a later rather
than earlier dating. As for *Aspro core* (265), it speaks of Laura as though
she were alive, but in fact was written, as we know on MS evidence,
more than two years after her death. Why then, we may ask, did
Petrarch (a) write it at all, and (b) place it where he did? But the
two questions can be answered together. On MS evidence[95] we know
that the writing of this sonnet was occasioned by Petrarch's chance

reading of a line from Arnaut Daniel, which in fact turns up, translated, in its second tercet: 'There is no heart so hard that...by praying, loving, cannot be moved'. Petrarch had only to insert the trite 'weeping' before the other two gerunds to have a phrase that would both recall and explain lines 3–4 of the preceding poem, *I' vo pensando* (264): 'a pity...for myself / leading me often / to *other* than my usual weeping [i.e. other than that caused by Laura]'. He had then only to compose the rest of 265, starting from the bit lifted from Arnaut[96] to have a sonnet ready to take a place in the *Canzoniere* precisely in function, as it were, of no. 264. This seems to me a reasonable answer to both of the above questions.

On rather similar lines I would explain the placing of 266, *Signor mio caro*, addressed, apparently early in 1345, to Cardinal Colonna, and revised much later. As 265 'pairs', as we have seen, with 264, so this sonnet 266, which mentions both the Cardinal and Laura as still alive, manifestly 'pairs' with 269 which is a double lament for their deaths (Laura's on 6 April, Colonna's on 3 July 1348): *Rotta è l'alta colonna e 'l verde lauro*. The coupling of the names in each sonnet sets up an obvious symmetry between, on the one hand the double celebration 'in life' (266.12–14) and on the other the double lament 'in death' (269.1; and note that this line repeats in reverse order the same pair of symbolic images, the column and the laurel, used in 266.12). The parallelism is of course the more striking for the two poems being placed so near one another. Nor would Petrarch have been the least deterred from patterns and symmetries of this kind by their requiring, in the circumstances, in the case of 265 the creation *ad hoc* of an apparently 'in life' sonnet when Laura was already two years dead, and in the case of 266, the transferring of an authentically 'in life' sonnet to an apparently 'in death' situation. Considered from this point of view the placing of 266 after 264 proves nothing as to the date of the latter.

In this as in all else that concerns the arrangement of these first half dozen poems in Part II, two things should be borne in mind: that the bipartite division of the *Canzoniere*, though related to, is not wholly determined by, the death of Laura; and that Petrarch was free to arrange his poems exactly as he pleased, and therefore, if he had a special reason for so doing, to break the expected chronological order. The MSS make it perfectly clear that the first poem in Part II is no. 264, but the post-Renaissance obsession with Laura's death caused all the printed editions (except Mestica's, 1896) down to and including the Carducci-Ferrari, 1899, to begin Part II with 267, *Oimè il bel viso*; thus needlessly obstructing, in effect, the task of those scholars – Rico above all – who have understood that behind the bipartite division was a period of profound (in intention at least) mental and moral change, a period beginning well before Laura's death (not later anyway than 1346–7)[97] and continuing into 1353; and that the change in question, though accelerated and in a sense precipitated by that death, is not to be explained simply in terms of it.

The precipitation I speak of is naturally most in evidence in Petrarch's Italian lyrics. Thus the greater part by far of *Canzoniere* II is dominated by Laura, now dead yet somehow more than ever alive – certainly more than ever present, in the poetry, as a centre of consciousness in her own right, as an 'I', a woman speaking, not merely spoken about. This aspect of her in Petrarch's later verse has been touched on in sections 1 and 2. Here it is necessary only to take note of the fact that, as mourned for or as lovingly contemplated, Laura dominates the *Canzoniere* from 267 to 359 inclusively. If from this long series we subtract the correspondence sonnet 322 and the penitential 355, we are left with 93 love poems dedicated to Laura 'in death'; 93 out of the total of 103 poems in *Canzoniere* II. With this in mind, consider Wilkins' theory that Petrarch divided the *Canzoniere* into two Parts *before* Laura's death and probably in 1346–7 (*The Making*, pp.152–3, 190–4, *The Life*, p.62). Now, even according to Wilkins, by the end of 1347 there existed of *Canzoniere* II only 264 and 266 (and just possibly the anyway irrelevant 322). On this view, then, the Part II that Petrarch already had in mind, at the latest by the end of 1347, was a Part II (a) minus Laura 'in death', (b) consisting of two poems only, one of which, 266, self-dated 1345, presents no grounds, on internal evidence, why it should *not* have found a place in Part I. It follows that 264 has to bear the *whole* weight of the theory; that is, that Petrarch's motive for planning a Part II at all – a Part II which in the event was to be 90 per cent dominated by the Laura attachment – has to be looked for exclusively in a poem that is radically a *renunciation* of that attachment (along with the cult of Fame); and the date of which, as we have seen is in any case very uncertain. A strangely improbable theory to put out with such assurance.

So much for the case against dating the bipartite division before Laura's death. The positive case for dating it after her death is set out in detail by Rico on pages 106–16 of the cited article – his attention being focused, not on 264 but on the Prologue-sonnet, *Voi ch'ascoltate*. It will suffice if I summarise the main heads of the argument. They are as follows.

1) The structure of *Canz*. 1 with its 'play of dichotomies, its binary construction ("la arquitectura bimembre"): *era | sono, piango | ragione* etc. (cf. R. Amaturo, *Petrarca*, pp.249–50)' is of itself indicative of the bipartite division of the *Canzoniere*; and this, as Rico says, not only for artistic reasons (correspondence of a work introduced to its introductory piece), not only because of the parallels with the 'conflict' that is the theme of 264, but because such bipolarity in construction corresponds of itself to the *partitio* [division of material to be treated] recommended for an *exordium* [the introductory part of a literary work or discourse] by classical and medieval rhetoric (art. cit., pp.106–7).[98]

2) There are a number of very close thematic and linguistic correspondences between *Canz*. 1 and the two introductory letters to the *Familiares* and the *Metricae* respectively, which we know to have been written between January 1350 and the summer of the same year; just as we know from V.L. 3196 that, along with those two Latin collections, Petrarch, between late 1348 and late 1351, was making and arranging an ordered (*in ordine*) collection of his vernacular lyrics.

3) It is in this period that the phrase *in ordine* makes its first appearance in V.L. 3196.

4) *Canz*. 1 is not in V.L. 3196, but all but one of the poems on which this MS shows Petrarch to have been working during this period, are in Part II of the *Canzoniere*; and the most important of these, and the one he was most assiduously working on at this time, 268, not only clearly represents the death of Laura as recent (espec. in stanzas 1, 4–6) but stands very close to the division of the *Canzoniere*, being only four places away from 264; which suggests, at least, an association in Petrarch's mind between that division and her death.

5) Another subsidiary but interesting point – relating this time directly to the date of *Canz*. 1, not to that of the division – emerges in a fragment of a poem, copied into V.L. 3196 on 30 November 1349 but apparently never completed: *Ché le subite lagrime* etc.;[99] line 4 of which has the phrase 'chi prova, intende', while line 6 runs 'pur chi non piange non sa che sia amore'; which, taken together, are highly suggestive, as Rico points out, of lines 6–7 of *Voi ch'ascoltate*: 'ove sia chi per prova intenda amore, | spero trovar pietà…' (in whoever knows love by experience, I hope to find compassion…). A note in Petrarch's hand attached to the fragment would lend strong support to Rico's view that its line 6 is *Canz*. 1, 7 'in germ', if one could be sure that his reading of the last word in the note as *versum* were the correct one; but the latest editor, Romanò, reads *verbum*. In any case, given

the date – late November 1349 – when Petrarch copied the fragment into V.L. 3196, its unquestionable verbal coincidences with *Canz.* 1. 7–8 are worth recording.

Of the arguments summarised above, the second is the weightiest; then the first; then the third and fourth. The fifth is suggestive, but even slighter as an 'indicio', to use Rico's term, than another which he couples with it (pp.114–15) drawn from a comparison of *Canz.* 1 with *Fam.* VIII, 3. This letter was drafted three times, first in May 1349, and the third time about a year later. A phrase in the first draft is to the effect that Petrarch is now ashamed of the love-poetry of his youth, and is distinctly reminiscent of lines 9–11 of *Voi ch'ascoltate*. In the third draft the phrase is expanded to stress the *youthfulness* of that poetry; and so its distance from Petrarch's present occupations and interests; which brings also into view the first quatrain of that sonnet: 'those sighs with which I fed my heart when I first went astray in youth, when I was, in part, other than the man I am now'. The phrase would have been expanded in the early summer of 1350.

What this argument has in common with those under the second 'head' above is, of course, the establishing of connections, external and internal, between *Voi ch'ascoltate* and Petrarch's known literary activities and moral attitudes during the year 1349–50. It is a matter of putting the sonnet into *that* time-context and noting how extraordinarily well it fits in – so well indeed as to make any other period suggested for the sonnet's composition seem, in comparison, hardly worth considering (and in fact the only other dating seriously maintained is Wilkins' – before the death of Laura and probably in 1347 – for which there is strictly no evidence whatsoever). The texts focused upon, besides *Canz.* 1 itself, are, as I have said, *Fam.* I, 1 and *Metr.* I, 1; the former written at Padua on 13 January 1350, the latter probably at Mantua, in the spring or summer of the same year.[100] Meanwhile, as V.L. 3196 testifies, in a note dated 3 April 1350, Petrarch was intermittently and somewhat impatiently busy on his Italian poems; an impatience motivated, it is clear, not only by the relative inferiority, in his eyes, of works in the vernacular but also by something of the same fury to order and organise his writings to date, which is apparent in the contemporary prefaces to the two collections, that in prose and that in verse, of the Latin letters.[101] So much for the external contacts between the three collections – now formally, as it were, incepted, as being now for the first time definitely decided upon and distinctly planned – : the *Familiares*, the *Metricae*, the *Canzoniere*.

Notice that it is in respect of these *external* contacts that an aspect of *Voi ch'ascoltate* comes into view which did not appear from the comparison mentioned above, that is the correspondence of motifs in the sonnet to phrases in *Fam.* VIII, 3, 13[102] – namely that this poem was to serve as 'preface' to the *Canzoniere* in a manner analogous to the relation of *Fam.* I, I and *Metr.* I, I to the two collections of work in Latin. This is one reason for the importance of *Fam.* I, I and *Metr.* I, I in Rico's argument; the other being the close verbal and conceptual correspondence linking the Prologue-sonnet to these two Latin compositions. It should be noted how careful Rico is not to overstate his case. What he aims at establishing – and perfectly, in my view, does establish – is a strong probability – no more, but also decidedly no less. These correspondences or points of convergence, conceptual and verbal, as between *Canz.* I on the one hand and the two Latin 'prefaces' on the other, are set out in detail on pages 111–14 of the article; beginning in each instance from a word or phrase in the sonnet: 'rime sparse', that is vernacular verse written at different times and in diverse circumstances (line 1); 'sighs' (2); 'weeping' (5); 'youthful error' and the contrast between *then* and *now* (3–4); diversity in style (5–6); the appeal to the reader's similar experience of suffering (7–8) and of being held up to ridicule by the vulgar (9–11). And Rico concludes: 'I think I can say with certainty that in the *opera omnia* of Petrarch there are no other two pieces that…have so close an affinity with *Voi ch'ascoltate* as the prefaces to those (two) collections of letters.' But before the demonstration in detail Rico had summarised the main points of his argument, at the same time carefully limiting its scope. Let his words here serve as conclusion to this section: 'The first of the *Familiares* and the first of the *Metricae* conform to a pattern ("esquema") rigorously parallel to that of the first sonnet of the *Canzoniere*, allowances made for the differences required by the *genre* and character of each compilation. Identity of concepts, reinforced by correspondences in verbal expression, combine to form an extremely close network of connections. Given these contacts, given the position of "proem" assigned to all three pieces, given the analogous treatment that Petrarch gave, in 1350, to the *Familiares*, the *Metricae* and the *Canzoniere*, the chronological nearness to each other of the two epistles inclines one to place the composition of *Voi ch'ascoltate* within the same period, or immediately before or after it' (pp.110–11).

4. METRICAL FORMS

In the *Canzoniere* Petrarch used only accepted Italian lyric forms: the sonnet (317 times), the canzone (29), the sestina – Dante's adaptation of the metre favoured by the troubadour Arnaut Daniel[103] – (9 times), the ballata (7), the madrigal (4). Each of these forms consisted of course of a given number of verse-lines, the number being fixed for the sonnet (14) and the sestina ($6 \times 6 + 3 = 39$[104] – see below) but not for the canzone or the ballata or the madrigal; in these forms the number of lines was left to the poet's choice (though madrigals by definition were short).

The Italian verse-line ('verso') is a sequence of syllables arranged to make a certain rhythm; arranged, that is, as a particular sequence of stressed and unstressed syllables. Such rhythms form themselves naturally in Italian because every Italian word of more than one syllable has a stress on one of the syllables (the 'accento tonico'). So Italian verse rhythm is markedly accentual – if less so than English or German. The poet has only to arrange such natural stresses, and their accompaniment of non-stresses in a certain order, and in a line of a given length, to produce a recognisable rhythm. The *rhythm* will result from the arrangement of stresses and non-stresses, while the *length* of any line that an Italian poet may choose to write is determined by the number of syllables that it contains. As to how *many* lines he uses for a given poem, and whether they do or do not vary in length, these are questions relating to the metrical form he happens to have chosen for his poem, questions that arise in particular with regard to the canzone. But to that we shall come later. Meanwhile a few elementary points still need to be made concerning (a) line-length and (b) rhythm. I keep to the bare essentials.

a) Consider these two lines from the *Canzoniere*: 'Voi ch'ascoltate in rime sparse il suono' (1.1); 'Qual piú diversa et nova' (135.1). Considered as bits of prose, the former has 13 syllables and the latter 8. But considered metrically, as pieces of verse exhibiting rhythm, the one is a hendecasyllable and the other a heptasyllable – lines, respectively, of eleven and seven syllables; and this because the first line loses two syllables by elision ('-te' eliding with 'in' and '-se' with 'il') and the second loses one ('-sa' eliding with 'et'). Such shortening by elision of vowels in different words is called 'sinalefe', and is normal in Italian verse, particularly since the time of Petrarch, who very seldom adopted the opposite procedure of keeping such vowels apart ('dialefe').[105] The shortening of lines for the purpose of metre is also commonly effected by coalescing successive vowels within the same word (sinèresi); thus 'mia' becomes one syllable in *Canz.* 80.37, 'capei' only two in 90.1, 'sue' one in 34.14. An important exception to this practice is when a diphthong in which the first of the two vowels is stressed occurs at the end of a line; when this happens each vowel forms a distinct metric syllable: thus 'noi' is a disyllable in 268.36, though a monosyllable in 128.35, and compare 'mai' in 9.14 with 'omai' in 62.5. Occasionally, however, a similar holding apart of successive vowels within the same word occurs in the body of the line; in which case it is called a 'dièresi' and is often – not always – typographically indicated by two dots over the first vowel: thus, in Petrarch, *Canz.* 109.9, 'L'aura söave che dal chiaro viso'; 263.1, 'Arbor victorïosa trïumphale'; 264.103, 'la ragione svïata dietro ai sensi'; 366.137, 'ch'accolga 'l mïo spirto ultimo in pace'. In the case of certain diphthongs the 'dièresi' is not permitted; but that is a refinement we need not go into here.[106]

The only complete lines used by Petrarch are the hendecasyllable and the heptasyllable. I say complete lines because very occasionally he makes use of 'rimalmezzo'[107] – making, that is, a hendecasyllable include a shorter line – of 3, 5 or even 7 syllables – in rhyme with a preceding line; see nos. 29, 105, 135, 366. The case of 29 is peculiar in that here the internal rhyme itself (in '-ella', line 4) is repeated from stanza to stanza through the poem.[108] But the cases that best repay study are those of 135 and 366.

b) Rhythm, as we have seen, is a matter of the distribution of stressed syllables in a given line; and its chief 'carrier', in Petrarch as in Dante and the Italian tradition generally, is the hendecasyllable with its eleven metrically relevant 'positions', to be occupied by stressed or unstressed syllables. Now every hendecasyllable – and heptasyllable – has a stress in the penultimate tenth position. This is the invariable rule. But the rhythm of most lines is chiefly determined by a principal stress falling, in the great majority of cases, on a syllable in either the fourth or the sixth position. I say 'of most lines' because of the evenness with which Petrarch at times balances the stresses on distinct syllables, e.g.:

> 2–6–10   Qual grátia, qual amóre, o qual destino (81.12)
> 2–6–(8)–10   Levómmi il mio pensér in parte ov'era (302.1)
> 3–6–10   l'odorífero et lúcido orïente (337.2)

In 285.9 the evenness extends into the second hemistich:

> 3–6–8–10   or di mádre, or d'amánte; or téme, or árde...

Far more often, however, a single principal stress is clearly heard:

4–10	e 'l vago lúme oltra misura ardea	(90.3)
4–10	et venga tósto, perché Morte fura	(248.5)
2–4–6–10	che quanto piace al móndo è breve sogno	(1.14)
2–6–10	la stancha vecchiarélla pellegrina	(50.5)

The normal hendecasyllable then, as represented by these last four
examples, has a fixed stressed syllable in the tenth position, and a
'mobile' one in either the fourth or the sixth; and this mobile stress
is the principal or dominant one. The norm also requires a third, subordinate stress 'falling between the beginning of the line and the
sixth position when this has the dominant stress, or between the
fourth position and the tenth when the dominant stress falls in the
fourth position. There may be more than three stressed syllables in
the line, but the norm requires a *minimum* of three, distributed in the
way just described'.[109] Another way of putting this is to say that a
third stress is normally to be found in the *longer* hemistich. Thus, to
cite the examples given above, it falls on the eighth syllable in 90.3
and in 248.5: 'misúra', 'Mórte'; on the second in 50.5: 'stáncha';
whilst in 1.14 there are, rather exceptionally, *two* stresses before the
dominant on the sixth syllable: one on the second syllable, 'quánto',
and one on the fourth, 'piáce'. Two further points should be noted.
The word bearing the dominant stress is usually – *not* always[110] –
followed by the pause, light or more marked, known as the caesura
('cesura'); and however light or slight the caesura, the position of the
dominant stress articulates the line into two unequal hemistiches. In
Italian metric the lines which begin with the shorter hemistich (i.e.
with the dominant stress in the fourth position) are termed *a minore*;
those which begin with longer hemistich (the dominant stress in the
sixth position) are termed *a maiore*.[111] Thus *Canz.* 90.3 is *a minore*,
1.14 is *a maiore*.

After the above introductory remarks, I pass now to Petrarch's actual
use of his five lyric forms: the sonnet, the canzone, the sestina, the
ballata, the madrigal. I begin with the last two.

1. The only rule for a MADRIGAL was brevity, and none of
Petrarch's has more than ten lines. A BALLATA could be much longer
(e.g. Cavalcanti's *Era in penser*), its one essential component, the
refrain, 'ripresa', being indefinitely repeatable. But here too Petrarch
favoured brevity. He was not, in any case, much drawn to this form.
The seven ballate are among the least original poems in the book.
No. 55, *Quel foco ch' i' pensai*, is biographically interesting, with its

allusion in line 6 to a moral relapse, but mostly these pieces read like echoes from the past. The ballata form, centred as it was on the refrain, was too open-ended to be congenial to such a master of the clinching final line or lines.

But he was perfectly at ease with the madrigal, knowing exactly how to melodise its brevity and turn to exquisite pictorial effect its association with idyll and pastoral. As to the auditory effect, much of this depends, given the brevity of the form, on the closing lines. Three of Petrarch's madrigals end with a couplet, and one, 54, *Perch' al viso d'amor*, with a deliberately isolated single line which rhymes nonetheless with the mid line of the preceding tercet: D E D; E (the invariable pattern, incidentally, of Dante's canto-endings). Thematically this is the weightiest of Petrarch's four madrigals and its dramatic effect depends entirely on the relative isolation of line 10, while at the same time its melody requires the rhyme-link between this and line 8. As to the pictorial effect, all four paint a rural scene involving Laura, under the forms, successively, of shepherdess, passing stranger ('pellegrina', 54.2), angel, girl seated barefoot in a flowering meadow. Two of the poems bring in a third 'agent': the Voice heard in 54, and Amor, invoked though not present in 121. The role of Amor is obvious, that of the Voice in 54 depends on the meaning of this little allegory, and to that I come presently. The role of the poet himself is mainly passive through 52, 54 and 106; he is successively chilled, moved, ensnared by love. Laura by contrast is active in these three poems, to the point of playing the temptress in 106, where the psycho-physical enchantment conveyed in the last line illuminates the material 'snare' of line 5. Yet in 121 she resumes the cold indifference implicit in 52. Hence Petrarch's prayer to the absent Amor, a prayer that plainly represents a movement *opposite* to the 'turning back' mentioned in 54.10; which is as much as to say, of course, that the Voice, as the cause of that turning back, and Amor are opposed and hostile forces. Amor is Cupid with his bow (121.6–8): what then, or rather whose, is the Voice? The opposition just noted gives the clue – clearly indicating that this allegory belongs with such explicitly penitential pieces as 62 and, above all, 80 and 81 (compare line 9 of 54 with 80 passim; 81.10; 54.4 and 10 with 80.16–17, 81.9–11; cf. 214.28–30). The Voice, in short, is that of God (as in 80) or Christ (as in 81); the same voice repeatedly heard by Petrarch's master Augustine (*Confessions* VII, x, 2, VIII, xii, 2, XII, x, XIII, i) who himself had gone astray in a 'wood' (cf. 54.6 and *Conf.* II, i. 2). Other echoes of Augustine in 54 have been plausibly proposed, but those indicated should suffice.

The point of this thematic digression is to suggest that Petrarch's four madrigals form a sequence which, in outline, tells a story: the poet falls in love and then repents of his love (52, 54); tempted, he falls again (106), only to encounter, in the end, cold indifference (121). A likely date for the first three poems is 1336–40; the last may have been added much later.

2. A SESTINA is a game played with six words, each at the end of a hendecasyllable. It consists in (a) arranging these lines as a stanza, as for example in 80, *Chi è fermato di menar sua vita*, the first six lines of which end, successively, on *vita, scogli, legno, fine, porto, vela*; (b) re-arranging these end-words by reversing the positions of words 1 and 6, words 2 and 5, and words 3 and 4; which gives the *next* order of end-words, as in 80, stanza 2: *vela, vita, porto, scogli, fine, legno*: (c) continuing to form new stanzas by new arrangements of the *same* end-words, using in each case a procedure corresponding to that used in the formation of stanza 2; with the result that each of the following four stanzas will exhibit an order different both from that of the other three and from that of stanzas 1 and 2; (d) with the completion, in this way, of stanza 6 the game is finished, for the next arrangement of end-words would only repeat that of stanza 1, and the point of the game was to exhaust the possibilities of *new* combinations of the six original end-words. At this point Petrarch, following Dante, adds a three-line *congedo* in which he continues to use all six end-words, one at the end and one in the middle of each line; as in 80: *fine, vita, | legno, scogli | porto, vela*.[112]

A successful sestina implies the choice of pregnant and resonant end-words; pregnant, that is, with a theme worth developing, and resonant, as setting, barely audibly perhaps, an appropriate emotional tone – a matter, of course, not only of the auditory effect of the six words chosen but of the visual images they call up. This said, I observe as follows on Petrarch's sestine.

i) His choice of end-words is made with a view to a greater or less thematic complexity in the poem as a whole. Compare for example the strongly erotic 22, *A qualunque animale*, with the penitential 80. The governing theme of 22 is the persistence of Petrarch's carnal desire for Laura; that of 80 the spiritual danger of such desires. But whereas in 80 the entire theme is expressed in terms of the single, relatively simple, linear metaphor of human life as a perilous sea-voyage, which is all that the chosen end-words suggest, the erotic theme of 22 is very soon complicated by the interlacing of at least

four motifs: that of wild nature (*terra*, *selva*) as both contrasted with
and enclosing the poet's human self, abruptly introduced in line 7,
'Et io'; that of the poet's solitude, as a man alone in a non-human
world – the wild beasts, the woods, the stars; as conveyed too in the
stressed recurrence of evening and night (lines 1–6, 11–12, 24, 29–
33); that of the incessant diurnal time-process, both terrestrial (*sole*,
giorno, *alba*) and cosmic (*stelle*); that, above all, of astral determinism,
the notion made quite explicit in the strong line 24, 'my firm desire
comes from the stars', which cancels, in effect, the poet's distinctive
humanity, making of his desire an ineluctable force of wild nature.
A similar contrast might be drawn, within the sequence of 'erotic'
sestine – 22, 30, 66, 237, 239 – between the complexity of 30 (which
is such as may leave one in doubt whether the finally dominant theme
is the same as that of 22, or is rather, as I think,[113] the transformation
of the Laura-Laurel into an idol (cf. line 27)) and the relative simplicity of the 'winter-poem' 66.

ii) Simplicity of a special sort is presented by 214, *Anzi tre dì creata*, for
only two of its end-words, *bosco* and *sciolta*, are at all suggestive,
initially, of the poem's theme, which is the poet's finding himself
caught in a magic wood as in a horrible prison from which he cries
to God to deliver him. Neither thematically nor tonally is this fine
sestina much affected by any but two of its initial end-words.

The unimportance in 214 of most of the end-words (except as
rhymes) may be accounted for by its being a narrative, not a psychological, poem; so that its movement is linear and not, like the erotic
poems, obsessively circular. It is true that the other two penitential
sestine are also narrative, as recounting stages in Petrarch's life, and
that in both all the end-words count, and count for much, all through.
But there are special reasons for this. In 80 the narrative is conducted
entirely in terms of the one voyage metaphor spelled out by the
initial end-words. The case of 142, *A la dolce ombra*, is more subtle.
The most overtly autobiographical of the sestine, 142 is also the one
in which Petrarch achieves his maximum liberation from the
'immobility', the near-absence of any ongoing theme at all, which
Contini found in Dante's seminal *Al poco giorno*. I cannot delay on
this achievement of Petrarch's; except to observe, first that 142 is
unique among his sestine in reaching its thematic climax *only* in the
congedo, in the statement of the poet's conversion from the Laurel to
the Cross; secondly, that with hindsight, but *only* so, we realise that
this statement was pre-contained, hiddenly, in the initial end-words,
especially the 'tree-words' *frondi* and *rami*, and in *cielo* and *lume*. In

other words, these terms had a double sense from the start; the point
of the poem being to bring that fact to the surface.

3. The essential unit of the CANZONE is the stanza. There were
normally several stanzas, the sequence being commonly rounded off
by the 'postscript or valediction' (P. Boyde), the *congedo*. None of
Petrarch's canzoni has less than five stanzas and only four have more
than seven (nos. 23, 29, 360 and 366); and to all but two, 70 and 105,
he added a *congedo*. In a given canzone, the stanzas all had to be of
identical design, that is have the same number of lines, arranged as
to their lengths in the same order, and exhibiting the same rhyme
pattern. The line-lengths generally used, and by Petrarch invariably,
were the hendecasyllable and the heptasyllable – lines, respectively,
of eleven and seven syllables. Dante liked to mix the two lengths, the
hendecasyllable predominating; and made it a rule to begin his
stanzas with the longer line.[114] Petrarch ignores this rule in nos. 71–3,
125, 126, 135, and in general makes rather freer use of the heptasyllable. Both poets occasionally use a three or a five syllable unit for
an internal rhyme (see *Canzoniere* 29.4, 11, etc. and 366.13, 26, etc.).
But, whatever their arrangement of lines and rhymes in a canzone,
the crucial thing for both poets was the choice of the stanza pattern;
as explained, from a purely technical point of view, in *DVE* II, ix,
2–3. From a wider point of view, we can say that both poets aimed at
the fullest possible manifestation of distinct forms of verbal beauty,
which, in the case of the canzone, meant one of the several possible
stanza patterns, arranged in a sequence of appropriate length.

The variety of possible stanza patterns is set out by Dante in *DVE* II,
x–xiv. The fundamental term he employs is drawn from music.
Every stanza is fashioned to contain a certain *oda*, 'melody', that is a
distinct rhythmic pattern which in turn will be either single and
continuous throughout the stanzas, or interrupted at a certain point,
called the *diesis*, by the introduction of a new melody contrasting with
the first one. Typical for Dante of the continuous kind of stanza is
that of the sestina (which for him counted as a canzone). Other
'continuous' forms were possible and one such, *Verdi panni*, no. 29,
appears among Petrarch's canzoni proper (i.e. taking this term as
excluding the sestina). All Petrarch's other 28 canzoni are of the far
more common 'discontinuous' type – the type Dante's analysis is,
in fact, mostly concerned with. It entails, as has been said, two contrasted melodies, and Dante insists that at least one of these must be
repeated *within the stanza*. The part of the stanza containing the first
melody (that before the *diesis*) he calls the *frons*; that containing the

second, the *sirima* (nowadays 'sirma'). If the first melody is repeated the resulting two equal parts of the *frons* are called *pedes*, 'feet'; if the second, the resulting parts are called by Dante *versus* or *voltae*, but this division is of little practical importance, most Italian canzoni having only the *frons* divided into its two *pedes* (only in the bizarre 105, *Mai non vo' più cantar*, does Petrarch divide the *sirma* into *voltae*). The usual canzone stanza may be represented as 1+1+11; but the best way to present schematically *all* the essential elements is (a) to show by a colon the division between the *pedes* and the *sirma*, and by a semi-colon that between the two *pedes*; and (b) to show the hendecasyllables by capital letters and the heptasyllables (and there is at least one in all Petrarch's canzone stanzas) by small letters. Thus the stanza pattern of 129 becomes A B C; A B C: c, D EeD F F. Note that the comma after the small c is to bring out the fact that here (as everywhere else except in 105) Petrarch is following Dante's usual practice – recommended as 'beautiful in *DVE* II, xiii, 6 – of rhyming the first line of the *sirma* with the last of the *frons*, that is of the second *pes*. Note too – a far more important matter – that as regards the repetition in the second *pes* of the line and rhyme pattern of the first one, it was not necessary to repeat the *rhymes* in the same order, and that Petrarch usually avails himself of this liberty – for example in no. 28: A B C; B A C; in no. 264: A Bb C; B Aa C.

Of this strict canzone form Dante and Petrarch are the undisputed masters; any consideration therefore of either poet's use of it entails some comparison with the other's. Here for obvious reasons such comment by comparison must be kept to the minimum necessary (which the reader is recommended to supplement with chapters 2 and 6 of Fubini's very useful *Metrica e poesia*). Here I confine myself to items of formal structure in the Petrarchan canzone, my principal aim being to supply the reader with just so much basic information as may stimulate intelligent curiosity. The items now to be added to those already mentioned concern, first the interweaving of long and short lines in the stanza, and secondly rhyming.

A) Remarking above that Petrarch uses the seven-syllable line rather more freely than Dante, I had three things in mind. First, that none of Petrarch's canzoni has less than one heptasyllable to the stanza (contrast Dante, *Rime* XIV and LXXIX) and that all but two, 28 and 53, have more. Second, in no less than seven canzoni (37, 50 – here with notably expressive effect in stanza 5 – 125, 126, 129, 135, 207) Petrarch begins the *sirma* with a heptasyllable; which Dante does *only* in his eccentric *Poscia ch'amor*. Third, there is the multiplicity of heptasyllables in nos. 125, 126, 37, 128, 50 – respectively 10, 9, 8, 7 and 4 (these last all in the *sirma*) to the stanza. Admittedly, the brilliance of the effects so achieved in these poems is such as to make one overlook the relative infrequency, in the *Canzoniere* as a whole, of this kind of patterning. The fact remains that those effects are absolutely characteristic: there is no real equivalent in Dante; the vivacity expressed by the recurrence of heptasyllables in Dante's *Le dolci rime* or *Poscia ch'amor*, or even *Doglia mi reca*, is more dialectical than emotional. A special interest, incidentally, is presented by *Canz.* 128, *Italia mia*. With Dante's *Tre donne* (*Rime* CIV) it has in common the expression of grave and weighty subject matter in stanzas studded with heptasyllables – seven to a stanza in both poems. Bembo was right, of course, to associate, in general, 'gravity' with the hendecasyllable (*Prose*, ed. Dionisotti, pp.156–7): these two great poems only show how a free but controlled use of the shorter line could conduce to the same effect.

B) In the *Commedia* Dante uses rhyme in ways certainly beyond Petrarch's capacity, but this is no judgement on Petrarch precisely as a rhymer. The difference has to do with content, not technique. Petrarch was neither a dramatist born, like Dante, nor a speculative thinker, but these obviously un-Dantean deficiencies are of no account on the level of the canzone – a form in any case quite unsuited to the expression in dialogue of interpersonal encounter, and only with difficulty adaptable to sustained philosophical argument; witness the rarity in the tradition of such poems as Cavalcanti's *Donna me prega* and Dante's *Le dolci rime*. In the canzone Petrarch, alternating between lyricism and meditation, was on his own ground: free to deploy a facility and ingenuity in rhyming that will bear comparison with Dante's. This statement I leave the reader to test for himself, with a few references and brief comments, glancing first at some of the varieties of rhyme used by Petrarch, and then at his placing and interrelating of rhymes.

Broadly there are two ways of distinguishing Italian rhymes: (a) by where the accent in the rhyme-word falls, the rhyme being called 'tronca', 'piana' or 'sdrucciola' according as the accent falls on the last syllable (*farà*), on the penultimate (*amóre*) or on the one before that (*cénere*); and (b) by whether the last two vowels in the rhyme-word are separated by one (*vena, lume*) or by two or even three consonants (*bocca, prende, aspro*). However, as almost all the rhyme words in the *Canzoniere* are of the 'piana' accentuation, we need take account here only of distinction (b), that is that between 'vocalic' rhyme-words (e.g. *vena*) and 'consonantal' ones (e.g. *bocca*), to which corresponds the distinction commonly drawn by Italian critics between rhyme *sounds*; as characterised, that is, on the one hand by 'soavità' or 'dolcezza', on the other by a certain 'asprezza'. These metaphorical terms were first used by Dante, in a quasi-technical sense, to mark off the contrasted auditory effects, smooth and sweet or rough and harsh, of lines, or groups of lines, of verse (*DVE* II, vii); but with special reference, obviously, to the rhyme sounds. And the same contrast naturally attracted other metaphors. Thus Bembo liked to trace the dignity of much of Petrarch's verse – a quality, for Bembo, no less characteristic of it than charm, 'piacevolezza' or sweetness – to the weight, 'gravità' given it by the free use of consonantal rhyme words. But if Petrarch's 'gravità' went with a moderate 'asprezza' – and Petrarch's 'asprezza' was usually moderate – he had also his moments of what Contini calls 'relative violence' (*Preliminari*, p.xxvi); occasions, that is, when he crowds a poem or sequence of poems with rare and harsh rhyme words; and does so either for the better expression of a particular theme, or occasionally perhaps as simply enjoying the verbal artistry involved. I take this distinction from E. Bigi, though he seems to me to draw it a bit too sharply. But a certain stylistic 'violence', anyhow, is evident enough in poems like *Verdi panni*, no. 29, or the 'frottola-canzone' 105, or in stanzas 1–3 of 125; to say nothing of such sonnets as 136–8, 83, 86–9, 173, 198, 318. To the influence of Arnaut Daniel and of Dante on *Verdi panni*, noted by Bigi, I would add that of Horace in his Odes. As for the bitter-sweet 125 – self-declared 'harsh' in line 16 – its most striking feature apart from the abundance of heptasyllables, is the very expressive reiteration of rhyme words beginning with 's' and a consonant: 'sforza', 'spoglia', 'scaltro', etc.[115]

The 'violence' of such poems may well seem 'relative'. Even so, it is exceptional; Petrarch's normal practice in rhyming, as in every part of versification, being marked by an overriding concern for harmony and balance. This concern operates broadly speaking in two ways. Whether in sonnets or in canzone-stanzas, he tends to avoid unbroken sequences of either 'sweet' or 'harsh' line endings. And in the composition of individual lines he likes to balance the weight of the rhyme word by a word or phrase preceding it in the line; in cases, that is, when it would otherwise too obviously claim attention; thus giving his rhymes that delicate unobtrusiveness which is certainly part of their charm. The former of these tendencies is discernible, for example, alike in the predominantly 'sweet' canzone no. 126, *Chiare fresche e dolci acque*, and in the predominantly 'grave' one, *I' vo pensando* (264). In 126 the 'sweetness' of the whole, a sweetness already apparent in stanza 1 and overwhelming in stanzas 4 and 5, is tempered by the relative 'gravity' of stanzas 2 and 3 – a gravity arising, of course, from the death-theme introduced at line 14, but owing much of its effect to the greater 'weight' of the rhyme words as compared with those in stanza 1 and, still more, stanzas 4 and 5. The case of 264 is rather different in that its theme is uniformly grave; making the avoidance of monotony that much more difficult. If it is triumphantly avoided – and by common consent this is among Petrarch's finest poems – this is due in part to the manifest urgency of its reasoning, but in great part also to the subtle tempering of its prevalent 'gravità' by a recurrent 'dolcezza' in diction and rhyming; most notably in the third stanza. In both poems the Petrarchan constant operates: distinction *within* unity – in these cases the unity of a whole poem. In the other characteristic of his rhyming mentioned above the unity immediately in question is that of the single line; the stylistic point being that this unity consists characteristically in a more or less marked equilibrium of diverse, often contrasted, elements. The point has been well analysed by E. Bigi with reference to *Canz.* 1, *Voi ch'ascoltate*. He shows how each rhyme word is related, in respect of emotive 'charge' as well as rhythm, to a word or phrase preceding it in the line – or, in the case of *vergogno*, following it as an 'echo' (lines 11–12). Each line is an equilibrium effected either by an anticipation within it of the emotive 'charge' of the rhyme word (1–3, 7, 9, 10, 12, 13) or by some other balancing device – antithesis (4) or pairing (5, 8) or both (6), or by echo and assonance (11–12, 14). Note that in this sonnet the diversity of the balanced elements is more than usually evident – diversity being, in a sense, its very theme ('*rime sparse*', line 1). But essentially the same procedure is found everywhere in the *Canzoniere*; if more visibly, as a rule, in the sonnets than in the canzoni. A beautiful example from the latter, which I leave the reader to study for himself, is stanza 4 of 129, *Di pensier in pensier*. An interesting point, incidentally, to emerge from the study of Petrarch's surviving work-sheets is that his definitive choice of the rhyme words for a poem was usually made at an early stage in the process of composition.[116]

The rhyme arrangement in Petrarch's canzoni usually conforms to the general type recommended by Dante: a *frons* divided into two *pedes* repeating the same rhymes (not necessarily in the same order); a *sirma* undivided but linked to the *frons* by its first line rhyming with the last of the second *pes*; for example in 126: abC; abC: c (the so-called 'verso chiave')...: the stanza usually ending with a rhymed couplet. The Petrarchan exceptions to this norm are of two sorts, major and minor. The major exceptions are: no. 29 which repeats the same rhyme sounds through eight undivided stanzas; 105, with its *sirma* divided and *no* 'verso chiave'; and 206, entirely constructed on three rhymes. The minor exceptions are: no. 70 which *twice* repeats in the *sirma* a rhyme in the *frons*: AB; BA: A, ccADD; and the more eccentric – and more interesting metrically – no. 135 where the interlacing of rhymes throughout the stanza almost smothers the *frons/sirma* division: aBbC; cDdA: aBEeBF(f)A. Here – apart from the internal rhyme in the last line, indicated by the bracketed 'f' – are two abnormalities: a new rhyme is introduced into the second *pes*, and two rhymes in the *frons* – not one only, as in 70 – are *twice* repeated in the *sirma*. Clearly, the aim has been to make the whole sound-pattern of the stanza move in a circle.

The remaining 24 canzoni play only slight variations on the norm. Seventeen have 3 lines to the *pes*, six have 4, one (359) has 2: the rhyme-order being often altered in the second *pes*; thus, in nos. 23 and 28, ABC; BAC: in no. 264, ABbC; BAaC: in no. 359, AB; BA. The *sirma*, usually longer than the *frons*, is often centred on a quatrain, with the rhyme-sounds reversed, as in 53 and 264, DEED, or in 129, DEeD, or in 366, CddC. Only in the following examples does the stanza *not* end on a couplet: 28, 50, 119, 128, 366; and in this last (as in 135) the place of the couplet is partly filled by an internal rhyme in the last line (and with singularly beautiful effect in the conclusion of this canzone, which is also that of the whole *Canzoniere*: 'Raccomandami al tuo figluol, verace/homo et verace Dio, / ch'accolga 'l mïo spirto ultimo in pace'.). The average length of the canzoni is just under 100 lines; the three longest are nos. 23, 360 and 366, with 169, 157 and 137 lines respectively. The number of stanzas in the canzone varies from 5 to 10; that most favoured is 7. Finally, as regards the variants from the norm, great or small, in stanza structure and rhyme-patterning, there are *more* of them in the first two-thirds of the *Canzoniere*. If anything, Petrarch, as a poet-craftsman, grew more conservative with age (simply from this *formal* point of view; there is nothing merely 'conservative' in the concentrated force of such sonnets as 302, 355, 364–5).

4. Since *c.* 1240 the SONNET had been the small change, as it were, of Italian poetry; widely used in verse correspondence and for brief statements, serious or jocose, on any and every topic. Its development

as an art-form was mainly the work of love poets: Cavalcanti, the young Dante, his follower Cino. These (especially the last three) were Petrarch's first masters in the use of this form: but he quickly went on his own way, a way marked on the one hand by incessant introspective analysis, and on the other by an unprecedented artistry in the balancing of part with part and in making the whole small composition converge on a pregnant and musically satisfying conclusion. And since the introspection never ceases to advert both to the flow of time and to the *quality* of the subject's use of a gift so precious and so transient, the sonnet, in Petrarch's hands becomes, for the first time in literature, an instrument of spiritual autobiography; and no more serious use could be made of it. No wonder then that when he came to construct the *Canzoniere*, Petrarch put his sonnets and canzoni on an equal footing – mingling the two forms, against all historical precedent, to make one book (the 'consistent practice', as E. H. Wilkins notes, 'in MS collections of pre-Petrarchan lyrics' having been 'the separation of canzoni and sonnets', *The Making*, p.266). Incidentally, any such mingling would have seemed a stylistic mishmash to the Dante of the *DVE* (II, iii, 2–5, iv, 1–6).

Petrarch took over the sonnet form much as the 'stilnovisti' had left it. Like them, but more exclusively, he preferred for the octet the double quatrain pattern ABBA ABBA (304 times in the *Canzoniere*); altering it once, in 279, to ABAB BABA. The older, continuous pattern ABABABAB he used 12 times. In the sestet he preferred, on balance, 3 rhymes to 2; his favourite 3-rhyme pattern (120 instances) being the simplest: CDE CDE; which of all the sestet patterns is considered the 'gravest', because of the number of rhymes, their relative distance from one another and their being arranged 'open-endedly'.[117] Appropriately, it is used in the Prologue-sonnet *Voi ch'ascoltate*; notably also in 35, 62, 189, 263. Petrarch was also fond (67 instances) of the slightly more complex pattern (rather favoured by Dante) CDE DCE. This reversal in the second tercet of the positions of C and D seem to have been aimed, most often, either at effecting a suspense before the final couplet (as in nos. 81, 90, 293, 316) or at emphasising the fourth rhyme-word (e.g. *sovente* in 32, *nostra* in 285, *Morte* in 298). Curiously, Petrarch uses only once (93) the elegant 'chiastic' pattern CDE EDC, of which both Cavalcanti and Dante were fond (see the former's *Chi'è questa che ven* and the latter's *Tanto gentile*). Of the 2-rhyme patterns, Petrarch's favourite by far was again the simplest: CDC DCD. Note that though this pattern is based on two rhymes twice repeated, it divides rhythmically into two tercets, the division being more or less distinctly marked – compare for example 193 or 292 with 361. If the last couplet is stressed there is a counterpoint effect, as in 254. Occasionally the first tercet is simply repeated with the rhyme in the same order, as in 78, 97 and 311. Two other rarely used patterns may be noted: CDD DCC (four times) and CDC CCD (once, in 38).

5. STYLISTIC SOUNDINGS : RHYTHM AND REPRESENTATION

Introducing the Prologue-sonnet *Voi ch'ascoltate*, Contini speaks of its 'shattering novelty' as something one is 'physically aware of at the first reading'.[118] The novelty immediately in question is Petrarch's sensitivity to the passage of time; in itself a matter of content and theme rather than of style. But it is, the critic tells us, above all in the 'tone' of the verse that this Petrarchan characteristic is so unmistakably evident; and what is 'tone' if not an effect of style? On the other hand, if Petrarch's stylistic distinctiveness is more or less self-evident, it has never been analysed systematically under all its aspects. There are excellent studies – by Contini himself, by M. Fubini, F. Chiappelli, M. P. Simonelli, D. Alonso and others – of aspects of his style, but nothing on the *Canzoniere* as a whole corresponding, for example, to Patrick Boyde's study of Dante's lyrics. However, there is more than enough good published work on the subject to justify my present modest undertaking, the purpose of which is to call attention to features of Petrarch's manner and diction which are certainly characteristic, even if the relative frequency of their occurrence in his lyrics, as compared with those of his Italian predecessors and contemporaries, has not been worked out systematically in detail.[119] I have in mind such features as the following:

1) His predilection for binary structures (whether in the form of parallel or antithetical phrases within the same line or group of lines, or of the pairing of nouns, adjectives, verbs, singly or in couples).

2) His decisive development of the sonnet as a balanced 'period',[120] together with his peculiar mastery, especially in the sonnets, of the art of concluding (as in *Canz.* 1, 9, 34, 35, 90, 180, 229, 292 and others).

3) His copious and subtle use of assonance.[121]

4) His fondness for polysyndetons (repetition of the copula, as at 32.11; 50.47–50; 204.2; 292.2; or of a preposition, as at 282.14, or a relative pronoun, as at 126.46–52).

5) His special interest in the sestina.[122]

6) His exquisite sense, in the canzoni, of the lightening or decorative, or even the oratorical effect of the 7-syllable line (125, 126, 128, 129).
7) More generally, his overriding concern for harmony and balance (see above in section 4, pp.115–16).

A fact often overlooked is that Petrarch saw style as intimately connected with meaning. If he was justly proud of the clarity of his Italian verse (cf. 293.8), this was because 'clarity is the very hall-mark of intelligence' (Prose, p.734). He would have agreed with Bembo, 'altro non è lo scrivere che parlare pensatamente', 'writing is simply well-pondered speech'.[123] To use a helpful distinction drawn by Simonelli, Petrarch as a stylist worked on two levels, the 'purely phonic' and the 'phonic-semantic'; on the first his concern was to render unnecessary any 'musical accompaniment in the strict sense'; on the second, and surely for him the more important level, his concern was to devise a musical, that is a rhythmic and tonal, representation of his meaning that would serve precisely as its right *interpretation* in a given passage – that is, as the indispensable aid to an intelligent reading of the passage.[124]

If poetry is a kind of verbal music, it involves two elements, rhythm and representation. Both of these imply of course in a given poem a given choice of words – a vocabulary or diction – but representation relates more directly and immediately to the words themselves, and rhythm to their arrangement. In attempting, in what follows, to illustrate leading features of Petrarch's style I have selected poems, or parts of poems, which seem to me to bring out qualities of rhythm and representation and the interaction of one with the other. In a first section I treat in some detail a single sonnet, the subject matter of which might be termed introspective – the poet communing with his own thoughts – and which exemplifies characteristically Petrarchan qualities of rhythm. In two following sections I concentrate rather on Petrarch's capacity for exciting the visual imagination, first in a group of poems in which aspects of nature are prominent, and then in another group largely concerned with describing Laura.

A sonnet of introspection (32)

Quanto piú m'avicino al giorno extremo
che l'umana miseria suol far breve,
piú veggio il tempo andar veloce et leve,
e 'l mio di lui sperar fallace et scemo.

I' dico a' miei pensier': Non molto andremo
d'amor parlando omai, ché 'l duro et greve
terreno incarco come frescha neve
si va struggendo; onde noi pace avremo:

perché co llui cadrà quella speranza
che ne fe' vaneggiar sí lungamente,
e 'l riso e 'l pianto, et la paura et l'ira;

sí vedrem chiaro poi come sovente
per le cose dubbiose altri s'avanza,
et come spesso indarno si sospira.

[The more I approach the last day that makes all our misery
short-lived, the more swiftly and lightly I see time run by, and
that the hopes I place in it are deceitful and empty. I say to my
thoughts: 'Not much longer now shall we talk of love, for this
hard and heavy earthly burden of ours is melting like new-fallen
snow, so that [soon] we'll have peace: for with it will die the
hope which has kept us raving so long, and all the laughter and
weeping and fears and vexations; and then we'll see clearly
how often things doubtful prove beneficial, and how often one
sighs for no reason.']125

There are two interconnected themes here, the shortness of life and
the end of illusions, the former predominant in the quatrains, the
latter in the tercets; these parts being clearly distinguished, so that
the line-pattern is 4+4: 3+3. The brevity of life, as individually
perceived ('veggio', 3), is dwelt on in the soliloquy beginning at
line 5. Note the effect of intimacy in the 'we' contained in 'andremo',
'avremo'. Then in lines 6–8 that faintly metaphorical 'veggio' is
reinforced by the melting snow simile which annuls, as it were, the
density of 'terreno incarco', the solid weight of which, with the stress
on the fourth 'position' in the line ('position' is a less misleading term
here than 'syllable'), is largely due to the preceding *enjambement*.
Meanwhile the second and deeper of the two themes – deeper as
representing a moral response to the mere *fact* of growing old – has
come to the surface in line 2, and again in 4–6, and finally in the second
hemistich of 8, 'onde…'. This last phrase draws the logical consequence of the described physical decline, in the light of the
generalisation enunciated in line 2, while leaving that consequence
ambiguous. For while the reader's attention has been forcibly caught
by line 2 – this 'catching' being due in part to the line's initial unclearness owing to the inversion of verb and object – the disconcerting idea

therein enunciated, the seeming identification of human life with unhappiness, this remains, down to line 8 inclusively, 'in the air' and unexplained. It is evidently connected with the illusions involved in human hopes (4), but what will be the effect of that termination of it implied by 'giorno extremo...'? What will be the resulting 'peace' in the expectation of which the octet ends? Will it consist in the mere cessation of life's fitful fever? Or in some positive good envisaged, after death? It is, in fact, to the latter position that the sonnet will finally point; but only in the final tercet, and then only indirectly. In the first tercet the field of vision is still bounded by death; lines 9–11 doing no more than explicate the metaphorical statement in the second quatrain to the effect that all our concern with 'amor' is a matter of life in the body and in time; merely spelling this out in terms of the emotions that love gives rise to; thus leaving in parenthesis the second half of line 8 which had looked beyond all this present fret and fury because it looked beyond death. Only with line 12 is that half-line resumed and expanded, in the form of an imagined *retrospect from the afterlife*; a retrospect which, it is now insinuated, will be an awareness *then* of a positive value in our perplexities and longings *now* (in this sense lines 12–14 here go beyond the conclusion of *Canz.* 1, where the retrospect is still from within the *present* life). There is a probable reminiscence here of Virgil's 'forsan et haec olim meminisse iuvabit', 'perhaps one day it will be pleasant to recall even this distress' (*Aeneid* 1, 203).

I dwell on these thematic points chiefly to bring out the three-fold *movement* of the poem: from the first quatrain to the second, and from the second, first to the first tercet and then to the second one. Notice how the first and third movements are interrelated by the characteristic binary patterning. In the first quatrain the governing verb 'veggio' has two objects, the infinitives 'andar' and 'sperar', each with its pair of adverbial adjectives. This pattern then recedes, except for the binomial in line 6, only to be resumed in the concluding tercet where the main verb – again a form of 'vedere' – governs two exactly parallel phrases. The effect of the reiterated binary patterning, reinforced by the use of the same main verb, in significantly different tenses, in lines 3 and 12, serves to hold this fairly complex little poem together.

Syntactically, the last three parts (lines 5–14) interrelate more closely than the first two (1–8); not so much because of the full stop at the end of line 4 as because all the rest is soliloquy expressly introduced as such (5), and also because of the prominently placed 'perché' in line 9, presenting all that follows as explanatory of the statement terminating the second quatrain. The result is a certain discrepancy between the sonnet's syntactic and logical movement and the rhyme-pattern of octet plus sestet; and it was perhaps to offset this that Petrarch added weight to the second quatrain – thus reinforcing its difference qua quatrain from the tercets – by slowing down the rhythm: note the halt after 'pensier' in line 5, the slighter yet still distinct pauses after 'omai' and 'incarco' (6 and 7), the strong caesura in line 8, the effect of which is enhanced by the subordinate stress on 'pace' in the second hemistich. These four caesural pauses are the more obvious factors in the process in question; but rhythmically, of course, they presuppose the accentuations which immediately or almost immediately precede them in lines 5–8; those on 'pensiér', 'omái', 'incárco', 'struggéndo'; each of which represents, in fact, the dominant stress in the line in which it occurs, and consequently the main factor in determining its particular rhythm. And since this main stress falls in lines 5 and 6 on the sixth metrical syllable, and in lines 7 and 8 on the fourth, the former pair of lines are of the *a maiore* type and the latter of the *a minore* (see section 4 above, pp.107–8). But this difference as such has nothing to do with alterations of pace or tempo as between any two lines. In this respect the determining factors may be expected to be (a) a caesura after the *dominant* stress in a given line,[126] and (b) in some cases a reinforcement of the effect of the caesura by *subordinate* accentuation, which as we have seen is the case in line 8. It is the case too in lines 6 and 7, with the difference that in these lines the relevant stresses are in the first hemistich – on 'amór' and 'parlándo' in 6, on 'terréno' in 7. In lines 5 and 8 the strength of the caesurae makes such reinforcement in the first hemistiches unnecessary.

There is no caesura of comparable strength in the first quatrain. Here the lines are all *a maiore* – even, as I read it, line 3. This of itself says nothing as to the 'pace' of any line, but it happens that each of these four has a subordinate stress the effect of which, *given its placing in the line*, is to quicken the tempo; I mean the stresses on 'piú' (1), 'umána' (2), 'velóce' (3) and 'fallace' (4). Take the case of line 3, to my ear the fastest-moving in the quatrain. The interesting thing here is that a certain 'rapidity' is achieved in spite of an inbuilt obstacle, namely the stress on 'tempo' in the fourth position. For at a first reading doesn't a doubt rather easily arise whether the main stress should not be placed here (thus making the line *a minore*) rather than on 'andar' in the sixth position? And the doubt is resolved, surely, only by the marked stress on 'velóce' in the eighth position, which so reinforces the otherwise rather light one on 'andár' as to cancel the delaying effect of 'tempo'. The result is that the complete verb 'veggio...andar' can all be contained within the first hemistich, before the caesura, leaving the second one for the adverbial phrase alone, 'veloce et leve', which makes, obviously, for a speedier line. My scansion here may be disputed, but not the general principle that the arrangement of subordinate stresses is a principal key to this aspect of hendecasyllabic rhythm.

I have stressed the logical and syntactical links between the second quatrain and the tercets. Yet to read this sonnet as an expression of feeling is to be struck by the way the tercets detach themselves from the octet to form a distinct musical unity with its own emotive charge. The first distinguishing feature is of course the obligatory change in the rhyme-pattern. But, here as elsewhere, the poetic effect of that change depends on the sound of the new rhyme-words chosen, and on their arrangement. The new rhymes are '-anza', '-ente', '-ira'; in that order in the first tercet. This order is important because of the new note struck by 'speranza', which with its open 'a' in the rhyme-syllables, in sharp contrast with the half-assonantal rhyming in '-emo' and '-eve' throughout the octet, serves to accentuate the detachment of the second main section of the poem from the first. This once effected, interest is focused on the three rhyme sounds in the sestet and on their arrangement, which changes from CDE in the first tercet to DCE in the second. The tempo of both '-anza' lines (C) is fairly quick, that of both '-ente' lines (D) rather slow, that of the first of the '-ira' lines (E) is *andante*, while the second is slow. And this last change, from *andante* to slow, means of course that the poem ends on a slow line, a 'dying fall'. Indeed the final tercet is predominantly slow, as compared with the first one, in that it both begins and ends with a relatively slow line. Moreover, to this slowing down of the second tercet corresponds a softening of the rhyme sounds: 'sovente' is softer than 'lungamente' (especially as preceded by 'sí') and while one might argue about 'avanza' and 'speranza', 'sospira' certainly calls for a softer enunciation than 'ira', both because of its meaning and because of its onomatopoeia. Thus the precondition of the 'dying fall' on which the sonnet ends is a pattern, involving the whole sestet, of various tempos and varying rhyme sounds.

While visual imagery is not absent from *Quanto più m'avvicino*, its sensuous effect is much more aural than visual; and this is in sharp contrast to *Apollo, s'anchor vive* (34), for example, where everything converges on the final brilliant image of Laura seated on the grass in springtime:

> sí vedrem poi per meraviglia inseme
> seder la donna nostra sopra l'erba,
> et far de le sue braccia a se stessa ombra.
>   (12–14)

[thus we shall then together see and marvel at our lady sitting on the grass, and shading herself with her arms.]

No. 34 is indeed a 'happy' poem, and this comes across chiefly pictorially; in the metaphors of lines 5–6 and 11, rendering the return of fine weather after the cold and clouds of winter, and in that final vision of the Laura/laurel in sunshine. It is this vision, this achievement of pure visualisation that holds all our attention, 'per meraviglia', at the end. In 32, by contrast, there is a minimum of objective visualisation; the poem makes a comment on experience, which is at the same time, inevitably, an expression of the poet's emotion. The difference between the two sonnets, the one a soliloquy, the other an address (to the sun-god, Apollo), is roughly that between a meditation and a picture.

And here a further, and deeper, contrast suggests itself; or rather it is suggested by a rather striking verbal correspondence between the closing tercets of these two sonnets: that at the same place in the last sentence of each poem, the same phrase is used to express an expectancy of 'vision', and so of some kind of 'visualisation': 'sí vedrem... poi' (32.12); 'sí vedrem poi' (34.12).[127] Only, in the one case the expectancy is fulfilled and in the other not. In 32, notwithstanding the reinforcement of 'vedrem' by the stressed 'chiaro' – so that verb and adjectival adverb together point towards some as yet unveiled brilliancy of vision – this last remains in the end out of sight. And of course it couldn't be otherwise; since here 'poi', 'then', refers to a moment *after* death; death is included within the time-perspective envisaged; whereas in 34 the thought of it simply doesn't arise. In other words, the vision at the close of 34, the epiphany of the Laura/laurel, proves this poem as *this*-worldly as the simultaneous expectancy and withholding of vision proves 32 *other*-worldly. The one ends on a triumphant affirmation of precisely that which the other had discounted: 'Not much longer now shall we talk of love' (32.5–6). The two poems indeed take up contrary positions; not with respect to the good in general – 32 is not a cynical poem – but with respect to the supreme earthly good, which in the *Canzoniere* is

Laura. The object of 'vaneggiar' in 32.9–11, she is the object of quasi-religious – paganly so, of course – contemplation in 34.12–14. Was it precisely to point this contrast that Petrarch introduced the *finale* of both sonnets – such near neighbours in the *Canzoniere* – with the same phrase in the same place?

So far it is the rhythmical aspect of Petrarch's style that has most concerned us, this being the most conspicuous aspect in 32. Before we turn to the other, representational element in the *Canzoniere* – that is to Petrarch's capacity for exciting the visual imagination – a few general remarks on his diction seem to be called for, and I return for a moment to sonnet 32.

The vocabulary of this poem is perfectly normal in the sense that there are no rare words.[128] If 'vaneggiar' (10) and 'indarno' strike the reader as characteristic, this may be only because each recalls a line of a better-known poem of Petrarch (e.g. *Canz.* 1.12; 62.2; or 62.7; 81.8; 159.9). Tonally, in any case, the words are in keeping with the 'disillusion' that pervades so much of the *Canzoniere*. The same feeling or attitude may perhaps be behind the figurative use of 'scemo' (4) in the sense of 'hollow', 'empty', for which there is no exact parallel in Dante, for example. But a far more pregnant comparison with Dantean usage is prompted by 'onde noi pace avremo' (8). Curiously, 'pace' occurs 36 times in both the *Commedia* and the *Canzoniere*; but whereas in Petrarch its connotations are chiefly negative – the *absence* of distress – its characteristic implication in the mature Dante is strongly positive; perfect self-fulfilment in the *active* vision of God.[129] This is not to say that spiritual 'peace' was not of the utmost importance for Petrarch; the last three lines of the *Canzoniere* are a passionate prayer for it; but only that he used the term to express sentiment rather than thought, a desire rather than an idea. Where Petrarch is subtle and precise is in his rendering of the 'inner world' of mood and feeling (as the foregoing analysis of 32 will, I hope, have shown); where vagueness and generality begin is where the external world begins, at the doors of sense-perception, or where the mind investigates the objective nature of things through abstractions and ratiocination. The concrete, sensuously perceived figure of Laura represents to some extent, it is true, an exception; to which I shall return presently; but in general Petrarch feels the sensible world far more than he tries to represent it. The countless evocations of natural objects in his verse – trees, hills, birds, sun, stars etc. – involve a minimum of objective curiosity and therefore of particularisation. His language, as Contini says, is 'non-naturalistic';[130] utterly different, in this respect, from Dante's or Montale's. To cite Contini again, in Petrarch's verse 'rhythm prevails over the semantic component' ('sulla semanticità'); though it is also true that its rhythms are always supported by a clear logical structure, after the model of the 'Stilnovisti'. This logically structured introspection is in Petrarch's verse that 'matter and meaning' which Hopkins called 'the element necessary to support and employ the shape', that is the poetry, 'which is contemplated for its own sake'.[131]

However, one must beware of over-pressing Contini's thesis on the 'prevalence of rhythm' in Petrarch unless one has taken care to define very closely that 'semanticità' over which, it is asserted, rhythm in Petrarch habitually prevails. In default of such a definition, the case remains open as regards this or that line or sequence. With regard to any line of poetry one can at least ask whether the rhythm determines the choice of words, or *vice versa*. In 'after life's fitful fever he sleeps well' it was surely the phrase 'fitful fever' that determined the eventual rhythm. The case would seem to be similar in line 10 of our sonnet, dominated as it is by 'vaneggiar'; the occurrence of which here is sufficiently accounted for by the preceding 'speranza', which it exposes as illusory, without any predetermining melody or rhythm. And 'vaneggiar' in its turn probably suggested the four nouns in line 11, as naming the usual components of Petrarch's 'raving' (cf. 1.12; 62.2); spelling out, as this line does, the classical fourfold division of the passions, compare *Aeneid* VI, 733, *Secretum* I (*Prose*, p.64). Where a preconceived rhythm probably was the determining factor was in the polysyndeton arrangement, 'e...e...et...et...', and in the *order* of the nouns; the combination of which factors gives line 11 its emotional tone, as the reader may judge for himself. Note that the word-order chosen results in a half-assonance of the first and the last noun, according to a distribution of assonance – or it might be of alliterations – in a given line of which the critic who has made the closest study of this matter, Simonelli, tells us that Petrarch 'was particularly fond'.[132] Of the many examples given by Simonelli, we may note here 'dove rotte dal vento piangon l'onde' (67.2); 'nocte et dí tiemmi il signor nostro Amore' (112.14); and the first quatrain of 141:

> Come talora al caldo tempo sole
> semplicetta farfalla al lume avezza,
> volar negli occhi altrui, per sua vaghezza [alliteration]
> onde aven ch'ella more, altri si dole...

[As sometimes in hot weather the simple butterfly, being

accustomed to seek the light, will fly into someone's eyes, attracted by their light, so that it dies and the person suffers.]

Four Nature Poems (33, 50, 180, 310)

Turning now to the matter of visualisation, and first to that of objects and scenes in nature, a nice example comes to hand in another early sonnet, 33:

> Già fiammeggiava l'amorosa stella
> per l'orïente, et l'altra che Giunone
> suol far gelosa nel septentrïone,
> rotava i raggi suoi lucente et bella...
>   (1–4)

[Already the star of love was aflame in the east, and that other constellation in the north which is wont to make Juno jealous was wheeling its rays, shining and beautiful.]

The first 'star' is of course Venus, rising before daybreak (1–2); the 'other one' (2) is collectively the Great Bear. The passing mythological allusion (2–3) is fairly typical (cf. 10.4; 129.43–4; 223.1; 310.6; 325.65), but in terms of the visualisation aimed at, lines 1–3 are all in function of the brilliantly pictorial line 4; and this in two ways: by directing attention to the *reality* of the night sky, first eastwards, then to the north (simultaneously putting into mere parenthesis the 'jealousy' of Juno); and by a slowing down of the rhythm, especially with the delaying, five-syllable word 'septentrïone', which enhances by contrast the quickened pace of line 4, especially in its first hemistich. Note that while lines 1–3 are all *a minore*, line 4 is *a maiore*; with its dominant stress on 'suoi' preceded by two subordinate ones in the second and in the fourth position, 'rotava' and 'raggi'; but the line is principally *visual*: 'raggi...lucente et bella'.

No. 50 (1337?), *Ne la stagion*, is a variation on a theme superbly handled by Dante in his canzone *Io son venuto*, which Patrick Boyde and I have described as 'the most sustained and brilliant working out of a *topos* common in the medieval lyric: the comparison or contrast of the feelings of the lover and the forces of nature, especially as... shown in the cycle of the seasons'.[133] We noted too this difference between *Io son venuto* and its probable Provençal model, Arnaut Daniel's *Quan chai la fuelha*, that the contrast, the turning point of each stanza, between the lover's feelings and the natural setting is in Dante's poem made five times in its five stanzas; a feature which Petrarch exactly reproduces. On the other hand whereas in Dante's poem the scene and setting is simply winter, from five points of view, in Petrarch's it is the oncoming of evening as the time of rest for man and beast – exactly the same situation, in fact, as that evoked in lines 1–3 of *Inferno* II (may not the exquisite 'e 'nbrunir le contrade d'oriente', 'and the eastern regions growing dark' (line 31) be a reminiscence of Dante's 'l'aere bruno'?). Hence in *Ne la stagion* the human figures in stanzas 1–4, and the tired oxen in stanza 5. A further difference is structural, that Petrarch varies the moment of the entry on scene of the love-tormented poet from stanza to stanza; it is three lines from the end of st. 1, four from the end of st. 2–3, no less than eleven from the end of st. 4–5. These variations, especially the major shift *upwards* in stanza 4 and the following prolonged polysyndeton ('e' repeated 7 times in 4 lines), powerfully affect the rhythm and tone of the poem. But no less effective poetically is the series of pictures in miniature – lines 4–11, 17–20, 29–32, 43–5, 58–9.

A brilliantly dynamic effect of movement in opposed directions is achieved in the sonnet 180 (1345?).[134] Petrarch is on a boat going down the Po, perhaps on his way from Parma to Verona; but his spirit simultaneously flies westward to and over the Alps, to Avignon where Laura is. The addressee throughout is the great river itself:

Po, ben puo' tu portartene la scorza
di me con tue possenti et rapide onde,
ma lo spirto ch'iv'entro si nasconde
non cura né di tua né d'altrui forza;

lo qual senz'alternar poggia con orza
dritto per l'aure al suo desir seconde,
battendo l'ali verso l'aurea fronde,
l'acqua e 'l vento e la vela e i remi sforza.

[Po, you may well bear along my outward shell with your powerful rapid current, but my spirit concealed therein spurns your and every other force; and – without tacking to port or starboard – straight through the breeze that yields to its desire, beating its wings towards the golden leaves [the golden-haired Laura-laurel], it overcomes the water, the wind, the sail and the oars.][135]

Rhythmically the pulse of this octet beats hardest in lines 6–8; lines 6 and 7 being *a minore*, while in 8 a caesura is barely discernible owing to the almost equal distribution of the stresses.[136] Visually – with the parallel glimpses of the river flowing one way (1–2) and the 'bird' flying in the reverse, westerly direction, drawn by the far-off gleam of the Laura/laurel (6–8) – the quatrains prepare us for the sestet; where the two opposed movements are restated, each with the maximum energy:

> Re degli altri, superbo altero fiume,
> che 'ncontri 'l sol quando e' ne mena 'l giorno,
> e 'n ponente abandoni un piú bel lume,
>
> tu te ne vai col mio mortal sul corno;
> l'altro coverto d'amorose piume
> torna volando al suo dolce soggiorno.

[King of rivers, proudly pre-eminent, who meet the sun as it brings in the day, and in the west leave behind you a lovelier light: you bear on your horns the mortal part of me; the other, covered with the feathers of love, flies back to its sweet dwelling.]

The Po, already personified (1), has become the king of rivers and, now viewed, as it were, from the zenith, is seen in its full west-to-east extent, from sunset to sunrise (10–11). It is then the turn of the poet's 'spirit', that is, for giving full scope to the bird metaphor of the second quatrain. Leaving the body far below, caught on the 'horns' of the eastward flowing river, the spirit-bird's immense flight back to the Alps and beyond is triumphantly re-affirmed (13–14). Note the pulsating rhythm of the concluding line; with the dominant stress on 'volándo', it has two strong subordinate ones, in the first and the seventh positions. Note too the assonances in lines 9 and 10, 'superbo, altero / 'ncontri, sol', and the half-assonances in 12 and 14, 'mortal, corno / torna, dolce'. Finally, note the force of line 9; *a minore*, with strong accentuation on the first and the sixth syllables and the marked assonance in the second hemistich.

My last example of Petrarch's pure nature-poetry is the octet of 310:

> Zephiro torna, e 'l bel tempo rimena,
> e i fiori et l'erbe, sua dolce famiglia,
> et garrir Progne et pianger Philomena,
> et primavera candida et vermiglia.
>
> Ridono i prati, e 'l ciel si rasserena;
> Giove s'allegra di mirar sua figlia;
> l'aria et l'acqua et la terra è d'amor piena;
> ogni animal d'amar si riconsiglia.

[The west wind returns and the fine weather with it, and its sweet progeny of flowers and grass, and chattering Procne and weeping Philomena, and spring, all silver-white and red. The

meadows laugh and the sky is clear again, Jupiter rejoices gazing
at his daughter, the air, the waters, the earth are full of love, every
living thing turns again to thoughts of love.]

Calling these lines 'pure' nature-poetry, I mean only that Laura has
no explicit part in the scene described. The description itself is, of
course, soaked in feeling and also in literary reminiscence. Yet, as
Contini says (*Letteratura*, p.617), the classical-mythological patina has
no dimming effect on the poem's 'bewitching charm'. The quatrains
are parallel, rhythmically and structurally; the first line of each is
a minore, and with an accent on the first syllable; and each moves
from the general to the particular and back again. Thus lines 1–4 tell
of the west wind bringing back fine weather with its *consequence* of
flowers, grass, bird-song; while line 4 synthesises the visual effect of
the whole spring landscape thus evoked. Again in lines 5–8, there is
first a glance taking in both earth and sky; then one at the night sky
lit up by the brightest of the planets, Jupiter and Venus; then a glance
back at the earth once more, with attention now focused on the love-
impulse reborn and all-pervasive; thus preparing us for the sestet with
its conventional contrasting of all that happy natural setting with the
poet's sad human heart. All the lines except 7 are *a minore*. The visual
nuclei are lines 4 and 6. Note the exquisite *vagueness* of line 4, on which
so much of the effect of the whole depends; it is infinitely more
evocative than descriptive.

Four Laura poems (90, 126, 198, 302)

In the earlier part of the *Canzoniere* Laura is linked through her name
with the tale of Apollo and Daphne as told by Ovid in *Metamorphoses*
1: the nymph, pursued by the god, turns into the laurel tree henceforth
sacred to him – and, in the *Canzoniere*, especially to him as the sun-
god and the patron of poets. But the fantasy of Laura in person as
Apollo's beloved, after a brilliant expression in 34, fades away;
recalled only briefly, here and there, as in 41, 51, 60, 188, 197. The use
of the Laura/laurel symbol, shorn of Ovidian trappings, is more
persistent, lasting well into Part II (269, 318, 327, 337). But already
far back in Part I it had begun to take second place to direct representa-
tions, more or less imaginative, of Laura (37, 71–3, 90, 126, 127, etc.).
Consider one of the most celebrated of these, 90: Laura, her youth
now past, is remembered as she once was:

> Erano i capei d'oro a l'aura sparsi
> che 'n mille dolci nodi gli avolgea,

e 'l vago lume oltra misura ardea
di quei begli occhi, ch'or ne son sí scarsi;

e 'l viso di pietosi color' farsi,
non so se vero o falso, mi parea:
i' che l'esca amorosa al petto avea,
qual meraviglia se di subito arsi?

[Her golden hair was loosed to the breeze, which turned it in a
thousand sweet knots, and her eyes burned with the loveliness
of the light which they show so sparingly now; and her face, it
seemed to me – truly or falsely, I know not – took on the colour
of compassion: I, who had love's tinder in my breast, it's no
wonder I at once caught fire.]

The inversion of subject and auxiliary verb in line 1, focusing
attention immediately on the *action* of Laura's hair flowing in the
breeze (the flow itself being suggested by the dactylic rhythm of
ērănŏ), at the same time places the entrancing experience recorded
here irrevocably in the past; re-lived – but how intensely – only in
memory. But it is only after the caesura in line 4 that this difference
between Laura past and present becomes explicit with the switch
to the present tense: 'ch'or ne *son*...'; which phrase at once introduces
the reflective, self-questioning second quatrain. The poet stands back
from the recalled enchantment to take the measure of it; first by
comparing past with present (4); then, with the cool 'aside' of line 6,
by raising a doubt even as to the past – a doubt, not, of course, as to
Laura's beauty then but as to its significance in his own regard (5–6).
After which these hesitations are shrugged off with the wryly resigned
reflection of lines 7–8. By now the original lyric elation is somewhat
deflated. The process in question – the penetration of the poem by the
rational factor can be traced in the changes of tense in the verbs:
three successive imperfects (1–3) have been followed by two presents
(4 and 6) and these again by two imperfects (6 and 7); until all comes
to rest in the past definite 'arsi' (8) concluding the rhetorical question
prompted by the original, lyrically recalled experience. Clearly, the
complexity of the poem so far (but the same will be true of the sestet)
is due to the rational factor; which is thus no less essential to it than the
brilliant word-play and assonantal patterning of the first quatrain.[137]

After the detached second quatrain the tercets return (with an
echo of *Aeneid* I, 327–9 and cf. 319) to the enchantments of memory:

Non era l'andar suo cosa mortale,
ma d'angelica forma; et le parole

sonavan altro, che pur voce humana.
Uno spirto celeste, un vivo sole
fu quel ch'i' vidi…

[Her walk was not that of a mortal being, but of some angelic
form, and her words sounded different from a merely human
voice: a heavenly spirit, a living sun was what I saw…]

Note how line 9 has linked up with line 1, verbally ('Erano' /'Non
era') and rhythmically (both are *a maiore*, with a subordinate stress
in the fifth position: 'capei', 'andar'). Assonantal patterning is
resumed: 'mortale / forma'; and, with alliteration, 'vivo /vidi'. But
rationality has the last word (13–14):

…et se non fosse or tale,
piagha per allentar d'arco non sana.

[…and if now things are otherwise, a wound isn't healed by the
slackening of the bow.]

But it is a reflective rationality made so to blend with the emotive
factor, reaffirmed in lines 9–12, as to bring the psychological complexity of the whole sonnet to final perfect equilibrium. In this sense
Petrarch wrote nothing more *typical* of his art than this sonnet-
ending. Note, in line 14, the assonances at each end of it *and* in the
middle, and the deliberately disturbing effect of juxtaposing the
accents in the sixth and seventh positions ('-tar' /d'arco'); finally,
the withholding to the end of the line of the emotionally crucial 'non
sana'.

This poem and that other sonnet of reminiscence, but written after
her death, *Gli occhi di ch'io parlai* (292), together present the whole of
Laura, physically considered. The resulting image is in itself both
conventional and fairly simple; the richness of Petrarch's lyrics is all
in the thought, emotion and artistry engendered by it. This is so at
least while Laura is still alive. After her death, as her corporeal image
gives place to the 'invisible form' that is her soul (268.37), a self-
aware, self-expressive personality shines through as never before. To
this I shall come presently; meanwhile something remains to be said
on the depiction of Laura in *Canzoniere* I.

The most celebrated picture of Laura in a natural setting is no doubt
Chiare, fresche et dolci acque (126). It will suffice to quote stanzas 4–5:

Da' be' rami scendea   40
(dolce ne la memoria)
una pioggia di fior' sovra il suo grembo;
et ella si sedea

humile in tanta gloria,
coverta già de l'amoroso nembo.   45
Qual fior cadea sul lembo,
qual su le treccie bionde,
ch'oro forbito et perle
eran quel dí a vederle;
qual si posava in terra, et qual su l'onde;   50
qual con un vago errore
girando parea dir: Qui regna Amore.

Quante volte diss'io
allor pien di spavento:
Costei per fermo nacque in paradiso.   55
Cosí carco d'oblio
il divin portamento
e 'l volto e le parole e 'l dolce riso
m'aveano, et sí diviso
da l'imagine vera,   60
ch'i' dicea sospirando:
Qui come venn'io, o quando?;
credendo esser in ciel, non là dov'era.
Da indi in qua mi piace
questa herba sí, ch'altrove non ò pace.   65

[From the branches was falling – sweet in memory – into her lap
a shower of blossom; and she sat there, humble in such glory,
already covered with the loving cloud; this flower fell on her
skirt, this on her golden locks, which that day seemed burnished
gold and pearls; this one came to rest on the ground, this one
on the water; this one, with a lovely wandering motion,
seemed as it spun to say: 'here Love reigns'. How often did I say
to myself then, full of fear and wonder: 'Surely she was born in
paradise!' So flooded me in oblivion had her divine bearing, her
face, her words, her sweet smile, and so distracted me from the
real image presented to my eyes, that with sighs I was saying:
'How and when did I come here?' – imagining myself in Heaven,
not there where I was. Since then I find no peace save in these
meadows.]

The effect of this poem as a whole very largely depends on two
structural features – the free use of the 7-syllable line (9 of the 13 lines
in each stanza) and the sudden change from future to past tense at
the beginning of stanza 4. As to the first, a natural effect of hepta-

syllables in series is to lighten the pause at the line-endings; while at the same time, where rhyme is used, that effect is continually offset by the rhyming. The result, in the hands of a master like Petrarch, is the kind of blend of delicacy and distinctness that we find here, especially in the stanzas quoted. Note, as contributing to this general effect, the *enjambements* at lines 7–8 and 34–5 (here following an alliteration) and 53–4, and the separation of auxiliary verb and past participle (inverted) in 56–9, with, between, the polysyndeton of line 58. Note too how in this canzone (but not in its companion piece no. 125) the *arpeggio* effect of the heptasyllables is balanced by the closing of each stanza on a hendecasyllable – a detail indispensable to the tone of the whole.

The hidden import of the change of tenses at the opening of stanza 4 is metaphysical and religious; from a mere dream of the future (st. 2–3) Petrarch passes to the contemplation of a *real* experience in the past, 'sweet in the memory', line 41; and then, in st. 5, to a *new* kind of unreality inasmuch as the resultant ecstasy has an illusory object. Isolating the Laura revealed in that moment of time, *from* time, he misconceives that experience as 'paradisal' (55), as though it were a glimpse of that Beauty which alone is both truly eternal (in contrast with the flux of time) and finally beatific (in contrast with all temporal joys). In short, misconceiving the 'transcendance' of memory with respect to the time-flow, he makes of Laura a false final end, a substitute for God. That this indeed is the implication of st. 4–5 – above all of '...diss'io / allor pien di *spavento*: / Costei per fermo nacque in *paradiso*. / Cosí carco *d'oblio* / il *divin* portamento...' (53–7) – cannot however be established by purely stylistic analysis, but only by a careful study of such key-words here as 'spavento' and above all 'oblio'; the former being, I think, equivalent here to the Latin 'stupor' as used in *Secretum* III (*Prose* p.152) to describe the first dazzling effect on Petrarch of Laura's beauty; and the latter to the consequent 'oblivio Dei', 'God-forgetfulness' (ibid. pp.265–71).[138]

The 39 sonnets of the series 159–98 are exceptionally rich in imagery and metaphor as also in rare and difficult rhyme-words; features indicative of a return here to the *leitmotiv* of 129–35, the 'strangeness' of the Laura-experience. It was a strangeness conducive to dismay and fear at least as much as to joy (compare 173, 194, 197–198 with 159, 193.9–14, and cf. 126.64–5). And it may be for the same reason that while Laura can still be placed, as in 126, in a rural setting – 160, 165, 190 (but here she is, emblematically, a white doe), 192 – Petrarch now tends to a preference for 'close-ups' (as in 173,

185 (but here she is a phoenix), 191, 193–4, 196–8). Yet the resultant image is always indistinct (I do not mean confused) except, significantly, in the two emblem-poems, 185 and 190, where the figures are shown in exact and lucid detail. By contrast, in all the showings of Laura's 'close-up' *in propria persona* a vivid visualisation of her eyes or hair, or of both, at once touches off a coruscation of subjective reflection, rapturous or fearful as the case may be.[139] Here is the highly wrought sonnet 198 (drafted probably in 1342–3, revised in 1367–8):

> L'aura soave al sole spiega et vibra
> l'auro ch'Amor di sua man fila et tesse
> là da' belli occhi, et de le chiome stesse
> lega 'l cor lasso, e i lievi spirti cribra.
>
> Non ò medolla in osso, o sangue in fibra,
> ch'i' non senta tremar, pur ch'i' m'apresse
> dove è chi morte et vita inseme, spesse
> volte, in frale bilancia appende et libra,
>
> vedendo ardere i lumi ond'io m'accendo,
> et folgorare i nodi ond'io son preso,
> or su l'omero dextro et or sul manco.
>
> I' nol posso ridir, ché nol comprendo:
> da ta' due luci è l'intelletto offeso,
> et di tanta dolcezza oppresso et stanco.

[The soft breeze spreads and waves in the sun the gold that Love, there in her lovely eyes, with his own hand spins and weaves, binding then with those same locks my weary heart and sifting my light spirits. There's no marrow in my bones or blood in my tissues that I do not feel a-tremble if I but approach the place where she is, she who so often weighs and balances on delicate scales both my life and my death; seeing the light burn by which I'm enkindled, and the knots that have bound me shining effulgent, now on the right shoulder, now on the left. I can't describe – it passes my comprehension – so overcome is my mind by the two such lights, so born down and exhausted by so much sweetness.]

At first the chief agent is Love who, dwelling in Laura's eyes (line 3) weaves a thong of her hair with which to bind the poet's heart (3–4); at the same time 'sifting' – dispersing, disintegrating – his soul as the seat of his 'spirits' (4), that is of all his vitality, vegetative, sentient and rational (cf. *Vita Nuova* II, 4–6). This latter detail anticipates the final state of the poet as described in lines 13–14. Nevertheless he is the experiencing subject in lines 5–6, and again from 9 to the end. Meanwhile Laura herself ('chi...', 7) has replaced 'Love' as the active, objective power, and this of course through her beauty, epitomised in her eyes and her hair; and in the first tercet her (or its) triumph is complete. The poet – subject of 'vedendo', 9 – is left a mere passive observer – so far as he can be, bedazzled and bewildered as he is – of his own prostration (12–14). Now this last state depends, evidently, on an action only completed in lines 9–11, which therefore *had* to follow – very unusually – from the second quatrain; which they do the less conspicuously as coming so soon after the drastic *enjambement* 'spesse / volte' (7–8). Meanwhile presages of that climactic first tercet may be felt in the language and patterning of the quatrains: in the six active, strongly metaphorical verbs in the first one; in the largely unfamiliar, consonantal rhyme-words ('tesse', the rare latinism 'cribra', 'm'apresse', 'libra'); in the repeated coupling of verbs (1–2, 4, 8) and nouns (3–4, 5, 7); in the physiological hyperbole of lines 5–6 (an echo of *Purgatorio* XXX, 46–7). Contributory to the general effect, are the frequent half-assonances and the alliterations in lines 1 and 4; not to mention the clinching, resonant paradox of line 14. It is all a triumph of style in the service of meaning.

I conclude these notes with a glance at a poem at the other, the unadorned end of Petrarch's stylistic range, the fifth 'apparition' sonnet, 302:

Levommi il mio penser in parte ov'era
quella ch'io cerco, et non ritrovo in terra:
ivi, fra lor che 'l terzo cerchio serra,
la rividi piú bella et meno altera.

Per man mi prese, et disse: 'In questa spera
sarai anchor meco, se 'l desir non erra:
i' so' colei che ti die' tanta guerra,
et compie' mia giornata inanzi sera.

Mio ben non cape in intelletto humano:
te solo aspetto, et quel che tanto amasti
e là giuso è rimaso, il mio bel velo'.

Deh perché tacque, et allargò la mano?
Ch'al suon de' detti sí pietosi et casti
poco mancò ch'io non rimasi in cielo.

[My thought lifted me up to where she was whom I seek and

find not on earth; there, with those whom the third circle
encloses, I saw her more lovely and less reserved. She took me
by the hand and said: 'In this sphere you will be with me, if my
desire doesn't deceive me; I am she who was so harsh to you and
who ended my day before evening. My bliss no human mind can
comprehend: I await now only you and that which you so much
loved, and which remained below, my beautiful veil'. Ah, why
did she then fall silent and let go my hand? For at the sound of
words so kind and chaste, I almost remained in Heaven.]

The opening is unforgettable, but the rest may seem at first a little
flat. Seven brief statements grouped in four segments; all in the
indicative mood and all except the last, following the question in
line 12, clear at first sight. Monotonously similarly rhyme-sounds in
the quatrains. Metaphors of course, but, apart perhaps from 'serra'
(3) and 'mia giornata…' (8), such as are either too conventional to
be noticed or come from the common Petrarchan stock: 'guerra' (7),
'bel velo' (11). All this is true but, in a sense, irrelevant. What in this
poem is of primary importance is not individual lines and phrases but
their interrelations; those, in particular, between the first quatrain
and the central section, lines 5–11. Now the latter relates to the former
in two ways: dramatically, as the woman's part in a lovers' dialogue –
the man having in the first place set the scene, reminiscently, in lines
1–4; and thematically, in that what she does (5a) and what she goes
on to say (5b–11) at once confirm, interpret and immeasurably
deepen his introductory statement. Note how crucial here is the role
of memory. The immediately past vision ('Levommi…') of Laura
imparadised recalls her absence from the earth and from him on
earth (2), the absence above all of that beauty of face and limb which
she had once possessed and which he in vain, by her choice, had
desired (4). *Now* that beauty is transformed (4a), that choice a thing
of the past (4b). Hence she can now promise to have him with her
forever 'in questa spera' (5b–6; cf. 3). Then in line 7 she confirms, at
once emphatically and compassionately, the veiled allusion (4) to his
prolonged suffering at her hands, and then (8) glosses his memory of
bereavement (2) with her own memory, which he could not share,
of premature death. Here Laura might have stopped; the rest of her
speech, the quiet yet wonderfully full tercet that follows (9–11) is
a further, unexpected confidence. Yet it does no more, rationally
considered, than explicate things already said or hinted at: compare
line 9 with lines 1, 3 and 5b; line 10a, 'te solo aspetto', with 5 and 6;
10b–11, 'che tanto amasti' etc., with 4a on Laura's now transfigured

beauty, and with line 8 on her death. The fineness of this first tercet is all in the simplicity and terseness with which so much is suggested – the sublime aspiration of line 9, the accumulated memories of 10–11. Note three further points. First, the Dantean ring of line 9 – cf. *Paradiso* III, 85, XXVIII, 108, XXXIII, 67–9. Next – a point at once structural, thematic and tonal – note how this first line of the sestet both answers to and enlarges *ad infinitum* line 1 of the octet. Note finally the effectiveness of the question, by no means merely rhetorical, in line 12; pointing as it does to the mysteriousness of Laura's present condition, and thus subtly corresponding with the pregnant negation in line 14.

Throughout the above analyses I have tried to relate the stylistic features noted to some presupposed 'matter' or meaning – taking this to include, along with concepts and their connections, states of feeling. It is not however suggested that Petrarch's 'meaning', even taken in this wide sense, will account for every characteristic feature of his style. For example, what I have referred to, following Contini, as his 'non-naturalistic' use of language in the rendering of natural objects can hardly be explained by his customary manner of envisaging the state itself of 'being in love' – seeing it, to quote Leonard Forster, as a 'conflict between physical and spiritual love, desire and frustration', expressible 'through a wide range of antitheses and paradoxes in a delicate balance of opposites'.[140] Implicit, obviously, in this excellent description of the Petrarchan manner is the propensity for binary structures, the propensity carried on, while the vogue for it lasted, by European 'Petrarchism'; though, as Forster goes on to say, Petrarch's later followers 'were less interested in the balance than in the antitheses', and to the point of tedious artificiality. The reaction was inevitable and it didn't always spare 'the sing-song, love-sick' Master himself. But this phrase of Lord Chesterfield's points at least as much to the content as to the style of the *Canzoniere*, indicating with 'love-sick' just that element in the work which its detractors from Bruno to Baretti tended to find particularly distasteful, the half-sensual, half-platonic cult of Laura. His artistry was universally admired, however, and by and large his high status as a poet conceded. Things changed with the rise of Romanticism, with its coolness towards the classical notions of poetic greatness. In this new atmosphere the very delicacy and brilliance of Petrarch's art could be and was held against him; the more so as he seemed, unlike Dante, lacking in moral depth and even in civic and patriotic feeling – a particularly damaging charge in

Risorgimental Italy.[141] And here one might go on to speak of the anti-romantic reaction of Petrarch's greatest nineteenth-century editor, Carducci; and then of subsequent reassessments, down to our own time, of Petrarch's extraordinary and ever-disputable achievement in lyric poetry.[142] But as literary criticism, not history, is my chief concern here, I will conclude these remarks on Petrarch's artistry by simply asserting the unique importance in this respect – whether 'artistry' be taken as simply an aspect of 'poetry' or as something quite distinct and potentially opposed to it – of the seminal utterances on the *Canzoniere* left us by the finest critical intelligence ever to have occupied itself, in depth, with Petrarch's lyrics. Need I say that I refer to Leopardi?[143]

III. The Philosophy

Two things combine to make Petrarch easy to find fault with as a man, apart from questions of literary merit: his habit of self-disclosure and the odd convergence of ambiguities, circumstantial or self-induced, that his life exhibits – this ardent Italian spent half his life in Provence; this cleric – no priest and having no care of souls – was virtually a layman; this scholar and intellectual never had to face a classroom of students; this lover passionately, yet platonically, loved another man's wife; this 'celibate' was the father of two children. Obviously, to some of these 'ambiguities' no blame, or little, can be attached; but the impression they surely convey is that of a man less committed than most to a definite role in society, whether religious or secular, and more than usually free from domestic or civic responsibilities. True, there was his job in the Colonna household at Avignon between 1330 and 1347; but the Cardinal was an indulgent employer, as the Visconti were to be later on. To a large extent Petrarch could generally do as he pleased – admirable conditions for a scholar and a writer, and Petrarch was both, enthusiastically, to the end of his days. 'When I cease to write,...I shall cease to live', he wrote in *Fam.* I, i; and, many years later, 'Nothing weighs less than a pen, and nothing is more cheering', and 'of all earthly delights none is nobler, sweeter, more lasting and dependable than that afforded by books' (*Sen.* XVII, 2, *Prose*, p.1156). Sweet idleness, however, was never Petrarch's temptation. Rather, the risk involved in his enjoying such exceptional independence came from the very promptness and versatility of his mind, the range and richness of his culture; the danger, in such an *embarras de richesse*, of losing his way; and what here needs to be stressed is the possessive pronoun. It is *his* way in life – the task of his truest self – that he seeks in the most introspective of his works, the *Secretum*. Now in this dialogue with his mentor 'Augustinus' the danger identified is not just Laura, it is the fascination of *all* created beauty and *all* human culture, with their power to distract from true self-knowledge and its correlative, a genuine awareness of God, that 'unique and most pure fountain-head of whatever is good', and especially of man's true self and quintessential title to 'nobility', the rational soul (*Prose*, pp.160, 186; cf. 198, 212). But the *Secretum*'s

exposure of this double fascination is above all *practical* – made in
view of a choice, a parting of the ways, a practical decision to be
taken, and taken here and now (ibid., pp.34–46, 150, 186–214).
Hence the importance of the date of the dialogue. But before we
come to that question, and to a closer look at the contents of the work,
let me recall things already said or implied touching specially
significant turning points in Petrarch's life.

Ignoring then Petrarch's youth and old age, and focusing on
external events and mental developments in the crucial middle period,
1340–55, I list the most important of these as follows. (i) The finding,
at Verona in 1345, of Cicero's letters; (ii) The writing, in 1346, of
De vita solitaria, the first of the prose works to make explicit use of
Christian themes and language; (iii) The death of Laura in April
1348; (iv) The inception of the *Familiares* and the *Epistolae Metricae*
(as collections) and the first organisation of the *Canzoniere*, between
1348 and 1352–3 (see above, pp.48–52); (v) The *Invective contra
medicum* of 1353, at once defending poetry and announcing Petrarch's
own farewell to it (above, pp.15–16, 41); (vi) The move from
Provence to Italy, effected finally in early summer 1353 but prepared
through the previous decade, as Petrarch's relations with the Avignon
Curia worsened, and especially in 1347, the year of Cola's seizing
power in Rome (above, pp.9–11).

We are concerned with a wonderfully gifted scholar-artist who in
middle life abandoned certain attitudes and interests in favour of
others he thought more appropriate. The temporal factor was of the
essence here, as it had been in Dante's case (*Inferno* I, 1–3). Petrarch
too, 'midway through life', found himself in a dark wood – 'Dear,
sweet, noble, difficult prize / which…drew me to that green wood /
where so often we lose our way *in mid course* / …But now, alas, I
see [that nothing] can heal the wounds I received in that wood /
thick with thorns.…But you, Lord, all-praised for mercy, / reach
me your right hand in this wood: / let your sun vanquish this my
strange *darkness*!' (*Canz.* 214.13–30) – even if the computation
behind Petrarch's 'in mid course' is less recognisable than the biblical
one[1] implied by Dante's 'Nel mezzo del cammin' (but see *Prose*,
p.1054). The point is that at roughly the same time of life both poets
awoke to find themselves off course and faced with the option either
of taking '*another* way' or of being eternally lost (*Inf.* I, 91, *Canz.*
142.35–8). Petrarch's too was a religious and moral predicament,[2]
the way out of which required a change on his part, not of basic
beliefs or ideas but of aim and direction. In fact, for all the continual

extension of Petrarch's reading during the 1340s and 1350s this period saw little if any change in his deepest ideas and sentiments. Thus when, on finally leaving Provence for Italy in May/June 1353, he felt this as a home-coming – 'agnosco patriam', 'I recognise my own country' (*Metr.* III, 24, cf. *Canz.* 128, stanza 6) – that sentiment represented nô change at all in his feelings about Italy, these having long been closely intertwined with that cult of Rome, stemming from his first grounding in Latin, which had had its first scholarly expression in his work on Livy in the decade following the return to Avignon from Bologna, as we saw in chapter I. Yet this very enthusiasm for ancient Rome and its history offers a convenient starting-point for a brief inquiry into the change of direction I speak of – one effect of which was in fact the gradual abandonment, in Petrarch's later years, of one of the two major literary undertakings to which that enthusiasm had first given rise, the epic *Africa*; whilst the other of these, the *De viris illustribus*, if never precisely abandoned, was never completed as originally planned (see section 4).

My inquiry divides into four sections, each distinguished by reference to a particular text.

I. THE PAGAN SOUL IN THE *AFRICA*

The laurel crown was conferred on Petrarch in Rome on 8 April 1341, in anticipation of the *Africa*, still largely unwritten. This is of course an historical poem, its theme the triumph of Rome over Carthage in the third century BC, its hero the younger Scipio Africanus. At a deeper level, however, the protagonist is the 'people of Mars', the Roman race itself, the race *par excellence* of soldiers, conquerors and rulers (*Tr. Famae* I–II). At a still deeper level it is pagan man driven by a craving for power and glory which – whatever his achievements – is doomed to final frustration. This is the message of the moving account of the death of the Carthaginian Mago at the end of Book VI, and also of the long colloquy in Books I–II of Scipio with his dead father Publius (respectively in *Rime*, pp.684–8, 626–636). In the latter passage the theme of the transience of all human glory is set in the perspective of the whole course of Roman history. The colloquy is recalled repeatedly by 'Augustinus' in the relevant part of the *Secretum* (*Prose*, pp.202–6, cf. 80).[3]

This clash between man's desire for permanence through fame and the brute fact of mortality is at the heart of the *Africa*. And the victor, inevitably, is mortality – not that of individuals only but of peoples

and institutions, and even, in the end, of all records of past achievement, all monuments, all literature even. Traditionally, the great men
of action, the heroes, attain immortal fame through the epic poetry
that treats of them. But this is an illusion; books too will all 'have their
death' (*Africa* II, 454–65). True, the same illusion reappears near the
end of the poem as we have it, in the conversation between Scipio,
after his final victory, and the poet Ennius (IX, 109–23, *Rime*, p.696).
But that flourish of fancy had been undermined in advance by the
cooler realism of Publius in Book II, which represents, unquestionably, Petrarch's more considered view – that *all* is subject to 'devour-
ing time'. Such was to be the message of the first five of the six
Triumphs: where triumphant Cupid (Carnality) is conquered by
Laura (Chastity), and then Laura herself by Death, and Death in
turn by Fame, and Fame by Time; leaving Eternity as the last and
absolute victor in the series. But towards Eternity the pagan epic
could only point vaguely from afar (II, 406–27, 470–82; *Rime*,
pp.632–6).

As an historical epic the *Africa* represents a broader and more
favourable view of poetry than that suggested in the preface to the
De viris illustribus (1351–3?) where poetry is opposed to history as
fiction to fact: the poet 'invents', the historian simply records (*Prose*,
p.220). What then of historical poetry? But here Petrarch had already
through the mouth of Ennius, insisted on 'a firm basis of truth',
meaning factual truth (*Africa* IX, 90–105) and much later, in a letter
to which we shall have to return, he was to insist that as regards
whatever the poet may make his personages do or say, he must be true
to historical verisimilitude.[4] Nevertheless, through all historical
changes the *nature* of man persists substantially unchanged, and it is
to this nature above all that great poetry bears witness, that of Virgil
in particular, who can be excused even the 'totally fictitious' Dido
episode of *Aeneid* IV since it shows him so 'expert in [human]
nature'.[5] The poet's task requires above all that he exclude from his
fictions whatever is not 'naturae consentaneum', 'consonant – consistent – with nature' (*Fam.* X, 4). Hence poetry's deep affinity with
philosophy, especially ethics, hence its permanent value as a source of
moral wisdom. This is the gist of the defence of poetry in Book III of
the *Contra Medicum*, written in 1353 when the *Africa* was already
being laid aside; and which, together with *Fam.* X, 4, sent with the
eclogue 'Parthenias' to his brother Gherardo in 1349, is Petrarch's
chief statement on the nature and purpose of poetry.

Now in neither of these texts is the poet himself said to be 'divinely inspired', as he had been in the Coronation Speech of 1341. Petrarch is now standing away from the line taken by the earlier humanist A. Mussato (1261–1329), who, defending poetry against a contemporary scholastic theologian, had declared poetry itself to be 'a kind of theology'. This might be true of the Bible, as containing 'poetic' language, but for the mature Petrarch classical poetry drew its material only 'from the lap of nature' – nature in all its amazing variety, but human nature in particular; and all this as humanly discerned.[6] In short, poetry conveys a human, not a 'divine' wisdom (there is a parallel here with Dante's final position as regards the origins of language, *Paradiso* XXVI, 130–8).[7] It follows – so I interpret Petrarch's position – that the *humanitas* which classical poetry both implies and discloses was something that Christianity impinged upon from *outside*: that in the nature of things there is a discontinuity between man and Christianity, even since the coming of Christ. Yet it is equally certain that man by nature is dimly aware of 'some higher Power governing all mortal things', and has a natural desire both to know that Power – hence the beginnings of philosophy – and to communicate with It – and hence religion arose, and, with religion, poetry, this being originally of a cultic character expressive of primitive man's sense of 'the divine'; a sort of pagan counterpart to the Psalms of David (*Fam.* x, 4). These ideas Petrarch could have found in Mussato, but with his more naturalistic view of poetry he set less store by any theory of its religious origins and focused rather on its links with philosophy, especially ethics. The moral component in classical poetry became increasingly, for him, its principal value. From the *Secretum* alone one might compile an anthology of 'moral texts' from the pagan poets, many of them cited by the severely Christian 'Augustinus' (see, e.g. *Prose*, pp.44, 64, 82, 90, 96, 124, 152, 186, 208). Naturally, the most favoured author in this respect is Virgil.

Inseparable from the moral sagacity of the old poets – especially Virgil and Horace – was of course their lasting example as artists in language. Petrarch, as he got older, came to set less store by this aspect of the classical poets, and therefore in a sense of poetry itself (*Prose*, pp.6 and 678). In 1352 he could even say: 'now my poet is David'.[8] Yet to the end he remained an enthusiast for the educative value, in the widest sense, of the classics.[9]

But, in and through the wisdom and the artistry of his loved poets, what Petrarch always in the last resort sought to make contact with was the individual man himself, his fellow-man, that human consciousness which – however long ago and however diverse the circumstances – had confronted life and expected death exactly as he, Francis Petrarch, now found himself doing. *Cor ad cor loquitur,* 'heart speaks to heart' – Newman's motto exactly designates Petrarch's attitude to all those, however long dead, who had left some memorable record of their passage through life. With them he instinctively tried to communicate; and not, in the last resort, as an historian of ideas nor even as looking for types of moral or artistic excellence, but simply as a fellow human being, which in the end is tantamount to reducing, or raising, all human souls to the same level. Now this manner of unifying human history was in its turn to have consequences for Petrarch's thinking about religion, of which he may well have been unconscious while constructing, with all the scholarly objectivity at his command, the pagan world of the *Africa.* For it was many years after describing the death-agony of the Carthaginian Mago (VI, 839–918) that Petrarch drew a Christian sense out of this episode, while at the same time asserting its strict conformity to its non-Christian setting. This was in 1363 in the letter to Boccaccio referred to above, *Seniles* II, I (*Prose,* pp.1030ss.), answering criticisms of this part of his epic (one of the very few to be made public in his lifetime), and in particular replying to the charge that he had made that dying pagan speak like a Christian. His reply to this 'calumny' is of great interest:

> What, I pray, is Christian here, and not simply, universally human?...What else but the grief and lamentation and remorse of a man at the point of death?...The name of Christ is not pronounced, there's no mention of any article of faith, of any sacrament of the Church, of anything Christian at all, nothing, in fine, that natural reason alone might not suggest to a man who feels himself hastening towards death...In that situation one does not have to be a Christian to recognise one's errors and sins and feel shame and remorse. Of course, such feelings are of less profit to an unbeliever than to a believer, but there need be no difference as to the repentance itself (*fructu quidem impari, penitentia autem pari*)...[For] granted that only a Christian knows to whom to confess his faults, and how to confess them, awareness of them and the pricks of conscience and repentance and self-accusation – all that is within the capacity of any rational being (*Prose,* pp.1050–2).

Rereading then, after more than twenty years, this fragment of his poem, Petrarch insists, (a) that he had scrupulously respected the

time-context of his personage, (b) that within that time-context it
was perfectly possible for a dying man, of necessity an unbeliever, to
repent of his sins, led by the light of reason alone. Note, however,
(c) that he is careful not to pronounce on the efficacy of such 'pagan'
repentance. Mago could not know, as Christians know, *to* whom and
how to confess his sins. Would he nonetheless have received forgive-
ness? As to this Petrarch is silent; only adverting to, but not explain-
ing, Mago's disadvantage, in this respect, as compared with any
Christian penitent ('fructu quidem impari...'). But, given Petrarch's
acute sense of people as individuals, it would seem out of character
for him to exclude the pagan world *as such* from any openness to
grace; though at times he may seem to imply such a view of it, as in
the conclusion of his first letter to Cicero (*Prose*, p.1024). Since, however, he never squarely faces the theological issue involved – as Dante
had done in *Paradiso* xix–xx – it is best to withhold judgement as to
his final position on this matter. What, at any rate, the passage just
cited suggests is that if there was a moment at which, in his view, the
pagan soul was likely to be open to grace, it was the moment of
nature's greatest weakness and desolation, the moment of death. It
is hardly too much to say that Petrarch's religion was, at bottom, a
cry to God prompted by fear and horror of death (see e.g. the last
lines of the *Canzoniere*). Of all his pagan personages the dying Mago
is the most religious, though he utters no explicit prayer; and with
Mago I would associate the dying Emperor Hadrian evoked in
passing, in the *De otio religioso* (1347), on the strength of the marvellous 'Animula, vagula, blandula' (*Prose*, p.600).

  With those reflections on the Mago episode Petrarch came as near
as he ever did to overcoming the 'discontinuity' noted above between
man qua man and Christianity. The gap cannot be entirely closed for
a Christian who retains any sense of the difference between nature
and grace; which Petrarch certainly did (cf. e.g. *Prose*, pp.590, 714–
716, 746). But there is more than one way of keeping that gap open.
A philosopher may argue that human nature is an end in itself; a
scholar, waiving that metaphysical point, may simply prefer to
confine his historico-literary interests to the pre-Christian classical
world. And such, it seems, was the line consciously and of set purpose
followed by Petrarch between about 1326 and the mid-1340s, so far
as his writing for the public was concerned. Modern scholarship
(G. Billanovich, B. L. Ullman, F. Rico) has uncovered his early interest
in the Bible and the Christian Fathers, especially Augustine. But the
face Petrarch chose to present to the public through those two decades

was exclusively that of a scholar-poet of the *pre*-Christian, classical, Roman world: the *De viris illustribus* (first series, 1338/9–43), the *Africa* (1338–9 and on through the 1340s). The term of this exclusively 'pagan' period seems to have come with his leaving unfinished, in 1345, the *Rerum memorandarum libri*. To this matter I shall return in Section 3 below. Meanwhile we have not quite finished with the Mago episode. Earlier I said of this that its 'message' was the 'doom' imposed on all pagan man's craving for power and glory by his subjection to time and mortality. And such indeed was the obvious message of the episode, as it had been that of much of *Africa* I–II. But now, having heard Petrarch, admittedly many years later, interpreting the episode in terms of Christian ideas like confession of sin and repentance, it becomes surely also possible to see the dying Carthaginian as a witness, certainly, to what St Paul calls the 'reign' of death (Romans 5.12–17), but also as a point of interrogation – and protest – raised *against* that reign by one in the act of succumbing to it; which, in the light of Petrarch's later interpretation, seems to give the protest at least a potential spiritual efficacy far beyond the reach of man in his moments of temporal power and glory.

Mago is suffering a twofold defeat – as Hannibal's brother, at the hands of the Romans, and as a man at the hands of Death. For Scipio, however, the latter defeat is the only one in question, and it is still far off. Meanwhile, of all the poem's protagonists, he is the victor *par excellence*, victorious not only over Carthage as the Roman general, but over himself as a paragon of virtue. If we are to make ethical sense of the *Africa*, the figure of Scipio is then of central importance. His virtue, as set out in the third redaction of his 'Life' in the *De viris* (*Prose*, pp.240–8), is extraordinarily complete. He possessed, we are told, all the qualities befitting not only a great soldier but a great gentleman: high courage, resourcefulness, energy, etc., but also modesty, courtesy, affability, clemency, even chastity (cf. *Tr. Pudicitiae*, 169–77; *Famae* I, 23–5) – a man for all seasons indeed, 'never less idle than when at leisure, never less alone than when alone' (Cicero, *De Officiis* III, 1; cf. *Prose*, pp.432, 552). And yet even in the *Africa* this perfect pagan rectitude raises difficulties. These arise in Books II and – less acutely – Book IX, in connection with the problem that so troubled Petrarch in the decade between the Coronation Speech of 1341 and *Secretum* III – that of defining the relation between Virtue and 'Gloria'; in other words that of the moral and philosophical validity of 'Fame', even if this be regarded, in Milton's words, as 'the spur that the clear spirit doth raise...' I shall return to this matter in section 4 below; here I do no more than touch on the complex issues involved. In the *Africa* itself Petrarch's self-questioning makes for a certain incoherence.[10] Briefly, what it comes to is this. All human things, with one exception, are subject to time. Rome itself will not outlast time. Fame, which at best is only Virtue's 'shadow' (*Canz.* 119.99; *Secretum* III, *Prose*, p.204) and of which the chief carriers are the poets (and Petrarch, of course, is Scipio's 'carrier' in this sense), will not outlast books, and they are mortal (II, 342–53, 428–34, 454–65). The one exception is Virtue; it alone can escape time by rising, as it alone can, to Eternity or Heaven (I, 214–21, 327–340, II, 471–82). Therefore the good man, be he poet or not, should renounce the pseudo-immortality of Fame – whether his own or that of his hero – and seek only that 'true glory' which is distinguishable from Virtue itself only as a good conscience and/or God's approval is from the goodness it bears witness to (II, 480–2; but most clearly in *Fam.* V, 17 (1343): 'God and one's conscience are witnesses …and this alone is real glory.'). All rewards but Heaven are ultimately worthless.

2. THE DE IGNORANTIA. DISCRIMINATIONS WITHIN PHILOSOPHY AND THE CRITIQUE OF SCHOLASTICISM

Of course the old poets and moralists would mean nothing to us had they not combined 'wisdom with eloquence'. The formula is Cicero's;[11] and it was natural that Petrarch's greatest defence of the classics, the *De Ignorantia*, 'On my own Ignorance and that of Many Others' (1367),[12] (which is also a passionate self-defence against four Aristotelians at Venice who had called him 'a good man, but uneducated'), should contain his warmest praise of Cicero, and at the same time a clear statement of Cicero's limitations, not indeed as an individual (Petrarch's judgement on him in that respect is to be found elsewhere)[13] but as a pagan. This qualified praise – where the qualification involves no disparagement of the merits praised – is typical of Petrarch's assessment of the pre-Christian mind at its best, expressing as it does his sense of the ambivalent relation of *humanitas* to Christianity to which attention was drawn above. What has now to be brought out is his understanding of certain philosophical aspects of that ambivalence (bearing in mind that he was anything but a professional philosopher).

Primitive man, he had affirmed in 1349 (*Fam.* X, 4), had a dim sense of God and a natural desire to discern Him more clearly. Four

years later, in the *Contra Medicum*, these primitive divines are identified as Orpheus and the other earliest poets; a memorable company,
yet one that came far short of the perfect knowledge of the true God
they instinctively desired, for that 'is a gift of grace, not the result of
study', and the time of grace had not yet come (*Prose*, p.674). With
these words Petrarch fixed the frontier that Greek philosophy, in the
account he went on to give of it in the *De Ignorantia*, could not cross.
This account, based largely on Cicero, supplemented by Macrobius,
St Augustine and a few texts from Aristotle, is of great interest for
the study of late medieval Christian humanism with its anti-
scholastic bias, its aversion to mere knowledge, *scientia*, divorced
from morals and piety, its impatience with logical subtleties, and
finally its desire to reunite philosophy with *eloquentia*.

Petrarch allows that for the most part the Greek philosophers, even
Aristotle, knew something of the existence and unity of God, though
none of them, not even Plato, had the courage to proclaim this truth
to a world darkened and debased by polytheism; of which cowardice
Cicero, their chief mediator to the Latin West, was especially guilty
(*Prose*, 724–8). But much worse was the intellectual weakness
affecting all the old philosophers except Pythagoras and Plato and his
followers, their incapacity to rise to the idea of creation *ex nihilo*,
leaving them with the damnable impiety of a world co-eternal with
God. Aquinas would have called this a *non sequitur* (*Summa theologiae*
1a.46), but Petrarch knew little or nothing of Thomism. Nevertheless
it was to his credit that he seized on, if not very lucidly, the importance of this point and the real difficulty it represented for Christian
Aristotelians. It was the chief proof for him of Aristotle's inferiority
to Plato as a philosopher, while the latter's incomparable – among the
pagans – insight into this and many other invisible and divine truths
made him the prince among pagan philosophers and in some sense a
Christian before his time, as of course Augustine had realised. Plato's
'sight' was as keen as any Christian's would ever be; he had only less
'light' to see by.[14]

Turning from metaphysics to ethics, Petrarch's interest shifted to
writers in Latin – Cicero, Seneca and, 'what may cause some surprise',
Horace (*Prose*, pp.744–6). The reason was the excessive intellectual-
ism of the Greeks. Artistotle, in the *Nichomachean Ethics* had defined
the virtues with endless subtlety, but never seemed to remember what
he himself had said at the start of the treatise that the end aimed at in
ethics was 'not knowledge but action' (*N.E.* 1, 3). 'It is one thing to
know, another to love, one thing to understand, another to will', and

what was the use of merely *knowing* about the difference between right and wrong? Petrarch had read all Aristotle's 'moral books', and heard lectures on some; they had not had the slightest effect on his morals. How different was the effect of reading Cicero or Seneca. '*Their* sharp, burning words penetrate the heart, rousing the torpid, warming the cold, awakening sleepers, encouraging the timid, lifting up the fallen, raising to lofty thoughts and noble desires minds attached to earthly things; so that vice is shown in all its hatefulness, and the form of virtue, appearing to the inward eye..., begets a marvellous love of wisdom and of virtue itself'. I know, Petrarch continues, that in fact 'no one deprived of the doctrine and the grace of Christ can be truly wise or good – no one who "has not drunk deeply, not of the fabled fountain of Pegasus...but of that one and only true fountain which has its source in heaven and wells up to life eternal" (John 4.14)...Nevertheless, to those who do have access to that fountain, the writers I have named [Cicero and Seneca] can be of great assistance'. And Petrarch goes on to cite a favourite passage from the *Confessions* (III, 4, 7) where Augustine tells of the marvellous change for the better that Cicero's lost work Hortensius had brought about in him when he read it in adolescence (*Prose*, p.746).[15]

All this commendation of the Roman moralists turns then on two points, their practical bent and their eloquence; Seneca excelling in the one respect, Cicero in the other. Petrarch's criticism of Aristotle as a moralist was on both accounts, but chiefly for his being too theoretical. The same charge was implicit in Petrarch's contempt for what he took to be the speculative philosophy current in the intellectual world of his time. But things were worse than ever because the theoretical interest itself had become petty, arid, pedantic, an endless exercise in dialectic punctuated by absurd and boring genuflexions to a quasi-divinised Aristotle (*Prose*, pp.718–22, 740–4, 750–6 – to cite only the *De Ignorantia*). Such was Petrarch's general view of 'scholasticism'. It contained an aesthetic judgment with cultural implications, and a moral judgement with religious ones.[16]

The aesthetic or literary element in his anti-scholasticism stemmed from his deep desire to keep philosophy 'human' by maintaining its connection with the art of verbal expression according to the Ciceronian ideal of 'wisdom combined with eloquence' (see above, p.149). Now since in the classical tradition wisdom, 'sapientia', was itself twofold, having both a speculative and an ethical aspect, the ideal implied in Cicero's formula was basically that 'three-sided' humanism which the Ancients transmitted to the Christian West (largely through the genius of Augustine) and was then, as the saying goes, 'rediscovered' by the Renaissance. For that humanism entailed a conscious directing of the intellect to truth, *veritas*, of the will to virtue, *virtus*, of language to *eloquentia*; the relevance of this last factor consisting in the fact that man alone among the animals uses speech.[17] Now the first requirement of speech is that it be appropriate; hence John of Salisbury's definition of 'eloquence' as 'a facility in expressing oneself in appropriate language'.[18] Clarity then is of the essence of eloquence, at any rate in prose and in difficult subject-matter. Indeed, says Petrarch, it is the very mark of intelligence and real knowledge, for only what is clearly understood can be clearly expressed. True, there is a distinct 'art' of clear expression, but this art (part of *eloquentia*) is of no use to one whose *mind* is confused (*Prose*, p.734). With this last distinction, incidentally, Petrarch is willy-nilly recommending the logic he so often blamed the scholastics for being obsessed with. Doubtless he would reply that he had never decried the study of logic as a *preparation* for philosophy; on the contrary, in this sense he had warmly recommended it (e.g. in *Fam.* 1, 7). The trouble was that nowadays most 'philosophers' were logicians and nothing else. They had turned a means into an end, taken a part, a small part, of philosophy for the whole; become so enamoured of the dialectical techniques they had picked up in youth as 'shamelessly to grow old in a study proper to schoolboys'; and in the event so confused themselves and everyone else with logic-chopping as entirely to lose the wood for the trees.[19]

All the same it is odd to hear the scholastics taxed with obscurity; if there is one thing certain about the great schoolmen of the thirteenth century it is that they used Latin with meticulous precision. But Petrarch ignored the thirteenth century, intellectually. What he saw was only scholasticism in decline – touched already with that desiccation and sterility against which he, and the humanists of the next generation, reacted so strongly and, sometimes, unjustly. That there was some such decline is generally agreed; how it came about, broadly speaking, I tried to indicate many years ago in words which may still serve at least as pointers to the historical situation they attempt to describe. 'The new Universities [in the thirteenth century], the Dominicans, the Aristotelian commentaries, Latin Averroism, the great *Summae*, even the *Divine Comedy* – the predominant notes all through are rationality, systematic distinction and organisation, and a great deal of novelty. There is an immense exercise of dialectic. Philosophy, conceived increasingly as distinct from theology, tends to autonomy and separation. Theology, becoming increasingly rational, tends to constitute itself as a science distinct from piety, and therefore, if *pietas* be *sapientia*, from wisdom…in the old [Pauline and Augustinian] sense of the term [cf. 1 Cor. 2.7–13, *Confessions* v, 5]. And both disciplines tend…as far as possible away from eloquence…Their outward form takes a logical, not a "literary", shape; following the laws of thought, not of verbal assonance and rhythm. The mould of rhetoric is shattered; the new thought had to find a new literary form, unciceronian and unaugustinian. So language is stripped to a system of abstract…signs, of technical terms. Each intellectual discipline, distinctly conceived under its own "formal object", must follow its own distinct and formal procedure. Wisdom breaks up into its component parts. The amateur gives way to the professional; and to the professional philosopher and theologian as such both virtue and piety…become professionally irrelevant…'. In short, 'the 13th century had lost something in gaining much…It had imperilled the harmony of thought, life and speech…And Petrarch reacted'.[20]

This diagnosis points to a disconnection between the different parts or powers of the psyche as the basic ailment in fourteenth century culture, a disconnection at once reflected in and exacerbated by the 'professional' separation of philosophy from theology and of this from piety. And in Petrarch's reaction I would distinguish three factors: his temperamental distaste for 'pure' logic ('My mind was well balanced rather than acute', *Epist. Posterit.*, *Prose*, p.6); his sense of wisdom as basically religious; his devotion to the classics, disparaged and neglected by current 'scholasticism'. It is especially in the first and third of these, of course, that the literary aspect of his polemic most appears. Petrarch's anti-dialectical bias is obvious in the way he persistently taunts and derides the *dyalectici* (though by this term he hardly ever means professional logicians, but rather doctors or 'natural philosophers') as puerile, vain, pedantic and contentious. These charges blend and overlap; thus the texts already cited apropos of 'puerility' serve to document the other charges, at least by implication. To those texts may be added the following, as variously illustrative of Petrarch's keen sense of the moral component in the intellectual life: the derisive picture of intellectual vanity and 'learned stupidity' in the *De vita solitaria*;[21] the insistence, backed by references to Cicero and Horace, that true philosophers, like true poets, are rare; that the only way to wisdom lies through awareness of one's ignorance, and definitely not through mere zest for argument, 'ardor disputandi' – a sure way to miss the truth. It is not controversy that enriches the mind, but truth itself, first silently contemplated, then quietly debated, 'for the well-ordered mind is always tranquil'.[22]

An interesting passage in the *Contra Medicum* shows Petrarch combining an appreciation of syllogistic reasoning with his classical sense of style. 'O you eternal schoolboy...read the works of the philosophers, or ask those who have read them: which of them ever wrote as you do? In their writings is an immense syllogistic force, certainly; but syllogisms themselves don't appear, or very seldom. Why? Because they were adults and spoke like men...' (*Prose*, p.682). The philosophers referred to would almost certainly not include any author later than, say, Boethius (d.524 AD) nor again any who wrote precisely as a Christian. In one sense indeed the Christian Fathers, as guided by a light that transcended reason, might be called the only 'true philosophers', compared with whom even Plato had walked in darkness (*Prose*, pp.736–42; cf. 722, 725, *Fam.* VI, 2), but Petrarch usually reserved the title to men guided by the light of reason alone. This was normal in the middle ages; what had not hitherto been normal was Petrarch's habit of using the term 'scholastic' to designate a pseudo-philosophy (*Prose*, p.524, 750; *Rerum memorandarum*, II, 47).

In effect Petrarch divided the history of European thought into four movements, one being supernaturally guided, the others following unaided reason. The first, that of minds illuminated by faith, began with the Incarnation, reached its peak in the fourth and fifth centuries and had gradually died out (cf. *De Remediis* I, 46). Of the other three movements, two had borne good fruit while one began badly and ended even worse. The two praiseworthy movements were those that issued respectively in Platonist metaphysics and in the moral wisdom of Seneca, both of which had greatly enriched Christian thought, thanks chiefly to the genius and humility of St Augustine (a few sample texts: *Prose*, pp.66, 102, 674–6, 746–750, 758, 820). The moral line, Ciceronian and Senecan, was of course of Stoic provenance, and Petrarch was ardently with the Stoa and against the Epicureans; between whom and Aristotle he went on to see an affinity in their common inability to rise to the idea of God as creator of the world *ex nihilo*, to conceive of matter as other than everlasting (*Prose*, pp.736–40). So we come to the fourth 'line'. This began perhaps with Aristotle's frontal attack on Plato (*Prose*, pp.754–756), but Petrarch is more interested in its results in his own time, which had been ruinous not only for philosophy, as we have seen, but for theology too. The very religious Orders are now riddled with rationalism and unbelief. This last and worst effect of the 'Aristotelian' line Petrarch tended in old age to associate especially with the pestilent influence of Averroes.[23]

Yet for all his mistrust of dialectic Petrarch set a high value on reason, especially in the practical conduct of life. Here *aequitas*, 'reasonableness' was supremely desirable. In this sense no work of his is more 'classical' than the huge *De remediis utriusque fortunae* (1354– 1366) throughout which Reason reigns as the only guide between the perils of favourable and adverse fortune, that is between the emotions of joy and hope on the one hand, sorrow and fear on the other. No work of his is more Stoic in temper. Yet we must not exaggerate. Petrarch was never a pure Stoic, even in theory.[24] Nor, of course, did he ever suppose that the only valid use of reason was the solution of ethical dilemmas in the manner of the *De Remediis*. Far from it; for him the primary problem, while it had immediate ethical implications, was not in itself ethical but rather anthropological: what is it to be a man? What am *I*? All moral questions went back in the end to that of self-knowledge. And so too did the historical investigations that Petrarch always delighted in, and no less keenly in old age – notwithstanding the objections raised against the *De viris illustribus* in the *Secretum* (see section 4 below) – than in early manhood. For clearly, all human history was in the last resort a study of *humanitas*, of human nature, and by the same token a form of self-investigation; the more so in that, as we have seen apropos of the *Africa*, all history for Petrarch tended to biography, to the study of individuals – a fact which for him (as was also implied in section 1) gave history its affinity to poetry. At the same time Petrarch was by instinct and training a scholar, one for whom the writing of history – and so also of historical poetry[25] – absolutely required the hitherto well-nigh unpractised art of historical criticism. In this art he was a pioneer; and it had nothing to do with the passing of moral judgments on its findings. This in itself didn't worry him. What did at times trouble him was when facts historically ascertained turned out to be morally ambiguous; particularly when his emotions were involved. The case *par excellence* was the career of Julius Caesar, studied with unprecedented thoroughness in the *De gestis Cesaris*.[26] By the time Petrarch wrote this work in the late 1360s the focus of interest for him in Roman history had definitely shifted from the earlier period, treated of in the *Africa*, to the first century BC, and in effect from Scipio Africanus, the greatest soldier of republican Rome, to Julius

Caesar, who ushered in the Empire. A factor in that shift had probably
been Petrarch's finding Cicero's letters to Atticus in 1345, leading to
his re-examining Caesar's part in the collapse of the Roman republic.
And this part, or aspects of it, he still found morally inexcusable – a
residue of his earlier republicanism. But what above all now drew his
fascinated, yet alertly intelligent, attention and admiration to Caesar
was the sheer greatness of the man. The admiration itself had been
expressed long before, in a chance remark thrown off in *De vita
solitaria*: 'I will not ask here with what justice he acted, but only
marvel at the force that was in that soul, the energy of it' ('sed animi
vim et acrimoniam illam miror', *Prose*, p.494). One is reminded of
words in the letter 'To Posterity' indirectly affirming the part of
imaginative sympathy in history-writing: 'I have given myself
particularly to the study of Antiquity...always striving to transfer
myself in spirit into [those] other times'. And the other, more purely
rational side of historiography, the sifting of evidence, is touched on
a bit later in the letter: 'In doubtful cases' – when testimonies disagreed
– 'I took verisimilitude as my guide, or else the authority of this or the
other writer' (*Prose*, p.6).

So much for the 'moral philosophy and history' which were two
of the three kinds of study that Petrarch in the same letter, declared
himself most naturally inclined to (ibid. p.6). The third subject,
poetry, he here discounts (as noted earlier); it used to delight him,
but now in his riper years he has come to prefer 'sacred literature',
that is, the Bible and the Christian Fathers. Some aspects of this
change will be touched on below. Its effect on his historical writing
was in one sense relatively small – a reorganisation in 1351–2, but
later abandoned, of *De viris illustribus* to include biblical figures along
with those from classical antiquity, and a good deal of Christian
historico-hagiographical material in the *De vita solitaria* and *De otio
religioso* (1346–7). In another sense the change in question was part
of the general shift in Petrarch's writing to be studied in the next
section. What remained unchanged was his congenital interest in
personalities rather than in tracing movements or defining abstract
ideas – the same tendency that, in a sense, found expression in the
dubiously historical figure of 'Augustinus' in the *Secretum*.

3. THE SIGNIFICANCE OF THE DE VITA SOLITARIA

The change that came over Petrarch's writing in his middle years
can be looked at from different standpoints according as one attends

to one or other of the three works that he began *before* 1345, but after-
wards discontinued gradually or abruptly – *De viris illustribus* and the
Africa (both from 1337–9) and the *Rerum memorandum libri* (1343–5)
– and then compares it with one or other or all of the prose works he
set his hand to between 1346 and 1353: *De vita solitaria* (1346), *De otio
religioso* (1347), *Epistolae Familiares* (from 1350), *Invectivae contra
medicum* (1353).[27]

The crucial date – we shall see why in a moment – is 1345–6.
Meanwhile it will be helpful to distinguish four aspects of the
'humanism' involved in all of these works (if only in that all, even
the *De otio*, imply a love of the classics), namely its historical,
aesthetic, ethical and religious aspects. For, as I use the term, humanism may be regarded: as a body of knowledge; as a care for the beauty
of words and verbal structures; as a source and measure of moral
values; and in close connection with this last, as a complex of human
achievement standing in ambivalent relation to the Christian message. Of these four aspects, the first is best represented, among
Petrarch's works begun before 1345, by perhaps the earliest of them,
the *De viris*. The second, aesthetic aspect predominates in the *Africa*.
The third factor, humanism under its ethical aspect, actively present
as it is in the *De viris* and the *Africa*, is most explicitly so in the unfinished *Rerum memorandarum*, planned as a systematic indoctrination,
through examples, on the four cardinal virtues.[28] Now – and this is
where the fourth, the religious factor comes in – the *Rerum*, abruptly
discontinued in 1345, was followed within a year by the inception of
De vita solitaria, also a moral treatise, but exhibiting a significant
linguistic and tonal difference. For whereas the *Rerum* was presented
as a *secular* work drawing only on the 'wisdom available to all men',
that is, on non-Christian sources, 'ex secularibus litteris' – Petrarch
professing himself 'ignorant of other', that is explicitly Christian,
writings, and unwilling to mix up 'things of their nature so dis-
parate'[29] – the *De vita solitaria* fairly teems with biblical and Christian
material. And in the epilogue he implicitly tells us why: quite simply,
he had found it pleasant to drop, after so long, the pagan mask and to
speak like the devout Catholic he had always at heart been: 'departing
here from the practice of the ancients whom I am accustomed to
follow…I have found it pleasant (*dulce michi fuit*) in this little work
frequently to introduce the sacred and glorious name of Christ'
(*Prose*, pp.588–90). But there was more in this than a passing
indulgence of pious feeling – there was a change in the aim and general
direction of Petrarch's writing.[30]

That ignorance, professed in the *Rerum memorandarum*, of any literature other than 'secular' was largely a pose; enough to recall what we saw early in chapter 1, that Petrarch had been well read in St Augustine since the 1330s.[31] The novelty he refers to in *De vita solitaria*, speaking of his pleasure here in using Christian language, can refer only to forms of expression, not to any belated discovery of new subject-matter. Nor, in particular, did this shift in language and tone involve any disparagement of the classical material to which he had hitherto confined his attention, as poet and moralist no less than as scholar. After 1346 Petrarch may, as he says in the *Contra Medicum*, have largely given up reading the Latin poets,[32] but this was because he now had other things to do. Meanwhile they remained in memory, an indispensable element in the 'ripeness', the maturity to which he now aspired: 'I read them at the proper time...and have learned by experience the truth of what Augustine, at the beginning of the *City of God*, says about Virgil: "little boys are made to read him, so that while their minds are still tender they may be so impregnated with this great poet – the most renowned and the best of poets – as never easily to forget him; as Horace says: *The scent a newly made pitcher is imbued with / long remains*"....But, as of fruit, so of...minds, ripeness is all. If then I don't now read the poets, you will perhaps ask me what it is that I do...I answer: I try to become a better man...You ask me what I do. I strive, not without difficulty, to correct my past errors...You ask me what I do. I don't read the poets, but I write what men who come after me may perhaps read...And if in the event what I am doing answers its purpose, so much the better; if not, there is some merit at least in having tried' (*Prose*, pp.678–80). What then were those new writings of his that Petrarch here refers to? Writings so evidently set in contrast with poetry, explicitly with the classical poets he had been indelibly imbued with in youth, but implicitly also, surely, with the neo-classical poetry he had himself for long been striving to win fame by? This question will recur when we come to consider the *Secretum*, Book III. But already, I think, the answer, in a general way, is not far to seek.

One thing is certain, that in middle life the scholarly and aesthetic sides of Petrarch's nature were taking second place to the ethical. One might say that the scholar-poet caught up with his own times. From being a spell-bound investigator of the past (the early work on Livy, the *De viris*) and transmutor of it into art redolent of the past both in form and content (the *Africa*); from being a moralist contemplating human kind from the standpoint of a Cicero or a Seneca; Petrarch, about this time, began to turn all this culture to account in a wide-ranging, highly critical assessment of his own medieval world – a critique not of its fundamental beliefs but of its culture in the sense of its intellectual fashions and pretensions, of certain widespread super-stitions, of the actual situation of its two chief transnational institu-tions, the Church and the Empire (witness the anti-scholastic and anti-aristotelian polemics, the critique of astrology, the diatribes against the 'illiteracy' of the pseudo-cultured, the 'Sine Nomine' campaign against the Avignon Curia, the repeated efforts to get both Pope and Emperor back to Rome).

This large shift of attention to contemporary matters and interests had been anticipated in a small way by sections added to Books I–II of the *Rerum memorandarum*, giving modern examples of the virtues treated therein (cf. *Prose*, pp.276–82). But this work was abandoned in 1345, and the date is important for it was in May/June of that year that Petrarch discovered at Verona Cicero's letters to Atticus and others,[33] and no other single event was to prove so decisive in fixing the general course and character of his future writing in prose. The personal (not private) letter was henceforth to serve as the chief medium through which he sought to act on the world of his time, and which we have no reason to think he would have adopted but for the stimulus of that find at Verona (even though nearly five years were to pass before the *Epistolae Familiares* really got under way in 1350). And that the personal letter had such a *focal* importance in Petrarch's later output in prose – from 1350 on – should be clear enough if we give due weight here to the term 'personal'. For what specially characterises all this later production is not the mere *fact* of its concern with a wide range of contemporary issues, but that this con-cern expressed one man's claim to speak on those issues on the strength of *his* unrivalled knowledge of the past experience of the most civilised part of mankind. It was *from* that knowledge – not merely or mainly *about* it, as hitherto – that Petrarch from now on addressed his contemporaries. In this sense one can say that the mark of all this later writing was 'subjectivity'.[34] In the huge epistolary collections, the *Familiares* and the *Seniles*, 'subjectivity' extends of course to the literary form itself, that of the personal letter; but personal letters, in a sense are also the four invectives: the *Contra Medicum* (1353), the *Contra quendam magni status*, etc. (1355), the *De Ignorantia* (written in 1367, and later sent, with a dedication, to Donato degli Albanzani), and the *Contra eum qui maledixit Italiae* (1373). In yet another sense the *Secretum* is obviously 'subjective'.

And even the remaining major work, the *De Remediis*, was a personal utterance for all its appearance of frigid impersonality; for Petrarch's aim here, besides being eminently practical, was to communicate to his contemporaries, in an easily assimilable way, that rational ethic of Stoic derivation on which he could and did claim to speak with exceptional authority, if only because he was exceptionally familiar with the relevant texts.[35]

In most of Petrarch's prose, then, after 1350, he aimed at bringing light from the past to bear on contemporary, mainly moral, issues. He made himself the mediator and champion of a tradition: affable, courteous, at times condescending in his letters; scornful, sarcastic, often insulting in the invectives. But in both *genres*, as befitted the upholder of a tradition, a tireless quoter of authorities. Naturally these differ according to whether the point at issue can be settled by reason or is a specifically Christian one, as is more often the case in the *De Ignorantia* or in the 'Sine Nomine' sequence. In such Christian matter Petrarch's chief authority by far was St Augustine, but pagan writers are by no means excluded. Official pronouncements of the Church are hardly ever invoked. Heresy, impiety and unbelief come in for furious attack,[36] but Petrarch never, I think, writes *as from* that clerical body to which he in fact belonged. If he is devout he is neither devotional nor theologically didactic. He writes simply as a believing and exceptionally cultured layman. And as such, while entirely uninhibited in the expression of his faith, he commonly rests his moral teaching either on experience and examples or on directives culled from his beloved Roman poets – Virgil, Horace, Persius, Juvenal (cf. *Prose*, p.670) – or from Cicero and, above all, Seneca. The paganism of these authors was irrelevant. Had not Augustine said that as the Israelites rightly despoiled the Egyptians, so Christians may freely help themselves to the spiritual wealth contained in the classics – 'elements of a liberal culture very serviceable to the truth and some extremely useful moral precepts' (*De doctrina Christiana* II, 145)? Moreover it may be questioned whether Petrarch ever took much interest intellectually in the specifically Christian virtues, faith, hope and charity. For him the difference that Christianity made to morals would seem to have consisted rather in its pointing to the true motive of virtue than in defining it more accurately *in se*. Christ revealed what the good life was ultimately *for*; he not only revealed this ultimate good, but made it, for the first time, really accessible (*Prose*, pp.746–8 and 790; 590). Nevertheless, granted that revelation, the pagan ethic at its best, as in Cicero and Seneca, could be of great assistance for a just definition of the virtues and, still more, in the practice of them (ibid., p.744; *Secretum*, passim). Moreover there was certainly a polemical motive behind Petrarch's very frequent reference to the pagan moralists. It was a part of his campaign to restore the classics to the place which he thought St Augustine, the 'Sun' of the Church (*Fam.* IV, 15), had in principle won for them, but which they had largely lost owing to the fatal triumph of scholasticism. As a result, Christendom was now exposed as never before to the linked diseases of barbarism and unbelief.

Petrarch found the link between these two evils in a debased Aristotelianism. The scholastics boasted of their indifference to poetry and eloquence – very different in this from the Church Fathers – and justified their illiteracy by the example, misunderstood, of Aristotle (*Contra Medicum* III, ed. Ricci, p.58, *Prose*, p.648; *Rerum memor.* II, 31). From Aristotle again – not, alas, misunderstood this time – the scholastics had learned to belittle the greatest philosopher of antiquity, Plato (*Prose*, pp.750–60).[37] This led to their reducing, or tending to reduce, all the knowable to sense-objects and the rules of logic (ibid., 718–22, 740ss.), and thus emptying philosophy of all ethical content – whereas Cicero had splendidly defined it as 'ars vitae', meaning moral wisdom, an understanding of and guide to the achievement of life's purpose[38] – and, by the same token, of all its relevance to religion – whereas Augustine (following Plato !) had defined the true philosopher as 'a lover of God' (*Fam.* XVII, 1).[39] The fact is, concludes Petrarch, that 'true wisdom can be neither understood nor loved by souls unpurified and lacking in piety. When all is said, "piety is wisdom" (*Prose*, p.718).[40] Whereas all that *your* philosophers are good for is wordy dialectic' (*De Remediis* I, 46).

4. THE SECRETUM

'Unchanging God, let me know myself, let me know You. That is my prayer.'[41] Thus St Augustine, not long after his conversion. And the prayer is at the same time a statement about himself and about God; about himself as declaring what he will henceforth *do* with his mind; about himself and God as declaring the fundamental *raison-d'être* of all such 'doing' – that a created intellect only exists in order to discover and delight in its Creator. Prior to any use of the created mind is the fact that it *is* created; and therefore has no other *raison-d'être* than its Creator. That is the primary Augustinian postulate. And the second is that the mind's way to God lies through that 'image' of Him which is itself; we know God through true knowledge of ourselves. As for the knowledge of the external world, the world of nature, some is of course needed in the practical business of life, and all or any such knowledge may be an object even of speculative inquiry provided that all such inquiry is taken into and subordinated to the quest for God. Hence there is an absolute prior requirement of humility, a requirement by no means congenial to the growing and expanding intellect. The successful astronomer, for instance, will infallibly find pleasure in the solution of his problems, and that is the precise moment when his science risks becoming irreligious; for then, while 'the ignorant marvel and are amazed, those who understand exult and are highly extolled; and through an impious pride deflect and fall away from Your light...' Why so? Because in their moment of triumph they fail to ask the crucial question about *themselves*: 'For they do not inquire, in a religious spirit, *whence* it is that they have the intelligence to inquire into these things.'[42] What inside them seem to justify self-complacency turns out to be precisely the trace of a Power to which they owe both it and everything else. This is one of a hundred examples one might give of the essentially religious cast of Augustine's thought about thought; and by the same token, of that ordering of the objects of human inquiry which his genius imposed on the West, and was to remain virtually unchallenged until the rise of Aristotelianism in the thirteenth century: 'from external things to what is within, and from what is below to what is above'.[43]

To this Augustinian method and scale of values Petrarch, as we know, responded with enthusiasm; he accepted the metaphysics involved in it more or less on faith but was eager to do battle for its ethical and cultural implications as he saw them. Here a difference appears. As we shall see, Petrarch's moral system, so far as he had one, is less Christian than Augustine's, both in itself and in the authorities adduced to support it. At its centre is the notion of a goodness proper to man. It is against such an ideal that he measures himself throughout the *Secretum* – where 'he' is the accusing-conscience figure of 'Augustinus', and 'himself' is 'Franciscus'. Petrarch's ideas then about himself as an actual moral agent are those that emerge in the course of the dialogue. But what of the ideal itself? The most important words used to denote it are *virtus* and *pietas* – *virtus* especially in the *Secretum*, while in the later *De Ignorantia*, *pietas* is particularly stressed. *Virtus* is the more general term. It is not any one of the four cardinal virtues, nor precisely a common term for them all, though it includes them all. Nor is it any of the theological virtues, faith, hope or charity. Let us call it undifferentiated human moral perfection; one advantage of this formula being that it relates the ideal to the two philosophical traditions on which Petrarch draws in his presentation of it in *Secretum* Book I; as an ontological perfection *virtus* relates to platonist metaphysics, as a moral perfection it relates, through the way it is presented, to Stoicism. The result of this dual derivation is something curiously hybrid about 'Augustinus' himself, especially in *Secretum* I where the Stoic aspect is to the fore (*Prose*, pp.30–44) for as long as this conscience-figure is urging 'Franciscus' to that decisive choice ('optare', pp.34–46) which alone can get him out of the misery which the whole dialogue presupposes (pp.22–6). But metaphysically 'Augustinus' is a Platonist, seeing the human soul as possessed of a God-given intrinsic nobility overlaid and besmirched by contact with the body its 'prison' (pp.24, 46, 64–6, 80, 98–102, etc.); and seeing the good life as a struggle against the body's 'contagion', the contagion which, taking effect through imagination and the passions, drugs the soul into forgetting its primordial nobility and divine origin (p.64, with the very effective citation of *Aeneid* VI, 730–4). At the ideal conclusion of the struggle a man would be able to say, 'with the body I have nothing in common' (p.46). This is hardly a Christian sentiment; yet Petrarch could of course find biblical and authentically Augustinian support for the aspiration to be 'out of' the body inasmuch as the bodily condition as we know it is incompatible with 'vision of the divine mysteries' (p.98). It remains true that throughout *Secretum* I and intermittently in the rest of the work, Petrarch inclines to a dualism which the Church has never approved. True, there was a touch of dualism in Augustine's definition of man: 'a rational soul using a body'.[44] Aquinas was the first theologian to come up with a strictly non-dualist anthropology. But Augustine was firm on the goodness of the material world and on man's duty of loving the body, his own and his neighbour's.[45] This was because he placed *caritas*, love, the reflection in us of God's love for man, soul *and* body, at the centre of his ethic.[46] And *caritas* is just what Petrarch leaves out of the *Secretum* – or at best presents only in a truncated way (notably at pp.156–60).

The dialogue starts from one man's unhappiness; but it proceeds with an ever clearer individuation of this man. 'Augustinus' opening words show that, in a sense, he is Everyman: 'What are you doing, poor little man?...Have you forgotten that you're mortal?' (p.28). Actually, 'Franciscus' is not doing anything, except worry over himself. The 'leisure and liberty' that he had always so cherished (cf. *De vita solitaria, Prose,* p.300) has become an occasion for mere brooding. At this point 'Augustinus' intervenes to change random self-pity into systematic, constructive self-examination, in the form of diagnosis aimed at finding a remedy, a cure. The diagnosis, comprising the first two books and much of the third, is of course already in a sense remedial. The proposal of remedies, as distinct from diagnosis, only clearly takes over in Book III, after the pitiless analysis of Petrarch's relations with Laura (pp.160–88); and it is resumed, less distinctly and decisively, at the close of the last matter examined, the poet's desire for fame (pp.206–14). The diagnosis itself proceeds in three stages: Book I, a general consideration of the invalid's 'sick' unhappiness, with a view to isolating the *moral* factor in it; Book II, a survey of his, that is Petrarch's, own moral life in terms of the traditional Christian schema (used by Dante in the *Purgatorio*) of the Seven Deadly Sins (more accurately, Vices); Book III, an exposure of his two pseudo-virtues, Amor, his love for Laura, and Gloria, his desire for literary fame. The connection between parts two and three of this diagnosis is clearer than that between parts one and two. For while the only difference, logically speaking, between Books II and III is that between vices that everyone admits to be such and vices that some people, and notably 'Franciscus', want to regard as virtues (this applies especially to Amor, see pp.132–52); it is not clear at first sight just what 'Franciscus' is being blamed for in Book I. Or rather, while it is clear enough, by the end of Book I, that 'Augustinus' is greatly concerned to get his patient to shake off a torpid unwillingness to think about death, it isn't clear at first sight what this has to do with the vices examined in the two following books. It might be thought that the connection lies in the Christian idea of Hell – that if 'Franciscus', who is after all a Christian, would only think of the afterlife punishment of sin, he would leave off sinning; and that this is why his mentor so earnestly recommends him to meditate on death (pp.28, 34, 48ss.). Now it is true that this aspect of death – as connected with a moral sanction in the form of so dire a penal consequence of sinning – is touched on in Book I (pp.56–8); but only in passing, as if reinforcing an argument which could do without it, as having its own independent persuasiveness. And this for two reasons: first, that the central line of argument throughout Book I explicitly draws on philosophical, not theological, sources; first on 'the teaching of the Stoics' (p.34) and then on Platonism (pp.46ss.); second, that the notion itself of moral sanction is only marginal to the moral argument of 'Augustinus' about his patient and pupil's unhappiness.

The argument is presented rather disjointedly and elliptically, but the sequence of ideas seems as follows.

i) Augustinus begins by asserting, to his pupil's astonishment, that Franciscus does not really want to be rid of his misery, for no one is unhappy against his will. Naturally 'Franciscus' protests at this in the name of experience and common sense, but his protest is brushed aside as unworthy of one who claims to have read the (Stoic) 'philosophers'; who have shown that a man is happy or unhappy simply and solely in so far as he is virtuous or vicious; and virtue and vice are states of the will (pp.28–36). To put the same Stoic point in another way, the only joy worth having is that engendered by virtue, the Stoics' *chara*, 'a rational state of exhilaration'.[47] All non-virtuous pleasure is at bottom irrational, and therefore evil. As for pain, the wise man cannot help feeling it sometimes but he will never allow it to rob him of his happiness, his rational *euthapeia*; for just as he knows that pain has no part in virtue, so he knows that neither is it *per se* an evil; and that to treat it as such, for example, by lamenting or raging at it, is irrational and therefore vicious.

ii) Implicitly, 'Augustinus' is adopting the Stoic view – known to Petrarch chiefly through Cicero's 'Tusculan Disputations'[48] – that all moral deviation involves culpable misjudgment, a voluntary assent given to error or folly. Which is why it *can* be corrected, why a vice once formed can, albeit with difficulty, be eradicated; for reason can always correct its own error, and the will can change direction. Hence it is in our power to reform ourselves, and so achieve or recover true happiness.

iii) The first step on the way of self-reform is deeply to desire it, the second is fully and decisively to opt for it, *optare* (pp.28–30, 38–44). All in the last resort depends on the will, but reason has a great part to play, not only, as we have seen, by clarifying the moral issues, but also by uncovering the root cause of human vice and folly. It is at this point – from p.46 on – that Petrarch's 'Platonism' comes into the picture. Evil is now not simply identified, as in authentic Stoicism, with irrational emotion; this in turn is now seen as a 'contagion' affecting the soul, especially through the imagination, from its union with the body. And precisely this is why 'Augustinus' so persistently recommends his patient to meditate on death (pp.28, 34, 46–58, 68, and finally, 210). The reason is not primarily to make 'Franciscus' think of what may happen to him *after* death, it is to induce in him a contempt for the body, an ever deeper sense of the ignominy of the bodily condition itself, which is revealed by nothing so much as by the physical horrors of death (pp.54–8). But these must be squarely faced and as far as possible visualised, for only thus will the sense-bemused soul be brought to realise the absurdity and indignity of an immortal nature's seeking its good in so transient and in the end repugnant a thing as life in the body. The whole argument turns on this contrast and is summed up in words which express with exceptional clarity the essence of Petrarch's humanism, minus only its Christian component (pp.52–4):

> Were you to find someone so vigorously possessed of his reason as to order his whole life by it, subjecting every desire, every impulse of his soul to its rule, in the full consciousness that reason alone is that which distinguishes him from brute beasts, and that he alone deserves to be called human who lives by its light; and who at the same time is so conscious of his mortality as to keep it daily in his mind's eye, regulating his entire life with death in view, so that, despising all the perishable things of this world, he aspires only to that life in which, grown to new heights of rationality, he will cease to be mortal; – then at last you could say that you had truly and profitably understood the definition of man' [as 'a rational, mortal animal' – the allusion is to some school-text of logic].

Before we leave Book I let us look more closely at 'Augustinus', in relation to his creator. The first thing to note is that this figure and that of his counterpart 'Franciscus' together express Petrarch's sense of a similarity between his own case and that of the young Augustine described in the *Confessions*; a sense he cherished and cultivated as the token of a real spiritual affinity. As he read the *Confessions*, especially its account of the interior struggles that preceded the saint's conversion in AD 386–7, it seemed to him, he tells us, as though he were reading his own story (*Prose*, pp.40–2, cf. 24). Now Petrarch had been familiar with the *Confessions* since the early 1330s, and it is natural to suppose that he was especially struck, to start with, by the author's brilliantly dramatic account of his struggles against the pull of the flesh (Books VII–VIII). By the end of 1335, however, having by then studied the *Soliloquia* and above all the *De vera religione*, Petrarch's attraction to the early Augustine already included a lively interest in the latter's debt to Platonism.[49] Thus in the years that preceded the *Secretum* – certainly finished after 1342 – he conceived an image of Augustine that combined moral with intellectual characteristics, both strongly marked – the image of a carnal sinner turned penitent, and such a penitent, of a philosopher turned believer, and such a believer! – one to whom the whole Western Church had for centuries turned as to a main source of Christian wisdom. And obviously both aspects of Augustine converge and blend in the *Secretum*, as they had already done, each reinforcing the other, in that sense of spiritual affinity which the work evidently presupposes. The *Secretum* takes the form of a master who guides his pupil in the light precisely of his *own* experience (the situation implicit, in fact, in the last extract quoted above).

Earlier we noted, from another point of view, that the two partners in the dialogue stand for two aspects of Petrarch himself, the one for his weakness and hesitations, the other for his conscience. The next step is to ask whether these two aspects have to be thought of as contemporary? Could they not represent respectively a less and a more mature Petrarch? In theory they certainly could; and, once suggested, such a *mise en scène* seems after all very plausibly in character – such as might naturally have occurred to a writer always so minutely concerned with time and his own passage through time. Yet no critic before Francisco Rico seems to have seriously considered the possibility.[50] For Rico 'Franciscus' is Petrarch as he was in 1342–3, 'Augustinus' is the same man ten years later. Now the *Secretum* is self-dated in 1342–3. Rico therefore dates it about a decade later, and I will later give an outline of his main arguments. At present I want to glance only at a subsidiary argument turning on the variations in Petrarch's attitude to Stoicism. This argument favours the view that in the *Secretum* two periods of his life are being simultaneously represented under the two proper names employed, and incidentally throws some light on the dialogue as a debate about the Stoic ideal (pp.28–44). The implicit point at issue is the difference between the Stoic and Aristotelian ('Peripatetic') conceptions of the good life. This is not the place for a close analysis of the difference.[51] Enough to say that, for Rico, 'Franciscus' voices the common-sense protest against the apparently inhuman demands of the Stoic ideal as expounded by 'Augustinus'. He speaks indeed very much as 'Peripateticus' does in Cicero's 'Tusculan Disputations', or like the Aristotelians cited in one of Petrarch's own later letters.[52] Yet in this same letter Petrarch, while conceding that the Stoic position is the more 'rational' one, hesitates between the two ethics: 'often enough my reason is Stoic, but my feelings are always Peripatetic'. The fact is that he never finally made up his mind. If in the person of 'Augustinus' he took sides in the *Secretum* with the Stoics, this was because that work was written at a time when – for reasons I shall indicate later – the Stoic influence on him was exceptionally strong – from the later 1340s to the late 1350s. This is Rico's contention, and he points out that whereas before 1350 Petrarch never adheres to Stoic positions explicitly, his letters during the next half-dozen years have frequent laudatory references to the Stoa (e.g. *Fam.* I, 7 and III, 6, as redated by G. Billanovich – cf. H. Baron's remark, 'modern criticism of the *Familiares* has helped to remove from their first books all traces of their later Stoicism'[53] –; and above all XI, 1). Within this period, too, falls the inception, c. 1354, of the prevalently 'Stoic' *De Remediis*.[54]

Later on Petrarch was to draw away from anything like pure Stoicism, being temperamentally inclined to more moderate and eclectic positions, but also, I think, because with age he became more sensitive to the hard pagan core, the irreducible anthropocentrism of pure Stoicism. Or better, perhaps, he recovered his Christian sense of proportion *vis-à-vis* any and every purely human ethic, the sense he had expressed, for example, in the *De Otio* (ed. Rotondi, pp. 93–4), and earlier still, rather magniloquently, in *Fam.* VI, 2, where, after commiserating with the ancient philosophers for their ignorance of 'the supreme, ineffable Good', he goes on: 'For our part, let us philosophise, as the word itself suggests, for love of wisdom. Now Christ is the true divine Wisdom; consequently to philosophise aright we must first love him. So in all things let us be Christians first and foremost; whether our subject be philosophy or poetry or history, let the ear of our heart be always alert to the sound of Christ's gospel...'. This was written in 1337–40, but it was in the *De Ignorantia*, written thirty years later, that Petrarch came out with his best formulation of the place of rational ethics in Christian life: 'For though our end does not consist in virtue, where the philosophers have placed it, nevertheless the right way to it lies through the virtues; the virtues, I mean, not only known but loved... Consequently they are far gone in error who spend their time trying to know what virtue is without practising it, and, worse still, to know God without loving Him. For while it is utterly impossible perfectly to know God in this life, it is possible tenderly and ardently to love Him... And granted that what is completely unknown cannot be loved... it is enough for us that we know God to be the... the Source of all that is good, and virtue to be the next best thing after Him' (*Prose*, pp. 746–8). One might question whether these last words quite measure up to Jesus' Double Commandment (Matthew 22: 37–9) but at least they firmly correct the man-centred Stoicism of *Secretum* I. With this last phrase I refer not to the aim 'Augustinus'

sets before his pupil but to the means on which – except in one respect
– he instructs him to rely; not, that is, to his telling his pupil to aspire
to a life transcending the bodily condition, but to his fierce emphasis
on the power of the human will, apparently unaided by grace, to
redress itself, master the passions, achieve perfect 'virtue'. What one
misses in all this is any allusion on the saint's part to prayer. The cry
on page 58, 'Jesus, have mercy, help me!' comes spontaneously from
'Franciscus'; on the subject of prayer 'Augustinus' is dumb throughout *Secretum* I. His first explicit mention of it comes half way through
Book II, and significantly with reference to sexual sin (pp.100–2).
In this sphere, at all events, virtue is not all will-power! 'Augustinus'
explicitly says as much, echoing the *Confessions* VI, 11, 20: 'No one
can be continent unless God grants it'. But this, as one might have
thought, basic point is left undeveloped, even in the long discussion
about Amor in Book III. Here, as we shall see, the main charge
brought against Petrarch's love for Laura is indeed a religious one,
but the *remedies* discussed are all human and, in this sense, secular
(pp.160–88); divine grace is virtually ignored. I shall suggest that
Petrarch had a reason for proceeding in this way; but what I wish to
underline here and now, as indicative of the kind of secular or humanist bias most in evidence in *Secretum* I, is the very strong stress on the
self-redressing power of the will (especially in pp.38–46). This in
turn involves an exclusive attention to the quintessentially *moral*
component in 'the good life' – an exclusiveness characteristically
Stoic and non-Peripatetic. This harshly austere Stoic (not Christian)
note struck in *Secretum* I is sustained implicitly through the rest of the
work. It is, I suggest, best explained biographically. Between the
death of Laura (spring 1348) and his settling down in Milan (summer
1353), Petrarch's moral life was characterised by a strong desire to
break with the past – with the world of Avignon, with the ties of the
flesh – now extended to include Laura – and even with the passion
for literary fame in so far as this had involved the desire to get himself
acclaimed as *the* Latin poet and Roman historian of his time (*Africa*
and *De viris illustribus*, first version). These last two renunciations – of
'Amor' and 'Gloria' – will be the subject of *Secretum* III.

One thing, however, was never to be renounced: attachment to
the classics. At times 'Franciscus' and 'Augustinus' seem like two
scholars engaged in a game of quotation-capping – each vying with
the other in giving proof of an easy familiarity with Virgil, Cicero,
Horace, Ovid, Terence and the rest. And all this in an atmosphere of
serene assurance that these writers together constitute the one

incomparable patrimony of human wisdom. It is this nuance that
distinguishes the classicism of the *Secretum* from that of both the
De Ignorantia and the *Contra Medicum*; these works being *inter alia*
passionate defences of that classical culture which the *Secretum* so
serenely takes for granted. There could be no polemic on that score
between the two interlocutors; 'Augustinus''s anti-scholastic and
therefore implicitly pro-classical outburst on pages 50–2 is inevitably
applauded by 'Franciscus'. And yet, more deeply considered, the
whole work *is* classicist propaganda. Not simply, of course, because
of its dialogue form, taken from Plato *via* Cicero (p.26), nor yet
because of the wealth of classical quotations, but above all because of
the strong tendency it evinces to find common ground between
ancient paganism and Christianity. This procedure takes different
forms. The pagan poets – much less often the writers in prose – are
repeatedly cited as witnesses to the human condition, and this always
in view, implicitly, of the dread moment of death when the soul must
meet its Judge – obviously a Christian concept, even if Petrarch's
allusions to it seem but little affected by such Christian dicta as 'perfect
love casts out fear' (1 John 4: 18). Occasionally the moral point is
made by allegorising the text.[55] The philosophers most cited are, as
was to be expected, Plato and Cicero. Plato offers precious glimpses
of an afterlife when the soul, freed from the body, that perpetual
bête noire, will explore 'the depths of the Divine' (p.98). And Plato's
metaphysic is strongly recommended by the moral consequence he
drew from it: 'For to what else does the heavenly teaching of Plato
incline us than to shun bodily desires...Above all keep ever in mind
what Plato said: that nothing is a greater hindrance to knowledge of
God than carnal desires and lechery' (pp.98, 102). Petrarch here
draws on a passage in the *De vera religione* (III, 3), which was probably
the work of St Augustine that most inclined him to regard Plato as
a Christian by anticipation. He took much the same view of Cicero,
and here again could invoke Augustine's approval.[56] But Cicero he
had read for himself, and, what counts for most in the *Secretum*, he
had read the 'Tusculan Disputations', where Cicero had taken sides
with the Stoics against the Peripatetics (Books III–IV). From the
standpoint of *Secretum* I this was to uphold the system of rational
ethics most consonant not only with Plato's but also with Christ's
'heavenly teaching'. What more could be asked of a pagan moralist?

In the light of all this it may come as a surprise to find the real St
Augustine decisively rejecting both Platonist dualism and the Stoic
idea of passionless virtue. This was in the *De Civitate Dei* XIV, 3–9

(after AD 415). These chapters provide a commentary on the same great passage in Virgil, *Aeneid* VI, 730–4, as that cited at the end of *Secretum* I and explained in terms precisely of Platonist dualism and Stoic *apatheia*. The difference between the two approaches to the same text is striking. St Augustine, waiving the question of what Virgil really meant, is concerned only with two errors that might claim support from his lines: that all sin is due to some sort of contamination of the soul by the body, and that all passion or emotion as such is perverse. The body, he insists, is good in itself; if we blame it for our sins, we wrong the Creator (chs 3–5). As to the emotions, in themselves they are morally indifferent. The morally decisive factor is a man's will: 'if the will is wrongly directed, the emotions will be perverse; if rightly, they will be not merely blameless but praiseworthy' (ch. 6). Again: 'The will rightly directed is good love, wrongly directed is evil love. Love, then, as a yearning to possess a loved object is desire (*cupiditas*), as delighting in its possession it is joy (*laetitia*); as shrinking from what is abhorrent, it is fear (*timor*), as feeling its presence, it is sadness (*tristitia*). All such emotions will be evil if a man's love is evil, and good if his love is good' (ch. 7).[57] For 'Augustinus', on the other hand, Virgil's 'inspired' lines confirm the truth of the view he has been urging on 'Franciscus' – that the body is opposed to the soul as a principle alien to the soul's 'primordial nobility', and indeed obnoxious to it through the working of the 'four-headed monster' of the passions arising out of the soul's 'intermingling with the body' ('ex corporea commistione subortas', *Prose*, p.64). So the saint seems to be contradicted on both points at issue: the goodness of the body and the assimilability of the passions into a life of noble virtue. And this is curious, for we can hardly doubt that Petrarch had read this part of *De Civitate Dei* (of which he had possessed a copy since the 1320s).[58] Yet it seems incredible that he should have deliberately contradicted Augustine. Perhaps – I make the suggestion only *faute de mieux* – perhaps he is tacitly only correcting Augustine as a reader of poetry; saying to him, in effect: 'Yes, revered and dear master, no doubt you are right about the abstract doctrinal points involved; but Virgil, don't you see, was a *poet* giving voice to human *experience*; and isn't it a fact that our bodies *are* burdensome to the spirit in us, and our passions for the most part deceptive and perverse?' The weakness of this suggestion, however, is that throughout *Secretum* I 'Augustinus' identified himself with *philosophical* positions drawn from the Stoics and Plato, and finally from the *De vera religione* of Augustine himself (p.66).

In *Secretum* II Petrarch's morals are sifted in terms of the traditional
Seven Capital Vices. Acquitted of envy, anger and gluttony, he is
charged, to his surprise, with pride and avarice, and, not to his surprise, with lust and with that 'disease of the soul which the moderns
call *accidia*' (p.106). This last evil might be called sloth except that
while this term suits, for example, the penitents on Dante's fourth
Terrace, it is far too unsubtle for Petrarch's case, involving as this
does a high dosage of melancholic depression. Another point of
nomenclature: by 'avarice' Petrarch means the desire for material
possessions, but also – as a kind of afterthought – worldly ambition in
general (pp.82, 94–6).

In this examination individual sins are not mentioned (whereas in
the *Inferno* for example, everything repeatedly gravitates to some bad
deed *in concreto*). Indeed, in contrast to the stress on the will in
Secretum I, here in Book II it is states of *mind* that are under criticism,
for the most part. This means that this part of the dialogue reflects the
Stoic analysis of vice in terms of mistaken assents, that is of false value-
judgements, 'perverse opinions' (cf. p.108).[59] Thus the procedure is
in the main psychological and curative; it is not so much the wicked-
ness of sin as its folly, indeed insanity, that is stressed, but not
exclusively, however. In three places the sin in question is given, if
only in passing, a religious dimension; it appears as an offence against
God, that is, as a *sin* in the Christian sense of the term. So it is on page
70 and, less directly, at the top of page 92, with regard, respectively,
to pride and avarice; and again, with far greater force, on pages 100–
104, with regard to lust – where significantly the philosophical pre-
suppositions are Platonist rather than Stoic. Lust is of all the vices the
most intellectually stultifying, and this in relation to the mind's
noblest capacity, that of rising to knowledge of God (pp.98, 102). In
this sense, as Petrarch presents it in the strange allegorisation of *Aeneid*
II, 361–9 (p.104), lust is especially dishonouring to God as blocking
the way to Him of man's highest faculty, a theme to be developed –
hence its introduction here – in the attack on the love for Laura in
Book III. But in the main, as I have said, the treatment in *Secretum* II
is psychological, not theological. 'Augustinus' argues from reason,
not faith, citing the philosophers, notably Seneca, and the Latin poets.
Seneca's moderated Stoicism even helps the interlocutors to reach a
partial agreement about 'avarice'. 'Augustinus' had begun by derid-
ing his pupil's concern to provide himself with a decent livelihood,
'with plenty of books and enough food for a year ahead' (Horace,

Epist. I, 18). But then he suddenly relaxes: he had not meant to urge real poverty on 'Franciscus'; let him be content with a modest sufficiency midway between wealth and penury (p.88). This sudden commendation of the Aristotelian 'golden mean' comes as a surprise after the intransigent Stoicism of 'Augustinus' in Book I. Then 'Augustinus' regains the upper hand by shifting his ground, momentarily, to religion. It is a question of what 'Franciscus' can mean when he says he wants 'to lack nothing': *Franc.* 'Neither to lack things, nor to have an abundance; neither to lord it over others, nor be subject to them – that's what I aim at'. *Aug.* 'If you want to lack nothing, then you'd better stop being a man and be a god'. And then, after an eloquent discourse on the ineradicable neediness of the human state, the saint concludes: 'Stop hoping for the impossible and, content with your human lot, learn to have things and do without them, to be above others and also below others... You can't shake off Fortune's yoke, kings themselves have to bear it. Only then will you know yourself free from it when, treading underfoot human passions, you submit yourself entirely to the rule of virtue' (pp.92–4). So a certain Stoicism has the last word, after all.

The charge of avarice is the only one that touches off a real debate between mentor and pupil. To that of lust 'Franciscus' at once pleads guilty; indeed he corroborates it with the Virgilian allegory, thus providing in advance, unwittingly, a foil to his violent reaction later on to the denial of the innocence of his attachment to Laura. As to the other two charges, 'Franciscus' protests against that of pride, but 'Augustinus' merely reiterates it and then drops the subject (pp.70–80). The theme of *accidia* is developed rather in a curative than in a condemnatory sense, with the two interlocutors putting their heads together to find a remedy, much as they will do in the latter half of the section on 'Amor' (pp.106–24, 160–88). This makes, then, another anticipation, but by likeness, not contrast, of things to be said in Book III. And the theme of pride has already offered the author the occasion of yet a third link with which to hold together these two parts of his work. For when 'Augustinus' taunts his pupil with 'wasting his time on the study of words, whose reproaches he is too blear-eyed to discern' (pp.72–4), he announces a theme that will return at the end of the work, in the section on Glory – the futility of literary work that is of no moral profit to its author (pp.192–4, 204–12). Appropriately, this section on pride brings out Petrarch's sense of his own intelligence and of his mastery of language. But equally – and with equal conviction – it brings out his sense of the relative smallness of human knowledge, and of what Eliot will call 'the intolerable wrestle with words and meanings'. Here, as elsewhere, 'Franciscus' clearly represents more than the individual Petrarch; he says what every intellectual and every writer ought to have the good sense and humility to say (pp.78–80). A final, characteristic touch at the end of Book II is the suggestion (p.128) that the pagan philosophers, and even 'my Virgil', had a premonition of the doctrine of the Trinity.

The first part of *Secretum* III, the argument about Amor (pp.130–88) is more than twice the length of the second, about Gloria (pp.188–214). This is one of two indications that the work was probably finished in haste; the other is the abrupt and rather imperfectly worked out conclusion. The ideas involved in both parts have already received fairly close attention at various places in the present essay, as regards Amor in chapter II, sections 1 and 2, as regards Gloria in chapter III, section 1. All that it remains for me to do here is to summarise the arguments in *Secretum* III, and indicate how they relate to the rest of the Petrarchan *œuvre*.

It is obvious that Amor and Gloria, as these terms are used by Petrarch, raise problems for the religious humanist. Once you have decided to place your final end in God, without renouncing human values, the question remains as to the degree and manner of your attachment to these. It would have still remained for St Paul's converts after he had encouraged them to think of 'whatever is honourable... just...lovely...gracious' etc., (Philippians, 4.8): a text 'Franciscus' might have, but didn't, cite in defence of his love for Laura. This defence comes back to his affirming the nobility and, for him, peculiar salutariness of the attachment. It is through Laura – not her beauty alone, he insists, but her virtue – that he has been given a fresh glimpse of the 'divine' in things, and so been inspired to put all his powers to their noblest possible use (pp.132–44). This affirmation includes, evidently, a general, if selective, reference to the *Canzoniere*; while the stress on Laura's virtue might seem best to correspond with the concluding sonnets of Part I and with most of Part II, down to no. 362. The counter-argument of 'Augustinus' focuses on two points: Laura's influence on his pupil has been in fact pernicious (however innocent *she* may be) and in any case his love of her has been objectively impious, a form of idolatry. 'Specifically, it had (a) robbed him of dignity and liberty, (b) enormously stimulated his perverse melancholy, (c) occasioned a general relaxing of his morals;

worst of all (d) deflected his desires from the Creator to a creature',
and consequently to a state of oblivion of God and of his own true
self, 'Dei suique pariter oblivionem...' (p.160, cf. p.154).

The substance of all these charges can be found frequently in the
Canzoniere.[60] Here in the *Secretum* the emphasis is mainly on the
religious motif (d) and on the coincidence of the *innamoramento* with
the beginning of Petrarch's moral decline (c), but in different ways.
The religious motif is basic and presupposed, whereas point (c) is all
in function of the dialogue itself as a trial of strength which has to end
in the victory of 'Augustinus', which in fact it ensures (pp.150–60).
Meanwhile there is an aspect of point (d) to be clarified. What is
'forgotten' is the human self no less than God: 'Dei *suique* oblivio'.
And the reason for this is not, or not in the first place – as I once super-
ficially suggested[61] – that Petrarch was obsessed by the 'endless
distress' his sin had involved him in. Of course this theme is not overlooked by 'Augustinus' (pp.154–60). But from the point of view of
authentic Augustinianism, which Petrarch is here certainly adopting,
the *primary* evil in the loss of true self-knowledge is that it entails the
loss of God-knowledge. The basic presupposition, in other words,
is that the way to the knowledge of God – wisdom in the full sense of
the term – lies through the traces of God's perfection in his effects,
and above all in that 'image' of Him which is the human mind; for
Augustine this included both understanding and volition, the power
to know and the power to love. And both powers are fulfilled only in
and by God. Hence the inner, true self of man is nothing other than
a certain need for God. So Augustine could say, and Petrarch echo
him (*Prose*, top of p. 728), that the true philosopher – that is lover of
wisdom – 'is a lover of God'. Hence to forget one's true, inner self is
by the same token to forget God.[62] And no less than this, according to
'Augustinus', has been the disastrous effect on Petrarch of his infatuation with Laura, leading in turn to his general moral decline. This
causal sequence 'Franciscus' is invited to verify for himself, in
memory. When he has done this, he admits defeat (pp.150–60).

The chief point of interest in the rather tedious discussion that
follows about 'remedies for love' is the decision, reached on p.174,
that 'Franciscus' had better put the Alps once and for all between himself and Laura – still alive according to the self-dating of the *Secretum*
in 1342–3 (pp.136, 98–100) – and settle down for good in Italy. As
F.Rico has shown, the discussion around this point (pp.164–74)
corresponds much better to Petrarch's situation in 1352–3 than to
any earlier period in his life.[63] The importance of this final option for

Italy as his habitat would also give point to the otherwise inexplicable prolongation of this part of the dialogue, which so much restricts the space left for the treatment of Gloria – 13 pages of the Latin text against 28 for Amor. The final preparations for the journey, with all they involved in the way of winding up affairs in Avignon, farewells to friends, a last visit to Gherardo at Montrieux in April,[64] would also help to explain the signs of hasty composition in the section on Gloria.[65]

The brevity of the section is itself such a sign. Another is a certain unclearness in the argument, especially at its close (unless indeed the ambiguity here was deliberate). The general presupposition, accepted by both disputants, is that the pursuit of fame ('gloria') is a desire for 'immortality'. 'Augustinus' opens his attack by distinguishing between true and false – 'empty', 'hollow' – immortality, and accusing his pupil of having set his heart on the latter, and so forgetting both God and himself in a hopeless craving, the end of which is perdition (pp.188, 196–200). 'Franciscus' counters – after a little sparring – by introducing the idea of 'postponement': he will aim at mortal, human glory for a time, and *then* set his sights on the immortal glory enjoyed by the blessed in heaven (a concept neither he nor 'Augustinus' defines). In thus projecting an achievement in two successive phases of all the glory he could hope for, 'Franciscus' certainly speaks for the historical Petrarch (whether as he actually *was* in 1342–3 or as he later *remembered*, or chose to *represent* himself as having been at that time). The project itself involves both an *idea* and a *fact*. The idea is basically that on which Dante constructed Book III of the *Monarchia*. If man is made up of mortal body and immortal soul, why then should he not order his activities accordingly, aiming *first* at temporal ends attainable here and now, on earth, and *then* at the eternal end corresponding to his immortal part? From the Christian point of view this idea of deferring the latter aim until after the achievement of the former is obviously unacceptable. But the basic reason why this is so – that God *can* be loved here and now, with perfect 'charity', in and through the things of this world[66] – never seems to occur to 'Augustinus', obsessed as he is with the dichotomy of time and eternity, concerned as he exclusively is to point out the perils of any postponing of one's interest in the latter (pp.194–204, 206–12). His eloquent preaching here contains little real theology.[67]

The fact involved in the project of 'Franciscus' was the still unfinished state, through the 1340s and beyond, of the two chief literary undertakings of Petrarch's early manhood, *De viris illustribus* and *Africa*. Brought early into the debate about glory by 'Augustinus' (p.192), they remain at the centre of it to the end. The question is, should 'Franciscus' finish them? Would their completion be worth the time and effort involved? It was not a question here of their intrinsic merit, but of the fame their author could expect from them; and in particular from the *Africa*. This work had already won him the signal honour of the Roman coronation in April 1341; an honour, however, given precisely in expectation of the poem's completion. After that date therefore all Petrarch's thoughts about literary glory centred perforce on the *Africa* and on its longed for completion. Hence the note of urgency, of impatience even, in the interventions of 'Franciscus' as the dialogue draws to its close.

But the urgency is no less moral than egoistic or aesthetic. 'Franciscus' has been genuinely impressed by his mentor's stress – reinforced significantly by three citations from the *Africa* itself (pp.202–6) – on the precariousness, indeed the ultimate nullity of mere worldly fame. Not only this, but he has fully accepted 'Augustinus''s deeper point, that fame has to be judged by the intrinsic moral worth of the work or deed which occasions it. That worth in turn has to be judged by reference to God – for, both interlocutors being after all Christians, what matters for both in the end is whether a work or deed is done in the 'grace', or as 'Augustinus' here calls it, the 'light' of God ('radiante Deo', p.204). So much is clear. What for many readers remains to the end unclear is just how each of the disputants goes on to relate this basic moral principle, on which they agree, to the practical matter in hand, that is whether 'Franciscus' is or is not to continue with the *De viris* and the *Africa*. Of the two disputants, 'Franciscus' is the more explicit and forthright at the end. He clearly says what he wants to do and – since he cannot 'rein in' this desire – that this is what he intends to do, only adding that he will finish the two works in question as quickly as he can, in order as soon as possible to devote himself exclusively to the task urged on him by 'Augustinus' ('studium hoc unum sectari', p.214). 'Augustinus' limits himself, in effect, to saying he would much prefer his pupil to set out at once on the 'right path'. That would certainly be 'more useful' (than to follow the path of poetry or historiography), for that is the path which sooner or later 'Franciscus' *must* follow if he is ever to reach his true end. However, if he is quite determined to stray down byways which *could* lead to perdition...well, he has been warned! Meanwhile 'Augustinus' continues to pray for him (p.214)

Understanding the conclusion of the dialogue in this sense, I would sum up the final position of the two speakers as follows. They are agreed that the only 'true glory' is that consequent on 'virtue', as its by-product or 'shadow'; and that this virtue has its source in God ('radiante Deo') and, by implication, is the only way leading to God (204–6). The nature of this absolutely obligatory 'virtue' is left unspecified by 'Augustinus', except that it implies assiduous 'meditation on death' (pp.210–12, cf. 186, 138–40, 52–62). It is clear, however, that he has in mind some definite task awaiting his pupil *in this life*, as his 'way to the Fatherland' (heaven). To discover the nature of that task, let 'Franciscus' only heed the promptings of his own 'spirit'; they will tell him clearly enough (pp.210–12). The task will then replace – better late than never – his sterile, perilous obsession with the *Africa* and *De viris*. For a moment 'Franciscus' seems to yield on every point, but then abruptly decides on a slightly different course. Certainly he will undertake those 'maiora' (p.206), those greater things – greater than the two Latin works – which 'Augustinus' is urging upon him. Such, he fully acknowledges, is the course required by 'virtue'. But first he will finish – he will do so with all possible speed – those other two 'great albeit secular' undertakings, not for any 'glory' they might bring him,[68] but simply because in the last resort he *cannot* give them up, his desire to the contrary is irresistible (p.214). So we return to the moral issue, as the dialogue presents it. Is this final option for a postponement of the better course presented as a *sin* on the part of 'Franciscus'? Clearly not – for 'Augustinus', albeit grudgingly, permits it: 'Sed sic eat, quando...' ('but so be it, since it has to be', p.214). But, equally clearly, it is not represented as virtuous. What then? I think it is envisaged, even by 'Augustinus', as a thing in itself neither right nor wrong, only dangerous. But 'Franciscus', in effect, declares himself prepared and resolved to take the risk. So the dialogue ends with both a concession and a warning.[69]

This conclusion of the section on Gloria is complementary to that of the longer one on Amor. In each case the conclusion is practical; in that of Amor it was the decision finally to leave Provence and settle in Italy; in that of Gloria it is a decision on what Petrarch, once settled in Italy, is going to do – since the question here is about future literary work, and all his 'doing' was, in the first instance, literary. The two arguments, then, run parallel; and together they comprise the whole of *Secretum* III. And while each terminates in its own conclusion, the unity of the Book requires that each conclusion be viewed in relation to the other – that each implicitly carries a *reference* to the other and cannot be understood without it. This surely can only be denied at the cost of denying the unity of this third part of the dialogue. Granted that unity however, it becomes surely equally clear that the two conclusions are parts or aspects of one and the same practical decision, and therefore relate to the same period of time: the time when Petrarch both decided on the final move to Italy and to have done, as quickly as possible, with the *De viris* and the *Africa*, in order henceforth to devote himself to something his conscience ('Augustinus') told him would be infinitely more worth while. What then *was* this period of time? *When* did Petrarch opt finally for Italy as his final habitat? Conversely, *when* did he come to so crucial a decision about his future literary work as the brief debate about Gloria bears witness to? Obviously any clear evidence on either point would help us to date the *Secretum*.

To this question we must now turn if we are to understand the complete evolution of Petrarch's thought in the latter part of his life. As regards the choice of Italy as his place of residence we should note that Petrarch left Provence for Italy in September 1343, and again in November 1347, and, for the last time, in May/June 1353. The first journey, to Naples, was undertaken at the Pope's behest and was purely diplomatic and political.[70] It had nothing to do with any such 'flight from Laura' as is envisaged in *Secretum* III, even if a year *later* we find Petrarch writing from Parma to say he intended to stay on in Italy and try to forget Laura.[71] The journey in 1347 was also political inasmuch as he was bearing an urgent message from the Pope to the lord of Verona, but in other respects it has some resemblance to the situation described in the *Secretum*, since it followed closely on Eclogue VIII, 'Divortium', in which Petrarch, though chiefly concerned with bidding farewell to Card. Colonna and his service, lays great stress also on his desire to settle down in Italy, and mentions the fascination of Laura as a reason why he has not put this desire into effect sooner.[72] But there is an important difference between the Eclogue and *Secretum* III. According to the Eclogue Petrarch's future Italian home is to be definitely at Parma, where he is expected by 'Gillias' (Azzo da Correggio), but in the *Secretum* it is emphasised that 'Franciscus', though certainly going to Italy, doesn't know *where* in Italy his journey will end: 'go wherever you please' is all the advice he gets from 'Augustinus' (*Prose*, p.172).[73] In this particular respect, then, the Eclogue, written in late summer or autumn of 1347, fails to tally with the situation reflected in *Secretum* III. But precisely this situation – combining a longing to go to Italy as soon as possible (and remain there) with an uncertainty as to where in Italy he will go – is expressed by Petrarch in four letters written between April 1352 and April 1353 (in chronological order, *Fam.* XV, 8, XII, 11, XV, 3 and XVI, 10). To no other passage in Petrarch's works do parts of these letters correspond so closely as to the debate about leaving Provence in *Secretum* III, while, as we have seen, there *are* good reasons for disconnecting this debate from the departures in 1343 and 1347. Those letters, then, point to 1352–3 as the probable date of composition of *Secretum* III.[74]

The same conclusion is suggested by comparing what is known of Petrarch's work on the *De viris illustribus* and the *Africa* after 1342 with what is said of these works in *Secretum* III (pp. 192–8, 202–6, 212–14). By 1343 the *De viris* consisted of 23 'lives', for the most part of heroes of republican Rome down to mid second century BC, and Petrarch had probably already thought of extending the book to include the first century BC and the earlier emperors (*Prose*, p.192).[75] At all events a main reason for his return to Provence in the summer of 1351 was an urgent desire to complete both the *De viris* and the *Africa*, a task he hoped to finish within two years and at Vaucluse.[76] In fact he quickly set to work on the *De viris*, but according to a new plan apparently intended to take in 'men of every age' (ibid., p.72); and, for a start, between 1351 and 1352, he wrote 12 new and 'pre-Roman' lives, beginning with Adam and ending with Hercules.[77] Turning now to the *Africa*, I note three distinct phases in Petrarch's work on it prior to his final return to Italy in May/June 1353: (1) a period of intense, very productive work, summer 1341 to January 1342; (2) a period of more interrupted, occasional, piecemeal work between late 1342 and 1347, during which, however, Petrarch's genuine interest in the poem and hope of bringing it to completion, seem to be steadily maintained;[78] (3) a period of disheartenment and of an increasing anxiety about whether he ever would finish the *Africa*, whether in fact he had not reached the end of his tether in its regard. This misgiving, already perhaps discernible in 1349, comes out clearly in the course of 1352.[79]

How far does all this help to date the *Secretum*? Does all or any of it support the usual dating in 1342–3? Or point rather to some time in the late 1340s? Or to Rico's dating, which is broadly 1347–53 but puts the main emphasis on Petrarch's last two years in Provence, 1351–3? But it is from within the *Secretum* itself that we have to consider the problem. Regarded then from that point of view, the question becomes, to which, if any, of those three datings does the evidence of the dialogue itself point? And here by the dialogue is meant, of course, that part of it, namely the section on Gloria, where the *De viris* and the *Africa* come into the discussion, and not just incidentally or implicitly (as on pp.72–6) but as a central, burning issue; the question, that is, whether Petrarch will or will not go on with these two works; the question thrashed out between himself and his conscience, 'Augustinus', on the last pages of the *Secretum*. The question was finally answered, as we have seen, with a qualified No: he will *not* go on with them except for just so long as is needed to bring them *speedily* to an end. And this because (a) he no longer regards them as worth spending time on, and yet (b) he very much *would* like to finish them. Now as between these two aspects of the dialogue's conclusion, much the weightier – as expressing the author's reasoned and decisive assessment of himself and of his whole task in life – is, it seems to me, aspect (a); compared with which the last-minute qualification (b) seems almost whimsical – its only motive being an unreasoned 'desiderium', 'desire' (p.214). Other, unspoken motives may of course have been at work here, above all perhaps that of enlivening an otherwise too one-sided conclusion to the three-day debate.[80]

As expressed, then, in the Gloria section of *Secretum* III, Petrarch's attitude to his own work as historian and poet is severely critical; it is not so on intrinsic grounds but because of the motive of vainglory that he sees inseparably attached to it, a motive which it is high time he got rid of once for all. So the dominant note here is renunciation, a renunciation which will be at the same time a conversion (as we have seen) to some unspecified task more befitting one who professes to love virtue (pp.192–208). Renunciation, a new direction, and, pervading this double decision, that sense of urgency, especially as regards Petrarch's future as a writer, that one feels in the closing stages of the dialogue. Tested against this state of mind and feeling, which of the three suggested datings of the *Secretum* seems the most plausible: 1342–3, the later 1340s, or 1351–3? As far as *De viris* is concerned, none of the three is strikingly plausible; yet on balance, I think, the evidence rather favours the last one. Let us glance again at the stages of that work's composition. Begun in 1338–9, by 1343 it comprised the 23 mostly Roman 'lives', including that of Scipio Africanus already in its second form of about 20,000 words.[81] Then a gap of more than seven years before the letter already mentioned a while back, of July 1351, expressing a 'vehement hope' of finishing both *De viris* and *Africa* within the next two years.[82] This was followed, through the winter of 1351–2, by the 12 pre-Romulus 'lives', of which the last, that of Hercules, was perhaps significantly left unfinished.[83] To 1351–3, 'or perhaps a little later', Wilkins assigned also the Preface (*Prose*, pp.218–26).[84] Then for about 15 years we hear no more of the *De viris* (still unfinished) apart from two allusions in 1354.[85] Finally, as from 1368 (?), Petrarch at the request of the lord of Padua wrote shorter versions of some of the original 'Roman' series of 'lives'. Meanwhile however, probably after 1353, he had made a third redaction of that 'Scipio', and after 1361 had begun the long 'Life of Caesar' (see above, pp.155–6) completed before his death.[86] But in the present context the most significant of these facts is Petrarch's strong desire to finish the *De viris* as soon as possible, and then the long interval, 1353 to the mid-1360s, during which, although it remained unfinished, we hear of no further work on it apart from a passing allusion in 1354.[87] The experts, it is true, date the third redaction of the 'Scipio' after 1353,[88] but apparently nothing else was done on the original Roman series, nor is anything more heard of the pre-Romulus series of 1351–2.[89] It was only in the 1360s that a creative interest in Julius Caesar took hold of Petrarch. Now Petrarch's eagerness, in 1351, to finish the *De viris*, followed by the new series of 1351–2, and this in turn by the long halt in the work (hardly interrupted by the re-writing of 'Scipio') – all this fits in with and is illustrated by *Secretum* III, as above analysed; but what has it in common with the situation in 1342–3? – when he was happily completing his original Roman series and, so far as we know, felt no such fretful urgency to have done with the whole work as he certainly felt eight or ten years later.

But the case for 1351–3 is clearer if viewed in relation to the *Africa*. Let us assume, what has been partly shown and will appear more clearly presently, that *Secretum* III (pp.188ss) represents a crisis in Petrarch's moral and artistic confidence in respect of his epic. The question then is one of determining, within the decade 1341–3 to 1351–3, the most plausible date for this crisis. And my argument proceeds as follows. (1) Between 1341 and 1348 the available evidence shows no serious falling off of his interest in the *Africa* or his confidence that he could bring it to a satisfactory conclusion.[90] (2) The first distinct signs of misgiving in this respect appear in 1349.[91] (3) July 1351 Petrarch, now back in Provence, wrote the letter already cited expressing a 'vehement' hope and desire to finish both *De viris* and *Africa* within the next two years.[92] (4) Yet if we are to believe E. H. Wilkins – always meticulously attentive to facts and dates – 'Petrarch seems not to have done any further work on the *Africa* either during this stay in Provence *or at any later time*' (my italics).[93] (5) In *Contra medicum* III, written in 1352–3, Petrarch says he is no longer a poet (meaning in Latin) and has even given up reading poetry.[94] (6) Three letters written in 1352 touch on the *Africa* and in doing so show striking similarities of thought or mood with things said or hinted in the Gloria section of *Secretum* III. In *Fam.* XII, 7 (20 Feb.) Petrarch tells his correspondent that he isn't at present working on the poem; he feels depression and irritation ('morositas') about it (cf. *Prose*, p.194, at top).[95] Let it lie fallow; it may ripen with time. Or perhaps he'll change his mind – give his work a final touch and publish it as it stands (cf. pp.206, 214). As such, after all, it may be the best he could ever hope to do as a poet. And he wouldn't remain idle, but always strive to become a wiser and better man (cf. pp.194, 206, 212–14).[96] In *Fam.* XIII, 12 (Sept. 1352) the stress is on the difficulties and vastness of the undertaking: it has proved harder than he anticipated, and there is still much left to do (cf. *Prose*, pp.192–4). The same ideas reappear in *Fam.* XIII, 7 (Nov. 1352), but now with a note of exasperation, almost of despair. Contrasting the 'length of time' and 'excessive toil' the poem has cost him ('inter manus *diutius* iam pependit...*immodico labore* confectum') with the 'burning' enthusiasm with which he began it, Petrarch is tempted simply to give up – only so can he hope to 'calm my panting heart'. All this, in the *Secretum*, pp.192–4, is transformed into a reminiscence: he had once been tempted to 'burn' the *Africa* rather than die leaving it 'half-finished'. This admission surely implies a half-assent to the charge just made by 'Augustinus' (p.192) that it was '*excessive* desire for glory' that had made him begin the work in the first place ('*immodice* gloriam petens'). The transformation, in any case, of present desire (in the letter) into reminiscence (in the *Secretum*) does not conceal the close similarity of mood and attitude in these texts. Both surely express, the one openly the other by suggestion, the same impatience to be rid of a burden and an obsession, now grown intolerable, that is implicit in the dialogue's conclusion.

Clearly, what items 4 and 6 in the above paragraph point to, and in part explain, is the same *negative* conclusion as that reached in *Secretum* III – a virtual renunciation of the *Africa*, that is, of the major *literary* undertaking of Petrarch's life. By contrast, what item 5 points to (viewed in its context – see especially *Prose*, p.680 – and with regard also to *Fam.* XII, 7, cited under item 6) is the dialogue's *positive* conclusion – that Petrarch will henceforth devote himself to some 'greater' work or works, more in line with virtue and the wisdom befitting his age (*Prose*, pp.194–8, 204–6, 210–14). And what all the items together seem to point to is that this major turning point in Petrarch's life occurred between the later 1340s and his final return to Italy in the summer of 1353. This is Rico's conclusion and I find it, to say the least, extremely cogent. I think Rico has shifted the *onus probandi* on to those who still hold the traditional view that (allowing for subsequent 'retouchings') the *Secretum* was written in 1342–3. As I wrote in a review of *Vida u Obra*, 'the weakness of the usual dating is that there is really very little to be said for it, except... that the *Secretum* is *self*-dated...between November 1342 and April 1343; and...there remains after all the possibility that that date is as fictitious as the conversation which contains it. We now know that ...many of Petrarch's letters, ostensibly written when he was young, were in fact composed many years later, and that the ostensible dating of poems in the *Canzoniere* is by no means always reliable. It cannot be simply assumed that a similar mystification...is not at work also in the *Secretum*.'[97]

In these last few paragraphs I have condensed a part, but only a part, of Rico's case for shifting the date of composition of the substance of the *Secretum* from the early 1340s to 1351–3. To the reasons given others could easily be added, drawn from what is now known of the growth of Petrarch's classical culture during the decade in question,[98] from mutual connections between the dialogue and other of Petrarch's works of the same period, from the *marginalia* in Fra Tedaldo da Mugello's transcript of the original autograph of the *Secretum*.[99] But enough is enough, for the present. Let me conclude with another self-citation apropos of *Vida u Obra*: 'Nevertheless this book does far more than fix a point in chronology. In and through the long discussion about dates a personality emerges...Petrarch in that crucial half-decade which followed the death of Laura and the break with the Colonna and with Avignon...years of deep self-criticism...which found expression in the *Secretum*, especially in Book III, that pitiless critique of the two ideals which had filled his young manhood, *Amor* and *Gloria*; years in which, from being the poet of Laura and of Rome, he aspired...to the status and dignity of a "philosopher".'[100] These words were written five years ago and they now, as the reader will doubtless have noted, call for two qualifications. First, Petrarch never left off being in some sense the poet of Laura (see ch. II, section 2, pp.80–92); secondly, the only kind of philosopher he ever seriously aspired to become was a moral philosopher, and that not in the theoretical way of an Aristotle (see above, pp.150–61) but in the practical, 'homiletic'[101] manner of Seneca in his letters, or better, after the manner – at however far a remove – of Augustine in the *Confessions*, gathering from his experience of life the bitter-sweet fruit of self-knowledge.

Bibliography and Abbreviations

I. PETRARCH'S WORKS
Editions referred to in this book and abbreviations used

1. COLLECTIONS
(1) Complete Works: *F.P. Opera quae extant omnia*, Basel 1554 (repr. 1581); referred to as *Opera omnia*; 'Edizione Nazionale delle Opere di F.P.', Florence 1926-00. So far 7 volumes have appeared: *Africa*, ed. N. Festa, 1926; *Epistolae Familiares* (4 vols.), ed. V. Rossi and U. Bosco, 1933-42; *Rerum memorandarum libri*, ed. G. Billanovich, 1943; *De viris illustribus*, vol. 1, ed. G. Martellotti, 1964. Referred to respectively as *Africa*, *Fam.*, *Rerum*, *De Viris*.

(2) Anthologies: *Opere di F.P.*, ed. E. Bigi (notes by G. Ponte), Milan 1963. *F.P. Rime, Trionfi e Poesie Latine*, ed. F. Neri, G. Martellotti, E. Bianchi, N. Sapegno, and *F.P. Prose*, ed. G. Martellotti, P. G. Ricci, E. Carrara, E. Bianchi – respectively vols 6 and 7 of 'La Letteratura Italiana, Storia e Testi', Ricciardi, Milan-Naples 1951 and 1955, referred to as *Rime* and *Prose*. Finally, the selections of P.'s verse and prose made by G. Contini for his *Letteratura Italiana delle Origini*, Florence 1970, pp.573-694.

2. INDIVIDUAL WORKS
A. *Italian*

All references to the *Canzoniere* are to the critical edition by G. Contini, with notes by D. Ponchiroli, Turin, 'Nuova Universale Einaudi', 1964. This edition is prefaced by an invaluable essay by Contini on P.'s language, referred to in the present book as *Preliminari* (reprinted in *Varianti e altra linguistica*, Turin 1970, pp.169-92). All modern editions of the *Canz.* are based on one MS, Vat. lat. 3195 (see below, ch. II, section 3). Also indispensable, however, for serious study of the *Canz.* is the MS, Vat. lat. 3196, of 20 autograph work-sheets used by P. in the composition of verse in Italian (see below, ibid., and A. Romanò, *Il codice degli abbozzi (V.L. 3196) di F.P.*, Rome 1955). The outstanding study of V.L. 3196, from the point of view of literary criticism, is still G. Contini's *Saggio d'un commento alle correzioni del P. volgare*, Florence 1943, now in *Varianti*, pp.5-31. I refer to it as *Saggio*. In translating poems cited from the *Canz.* I have made some use of the scholarly version by R. M. Durling, *P.'s Lyric Poems* etc., Harvard University Press 1966.

For the *Triumphs* I have used the text edited by F. Neri in F.P. *Rime, Trionfi e Poesie Latine*, pp.481-578 (see under Collections). There is a good translation of the *Triumphs* by E. H. Wilkins, University of Chicago Press 1962.

B. *Latin*

(a) Verse

(i) *Africa*. See under Collections the 'Edizione Nazionale' and the anthologies ed. by E. Bigi and by F. Neri *et al.* Most of my direct allusions are to extracts printed in the latter compilation, pp.626-702. There is a translation in verse by T. G. Bergin and A. S. Wilson, Yale University Press 1977. (ii) For the *Bucolicum Carmen* (or 'Eclogues') I have chiefly made use of the edition by T. Mattucci, with an Italian version *en face* and Introductions to the various Eclogues, Pisa, Giardini, 1970. Of *Carmen* x, 'Laurea occidens', G. Martellotti has published the text, with transl. and notes, Rome 1968. There is an English transl. of the complete *B.C.* by T. G. Bergin, Yale University Press 1974. (iii) *Epistolae Metrice*. There is no complete modern edition. I have used the Ricciardi 'Storia e Testi', vol. 6 (see above under Collections) supplemented by the *Opere*, ed. E. Bigi (which e.g. gives the important introductory epistle I, I, to Barbato da Sulmona, not printed in the Ricciardi volume).

(b) Prose

Opere Latine di F.P., ed. and transl. by A. Bufano, 2 vols, Turin 1975. This compilation includes all the works listed under (ii) to (iv) below except the *Rerum memorandarum libri* and the *De Remediis*; and with the addition of two orations, of P.'s Will (1370) and of his transl. (1373) of Boccaccio's tale of Griselda, *Decameron* x, 10. The orations are (a) the *Collatio laureationis* delivered at Rome, April 1341, when P. was crowned as poet laureate, (b) one spoken before King John II of France, at Paris in Jan. 1361.

Particular works. (i) Historical. The chief authority on the *De viris illustribus* and *De gestis Cesaris* is G. Martellotti, and it is on his edition of the fairly ample passages from these works printed in the Ricciardi vol., *Prose* (see under Collections) – as also on his 'Critical Note', ibid., pp.1161-6 – that my judgements on P.'s historical writings are mainly based. There is no modern edition either of the complete *De viris* or of the *De gestis*; but, besides the partial edition of the former in the 'Edizione Nazionale', Martellotti has edited the 'Life' of Scipio Africanus, Milan-Naples 1954.

(ii) Moral Treatises. Apart from G. Billanovich's ed. of *Rerum memorandarum libri* ('Ediz. Nazionale', vol. xiv, 1943) we have good editions of *De vita solitaria* – ed. G. Martellotti in *Prose*, cit., pp.286-591, with transl. by A. Bufano – and of *De otio religioso*, ed. G. Rotondi, 1958. There is no modern edition of the *De remediis utriusque fortunae*, excepting the fragments printed in *Prose*, cit., pp.606-45.

(iii) For the *Secretum* I use the text edited by D. Carrara in *Prose*, cit., pp.22-215. In the matter of dating the dialogue I follow F. Rico, *Vida u Obra de P.*: I, *Lectura del 'Secretum'*, Padua 1978.

(iv) Polemical. For the *Invective contra medicum* I have used the critical edition of P. G. Ricci (with a 15th century transl., and an Appendix by B. Martinelli), Rome, 'Storia e Letteratura', 1978. Book III is also in *Prose*, cit. pp.648-93. The other two 'Invectives' are also in *Prose*, cit., respectively on pp.694-709 and 768-807; and in vol.2 of *Opere Latine di F.P.*, ed. A. Bufano, 1975.

(v) Epistolary. I have made considerable use of the anthologies mentioned above under Collections; to which should be added the fuller selection given, with translations *en face*, by U. Dotti, *Epistole di F.P.*, 2 vols., Turin 1978. Dotti's special interest is in the social setting and ideological significance of P.'s letters; and his views, set out in a lengthy Introduction to these volumes, deserve far more attention than they have received, I fear, in the present book. In all these compilations the text of the *Epist. Familiares* is that given in the 'Edizione Nazionale' (see under Collections), while for most of the *Seniles* included the editors have still had to depend on the Basel edition of 1554. The case is different with the 'Sine Nomine' letters, of which there is the critical edition by P. Piur, *Petrarcas 'Buch ohne Namen' und die päpstliche Kurie*, Halle 1925. See also the very useful edition with Italian transl., by U. Dotti, Bari, 'Universale Laterza', 1974. Of the *Epist. Variae* only no. 48 (to Cola di Rienzo, summer 1347) is given in any of the anthologies I have mentioned – in vol. 2 of Dotti's *Epistole di F.P.* Of great utility throughout has been the precise chronological information contained in *P.'s Correspondence* by E. H. Wilkins, Padua 1960. I have used the following abbreviations: *Fam.* and *Sen.* (with roman numeral for the book and arabic for the particular letter), 's.N.' and *Variae* (followed in each case by an arabic numeral). I should add that there is an English translation of Books I-VIII of the *Familiares* by A. S. Bernardo, State University of New York Press 1975.

II. STUDIES

A. BIOGRAPHICAL (N.B. Of the works listed under this head, those by Wilkins are the more purely biographical. The others include much critical comment).

E.H.WILKINS, *Life of P.*, Chicago University Press 1961.
— *Studies in the Life and Works of P.*, Cambridge, Mass. 1955.
— *P.'s Eight Years in Milan*, Cambridge, Mass. 1958.
— *P.'s Later Years*, Cambridge, Mass. 1959.
U.BOSCO, *Francesco Petrarca*, Turin 1961.
N.SAPEGNO, *Storia della letteratura italiana*, Milan 1965, II, pp.187-313.
A.E.QUAGLIO, *Francesco Petrarca*, Milan 1967.
T.G.BERGIN, *Petrarch*, New York 1970.
Il P. ad Arquà. Atti del Convegno di Studi nel VI Centenario (1370-1374), Padua 1975.

B. CRITICAL
1. Petrarch as Poet
(a) P.'s idea of poetry, and aspects of his poetical practice in general:
G.BÀRBERI SQUAROTTI, 'Le poetiche del trecento in Italia', in *Momenti e*

problemi di storia dell'estetica, Milan 1959, I, pp.255-303.

R. MONTANO, *L'estetica del Rinascimento e del Barocco*, Naples 1962, pp.27-38.

H. GMELIN, 'Das Prinzip der Imitatio in den romanische Literaturen der Renaissance', in *Romanische Forschungen*, 46 (1932), pp.83-192.

G. RONCONI, *Le origini delle dispute umanistiche sulla poesia: Mussato e P.*, Rome 1976.

G. VELLI, 'La memoria poetica del P.', in *Italia medioevale e umanistica* (*IMU*) 19 (1976), pp.173-207, repr. in *P. e Boccaccio*, Padua 1979, pp.1-37.

E. RAIMONDI, 'Ritrattistica petrarchesca', in *Metafora e storia*, Turin 1970, pp.163-87.

(b) The *Canzoniere*
(i) *The 'Canzoniere' form, and the composition of P.'s 'Canzoniere':*

M. SANTAGATA, *Dal Sonetto al Canzoniere: Ricerche sulla preistoria e la costituzione di un genere*, Padua 1979.

G. CONTINI, *Saggio d'un commento alle correzioni del P. volgare*, Florence 1943; repr. in *Varianti e altra linguistica*, Turin 1970, pp.5-31.

A. SCHIAFFINI, 'Il lavorio della forma in F.P.', in *Momenti di storia della lingua italiana*, Rome 1953.

E. H. WILKINS, *The Making of the 'Canzoniere' and other Petrarchan Studies*, Rome 1951.

F. RICO, '"Rime Sparse", "Rerum Vulgarium Fragmenta". Para el titulo y el primer soneto del "Canzoniere"', in *Medioevo Romanzo*, III (1976), I, pp.101-38.

V. BRANCA, 'Il momento decisivo nella formazione del "Canzoniere",' in *Studi in onore di M. Marangoni*, Pisa 1957, pp.30-42 (cf. *Tradizione delle opere di G. Boccaccio*, Rome 1958, pp.289-304).

B. MARTINELLI, *P. e il Ventoso*, Minerva Italica, Bari 1977, chapters 1-3, and ch. 4, pp.217-25.

(ii) *General studies, thematic and stylistic:*
Under this head should be included the critical sections of the works cited above, under A, by Bosco, Sapegno and Quaglio; to which may be added, of Sapegno, his Introduction to the Ricciardi selection of *Rime, Trionfi e Poesie Latine*, ed. F. Neri *et al.*, cited above in Part I; and, of Bosco, *La lirica del P.*, Rome 1965. Also the following:

F. DE SANCTIS, *Saggio critico sul P.*, ed. N. Gallo and N. Sapegno, Turin 1952.

C. CALCATERRA, *Il P. e il petrarchismo*, in *Questioni e correnti di storia letteraria*, Milan 1949, pp.167-273.

E. BIGI, *Dal P. al Leopardi*, Milan-Naples 1954, pp.1-22.

G. CONTINI's Introduction to the 'Nuova Universale Einaudi' ed. of the *Canz.*: 'Preliminari sulla lingua del P.'; repr. in *Varianti e altra linguistica*, Turin 1970, pp.169-92.

F. MONTANARI, *Studi sul Canzoniere del P.*, Rome 1958 (but see the pertinent criticisms in A. Noferi, *L'esperienza*, cited below, pp.290-7).

A. NOFERI, *L'esperienza poetica del P.*, Florence 1962.

R. AMATURO, *Petrarca*, Bari 1971, pp.240-359.

M. FUBINI, *Metrica e poesia*, Milan 1962, chapters 6 and 7.

D.ALONSO, 'La poesia del P. e il petrarchismo (Mondo estetico della pluralita),' in *Lettere italiane*, 11 (1959), pp.277-319.

M.P.SIMONELLI, 'Strutture foniche nei *R.V.F.*', in *F.P. Six Centuries Later*, ed. A. Scaglione, University of Chicago Press 1975, pp.66-104.

B.MARTINELLI, 'l'ordinamento morale del *Canzoniere*', in *P. e il Ventoso*.

N.ILIESCU, *Il Canzoniere petrarchescho e Sant' Agostino*, Rome 1962.

R.MONTANO, *Lo spirito e le lettere. Disegno storico della letteratura italiana*, Milan 1970, I, pp.202-17.

R.M.DURLING, 'Petrarch', in *The Figure of the Poet in Renaissance Epic*, Cambridge, Mass. 1965, pp.67-87.

B.T.SOZZI, *Petrarca: storia della critica*, Palermo 1963.

(iii) *Particular studies, thematic and stylistic:*

E.CHIORBOLI, 'I sonetti introduttivi alle "Rime Sparse"', in D. Bianchi *et al.*, *Studi Petrarcheschi*, Arezzo 1928, pp.65-77.

On *Canz.* 1 in particular, see R.AMATURO, *Petrarca*, pp.248-51; A.NOFERI in *Lettere Italiane*, 26 (1974), pp.165-79; C.KLOPP in *Lingua e stile*, 12 (1977), pp.331-42; F.RICO in art. 'Rime Sparse', etc. cited above in (i), pp.116-38.

On the Apollo/Daphne theme: C.CALCATERRA, *Nella selva del Petrarca*, Bologna 1942, chapters 1-3; U.DOTTI, 'Il mito dafneo', *Convivium*, 37 (1969), pp.9-23; D.DUTSCHKE, *F.P., Canzoniere XXIII*, etc., Ravenna 1977; B.MARTINELLI, *P. e il Ventoso*, ch. I, 'La canzone delle metamorfosi...'; R.M.DURLING on *Canz.* 30, 'Giovene donna sotto un verde lauro', *Modern Language Notes*, 86 (1971), pp.1-20; M.COTTINO-JONES, 'The Myth of Apollo and Daphne in P.'s *Canzoniere*', in *F.P., Six Centuries Later*, ed. A. Scaglione, pp.152-76; P.R.J.HAINSWORTH, 'The Myth of Daphne', etc., *Italian Studies*, 34 (1979), pp.28-44; R.AMATURO, *Petrarca*, pp.248-75.

In connection with *Canz.* 35, 'Solo e pensoso', see M.PASTORE STOCCHI, 'Divagazione su due solitari, Bellerofonte e P.', *Dal Dante al Novecento. Studi offerti a G. Getto*, Milan 1970, pp.63-83; M.GUGLIELMINETTI, 'P. fra Abelardo e Eloisa', ibid., pp.87-107.

For the theme of time and memory in the *Canz.*, viewed in the light of P.'s Augustinian platonism, see the fine analysis by A.NOFERI, *L'esperienza poetica del P.*, op. cit., pp.260-84; and in relation to classical Latin sources, J.PETRIE, *Petrarch*, Dublin 1983, ch. III. Also F.BETTI, 'Motivo della fuga del tempo nei "Trionfi" e nel "Canzoniere" di F.P.', *Forum Italicum*, 2 (1968), pp.206-13.

On the political poems: G.PETRONIO, 'Storicità della lirica politica del F.P.', *Studi Petrarcheschi*, 7 (1961), pp.247-64. On *Canz.* 128, *Italia mia*, Carducci's commentary is still immensely worth reading (*F.P., Le Rime*, ed. Carducci-Ferrari (cited in Part I), pp.193-205). See also that by G. Contini, *Letteratura...delle origini* (cited in Part I), 598-603.

For the background to the anti-Avignon sonnets, *Canz.* 136-8, see

P.PIUR's introduction to his edition of the *Sine Nomine* letters (cited
in Part I), pp.3-132; and U.DOTTI's translation of the same (cited
ibid.), pp.vii-xlvi. N.ILIESCU, *Il 'Canzoniere'...e Sant' Agostino*,
Rome 1962, pp.133-9.

On the treatment of 'nature' in the *Canz.*, see G.CONTINI, 'Preliminari'
in *Varianti*, etc., pp.169-92, and ibid., pp.193-9, 'Préhistoire
de l'*aura* de Prétrarque'. For classical influences on this aspect of the
Canz. – with references to previous work on the subject – see
J.PETRIE, *Petrarch*, pp.51-102, 216-22.

On the penitential element in the *Canz.* as a whole, see B.MARTINELLI,
P. e il Ventoso, pp.217-300; K.FOSTER, 'Beatrice or Medusa' in *Italian
Studies presented to E. R. Vincent*, ed. C. P. Brand and U. Limentani,
Cambridge 1962, pp.41-56. Also M.CASALI, 'P. penitenziale: dai
Salmi alle Rime', *Lettere italiane*, 20, 1968, pp.366-82; N.ILIESCU,
Il 'Canzoniere', etc., pp.15-27, 69-131.

F.CHIAPPELLI, *Studi sul linguaggio del P.: la canzone delle visioni*
(Florence 1971) (*Canz.* 323) is an excellent analysis of a sample of
P.'s mature poetry.

On the concluding poems in *Canz.*, Part I, and the *post mortem*
appearances of Laura the best fairly detailed stylistic treatment
available is probably that of R.AMATURO in *Petrarca*, pp.319-45.
Amaturo is also worth reading on the concluding poems in Part II
(ibid., pp.245-52) though he is weak on the moral and religious issues
involved; on which see B. Martinelli, pp.225-39, 283-98.

  (iv) *Literary influences on the 'Canzoniere':*
For the classical Latin sources, consult *passim* the Carducci-Ferrari
commentary. A helpful outline of this subject is given by J. Petrie,
passim.

On Petrarch in relation to earlier vernacular poets, it will be enough
here to cite the following: M.CASELLA, 'Dai Trovatori al P.', in
Annali della Cattedra petrachesca, 6 (1935-6), pp.151-74; D.PIERANTOZZI,
'Il P. e Guittone', *Studi petrarcheschi*, 1 (1948), pp.145-65; F.SUITNER,
P. e la tradizione stilnovistica, Florence 1977; F.NERI, 'Il P. e le rime
dantesche della Pietra', *Cultura*, 8 (1929), pp.389-404; A.S.BERNARDO,
'P.'s Attitude toward Dante', *Publications of the Modern Language
Association*, 70 (1955), pp.488-517; M.SANTAGATA, 'Presenze di Dante
"comico" nel "Canz." del P.', *Giornale storico della letteratura italiana*,
146 (1969), pp.163-211; P.TROVATO, *Dante in Petrarca*, Florence 1979;
and the now classic comparison of the language of P. with that of
Dante in G. Contini, 'Preliminari', espec. pp.8-14.
As regards the *Triumphs* let it suffice here to mention G. Contini's
notes in the relevant section of *Letteratura...delle origini*, pp.626-33,
those on pp.359-77 of R. Amaturo's *Petrarca*; and the substantial
monograph by A. S. Bernardo, *Petrarch, Laura and the 'Triumphs'*,
State University of New York Press 1974.

2. Petrarch as Humanist

  (i) *Sources of P.'s Humanism:*

P.DE NOLHAC, *Pétrarque et l'humanisme*, Paris 1907.

    Among living scholars, G.BILLANOVICH is pre-eminent in this field of Petrarchan study. There is a complete bibliography of his work down to 1975 in the *Anuario de estudios medievales* (Madrid) 9, 1974-5. Here we may mention: *P. letterato: I, Lo scrittoio del P.*, Rome 1947; 'P. and the Textual Tradition of Livy', *Journal of the Warburg and Courtauld Institutes*, 14 (1951), pp.137-208 (and cf. *Italia medioevale e umanistica (IMU)* 2 (1959), pp.103-78); 'P. e i classici', *Studi petrarcheschi*, 7 (1961), pp.21-33; 'Nella biblioteca del P.', *IMU*, 3 (1960), pp.1-59, comprising fundamental studies of P.'s acquisition of works of St Augustine, in particular the *Enarrationes in Psalmos*, and of the Roman historian Suetonius; 'Tra Dante e P.', *IMU*, 8 (1965), pp.1-44; 'P. e gli storici latini', in *Tra latino e volgare. Per C. Dionisotti*, Padua 1975.

U.BOSCO, 'Il P. e l'umanesimo filologico' in *Saggi sul Rinascimento italiano*, Florence 1973; 'Il P. e il Rinascimento', *Cultura e Scuola*, April-June 1975.

G.MARTELLOTTI, 'Alcuni aspetti della filologia del P.', *Lettere italiane*, 6 (1974), pp.288-96.

B.L.ULLMAN, 'P.'s Favorite Books', in *Studies in the Italian Renaissance*, Rome 1973 (2nd ed.), pp.113-33.

L.D.REYNOLDS and N.G.WILSON, *Copisti e filologi. La tradizione dei classici dall' Antichità al Rinascimento* (tr. of *Scribes and Scholars*, OUP, 1968), Preface by G. Billanovich, Padua 1969, Part IV, ch. 1-3.

R.WEISS, *Medieval and Humanist Greek. Collected Essays*, Padua 1977, pp.136-203.

A.TRIPET, *Pétrarque, ou la connaissance de soi*, Geneva 1967, pp.117-56.

A.SCAGLIONE, 'P. 1974…', in *F.P. Six Centuries Later*, ed. A. Scaglione, pp.1-24.

F.RICO, 'P. y el *De vera religione*', *IMU*, 17 (1974), pp.313-64.

  (ii) *The Development of P.'s Humanism:*

G.MARTELLOTTI, 'Linee di sviluppo dell'umanesimo petrarchesco', *Studi petrarcheschi*, 2 (1949), pp.51-80.

— 'Le ultime fatiche letterarie del P.', in *Il P. ad Arquà. Atti del Convegno di Studi nel VI Centenario (1370-1374)*, pp.165-75.

C.GODI, 'La *Collatio laureationis* del P.', text and commentary, *IMU*, 13 (1970), pp.1-27.

    This 'Collatio' – the oration with which, at Rome on the 8th of April 1341, P. publicly signified his acceptance of the office and title of Poet Laureate – is obviously an important event in the history of European humanism, if only as P.'s first public statement of his ideal of a culture based on the classics. On the other hand it represented only the first stage in his own career as humanist and champion of humanism, the stage in which he still saw himself chiefly as a Latin poet and a connoisseur of Antiquity ('notitia vetustatis'). From this stage he would pass, in the course of the following decade, to the second and

final period in his career as a man of culture and a writer, the period
characterised broadly by a shift of attention from poetry to ethics,
from antiquity to the contemporary world, and, at the same time, by
that explicit affirmation of traditional Christian values which marks
so much of both his anti-Curial and his anti-Scholastic polemic (the
Sine Nomine letters, the *Contra Medicum*, the *De Ignorantia*). For a lucid
and well-documented account of this development, see F. Rico's
Introduction to the selection of P.'s prose published in 1978 by
Ediciones Alfaguara, Madrid (*P. Obras I. Prosa*, pp.xv-xxix).
To return to the Coronation Speech, its background and circum-
stances are set out in detail by E. H. Wilkins in pp.9-69 of *The Making
of the 'Canzoniere'*, Rome 1951. Its wider background and implications
may be studied in the two introductory chapters, respectively by
C. Muscetta and F. Tateo, to vol. 6 of the *Lett. ital. Laterza* series
(R. Amaturo, *Petrarca*); espec. Tateo's contribution, *L'incremento degli
studi classici*, pp.39-70. See too the works by Bosco, Sapegno, Quaglio,
Bàrberi-Squarotti, Montano, Gmelin and Ronconi, cited above under
A and B, 1. To these should be added vols. 1 and 2 of G. Toffanin's
Storia dell'umanesimo, Bologna, 3rd ed. 1942, repr. 1964. For other
aspects of P.'s humanism, as it developed after the early 1340s, it may
suffice to mention the following works (without forgetting Billanovich's indispensable *P. letterato. I, Lo scrittoio del P.*, cited above):

H. BARON, *From P. to Leonardo Bruni*, Chicago 1968, pp.7-50.
— 'P.: His Inner Struggles and the Humanistic Discovery of Man's
   Nature,' in *Florilegium Historiale. Essays presented to W. K. Ferguson*,
   Toronto 1971, pp.18-51.
J. H. WHITFIELD, *P. and the Renascence*, Oxford 1943.
P. GEROSA, *Umanesimo cristiano del P.*, Turin 1966.
W. J. BOUWSMA, 'The Two Faces of Humanism. Stoicism and Augustinian-
   ism in Renaissance Thought', in *Itinerarium Italicum. The Profile of the
   Italian Renaissance in the Mirror of its European Transformations*, ed. H. A.
   Oberman and T. A. Brady, Leiden 1975, pp.3-60.
K. HEITMAN, *Fortuna und Virtus. Eine Studie zu Petrarcas Lebensweisheit*,
   Cologne 1957.
C. VASOLI, *La dialettica e la retorica dell'Umanesimo*, Milan 1968, pp.9-16.
C. TRINKAUS, *'In Our Image and Likeness'. Humanism and Divinity in
   Italian Humanist Thought*, Chicago 1970.
E. GARIN, *L'età nuova*, Naples 1969, pp.139-60.
P. O. KRISTELLER, *Eight Philosophers of the Italian Renaissance*, Stanford
   1966.
— 'P.'s Averroists', in *Bibliothèque d'Humanisme et Renaissance*, 14 (1952),
   pp.59-65.
J. E. SEIGEL, *Rhetoric and Philosophy in Renaissance Humanism. The Union of
   Eloquence and Wisdom. Petrarch to Valla*, Princeton 1968, pp.3-98.
E. GILSON, *La philosophie au moyen age*, ch. X, 'Le retour des belles-lettres
   et le bilan du Moyen Age', espec. pp.720-30.
U. DOTTI, *P. e la scoperta della coscienza moderna*, Milan 1978.
B. MARTINELLI, 'Il P. e la medicina', pp.205-49 of the 2nd ed. of *Invective
   contra medicum*, ed. P. G. Ricci, Rome 1978.

F. TATEO, *Dialogo interiore e polemica ideologica nel 'Secretum' del P.*,
    Florence 1965.

F. RICO, *Vida u Obra de Petrarca. I, Lectura del 'Secretum'*, Padua 1974.

Notes

PREFACE

1. This tradition, considered as a body of knowledge, is what Petrarch called *notitia vetustatis*, 'knowledge of antiquity'; see 'Letter to Posterity' in *Prose*, p.6. Petrarch in fact knew hardly any Greek, but his knowledge of the Latin sources was unrivalled in his time.

2. cf. R. Hague, 'David Jones: a Reconnaissance', in *Agenda*, 5, nos 1-3 (1967), p.59.

3. *Secretum* I, in *Prose*, pp.40-2, and cf. p.24, the last 8 lines.

4. *Vida u Obra de Petrarca: I, Lectura del 'Secretum'*, Padua, 1974.

CHAPTER ONE

1. *Seniles* XVI, I, in *F. P. Opera omnia* (Basel 1554), p.1046.

2. *Paradiso* VIII, 147.

3. *De vulgari eloquentia* II, iii, 7.

4. For the *De vita solitaria*, see *Prose*, pp.286-590; and for an excerpt from the *De otio religioso*, ibid., pp.594-602.

5. E. H. Wilkins, *The Life*, p.54.

6. *Prose*, 890-4.

7. cf. G. Martellotti in *Prose*, introd., pp.xix-xx.

8. See especially the letter to Charles IV, *Fam.* X, I, in *Prose*, pp.904-14.

9. 'Lince di sviluppo...' in *Studi Petrarcheschi*, II (1949), pp.51ss; cf. *Il P. ad Arquà* (1975), pp.170-2.

10. See especially *Fam.* I, I (1350-1), IV, I, X, 3 (*Prose*, pp.830-42, 916-938); *Sen.* V, 2, X, 2 – Petrarch's most detailed account of his childhood and youth (*Prose*,

pp.1090-1124); XVI, I; and of course the unfinished 'To Posterity', planned as the conclusion to the *Seniles* (*Prose*, pp.2-18).

11. Text, ed. C. Godi, in *Italia Medievale e Umanistica* (*IMU*), XIII (1970), pp.1ss.

12. Text, with valuable introduction and notes, in *Bucolicum Carmen*, ed. T. Mattucci, Pisa (1970), pp.1-44.

CHAPTER TWO

1. See G. Contini, 'Preliminari sulla lingua del P.' in *Varianti e altra linguistica* (Turin 1970), p.173.

2. *Convivio* I, xii-xiii.

3. *De vulgare eloquentia* I, i, 2-4.

4. ibid., I, i, 4.

5. cf. *Inferno* XI, 97-105; Aristotle, *De Coelo* II, 3: 286a; Aquinas, *Summa theol.* 1a2ae. 49, 2.

6. *DVE* I, iv-vi.

7. As *DVE* I, vi, 4 is commonly interpreted; for the contrary view see M. Corti, *Dante a un nuovo crocevia* (Florence 1981), p.47.

8. *Convivio* I, xiii, 12.

9. Contini, *Letteratura Italiana delle Origini* (Florence 1970), p.577.

10. *Letteratura*, p.577.

11. *DVE* I, x, 3-xix.

12. *Convivio* I, xi, 21.

13. See the scrupulously documented pp.150-73 in E. H. Wilkins, *The Making of the 'Canzoniere'*, Rome, 'Storia e Letteratura', 1950).

14. *Opera omnia*, p.879: improved text in Branca, *Tradizione*, p.301.

15. *Letters from Petrarch* (1966), p.245.

16. *Tradizione*, p.303 n.1.

17. cf. Seneca, *Ep. ad Lucilium* 88, 32.

18. *Consolatio Philosophiae* I, pr. 26–41; for the influence of Boethius on Petrarch, especially in the *Secretum*, see F. Rico's summary in *Vida u Obra* (Padua 1978), pp.519-20.

19. E. Bigi, *Opere di F.P.*, ed. E. Bigi and G. Ponte (Milan 1963), p.xxv.

20. cf. Aquinas, *Summa theol.* 1a 2ae.74, 6.

21. E. H. Wilkins, *The Making*, pp.175-6.

22. I give my reasons for dating *Canz.* I after the death of Laura in section 3 below.

23. cf. *Secretum*, in *Prose*, pp.108, 132; Cicero, *Tusculan Disp.* III, 1-3, IV, 26, 38, 57, 82-3.

24. *Sen.* V, 2 and XIII, 10; see above pp.29-37,; and cf. *Metr.* I, i, 70-84, for an exact parallel in his verse in Latin.

25. See in *Fam.* II, 12, written shortly before his arrival in Rome, the possibly significant phrase in this connection 'me sepe per hos colles vagum videas', 'you would often see me wandering over these hills', etc. *Opere di F.P.*, ed. E. Bigi, p.722.

26. *Rime*, ed. F. Neri *et al.* (Milan-Naples 1951), p.502.

27. *St Petr.* VII (1961), p.164.

28. *DVE* II, iv, 7.

29. e.g. in canzoni nos 264, 359, 360, and in sonnets like 285, 307, 319, 355. Nos 264 and 360 stand very close to Book III of the *Secretum*, as is generally recognised in the case of 264; as regards 360, see F. Rico, *Vida u Obra*, pp.261-2.

30. *Confessions* IV, 4-11, VIII, 5, 9 and 10.

31. *St Petr.* VII (1961), p.124.

32. cf. *DVE* I, x, 1-2; II, vi, 8, etc.; *Inferno* I, 87, XXV, 94-102; *Purgatorio* XI, 97-9; *Paradiso* I, 22-7.

33. cf. M. Fubini, *Metrica e poesia* (Milan 1962), pp.236-61.

34. See section 3 below, pp.98-102. For the date of P's getting news from Avignon of the death of Laura, see E. H. Wilkins, *The Life*, p.77.

35. *Medioevo Romanzo* III (1976) i, pp.101-38.

36. See below section 3, pp.95-6.

37. The autograph MS in the Vatican Library containing drafts and fragments of P's lyrics. See below, section 3.

38. See *Fam.* I, I, from Padua, January 1350; *Metr.* I, I, from Modena in the spring or early summer of 1350.

39. *DVE* I, x, 2; cf. *Vita Nuova* XXV, 3-5.

40. *Inferno* XXVII, 81.

41. The MS in the Vatican Library, about one third autograph, of the *Canzoniere* as Petrarch left it at his death; see below, section 3.

42. E. H. Wilkins, *The Making*, pp.265-7.

43. B. Martinelli, *Petrarca e il Ventoso* (Bergamo 1977), pp.137-8.

44. E. H. Wilkins, *The Life*, p.77.

45. E. H. Wilkins, *The Making*, p.174.

46. E. H. Wilkins, *The Life*, p.77.

47. Genesis 1.26-31; Dante, *Par.* XXVI, 139-42; Mark 15.33 and parallels; St Bonaventure, *Breviloquium*, Proem.

48. See B. Martinelli, 'Feria sexta aprilis' in *P. e il Ventoso*, pp.103-48.

49. E. H. Wilkins, *The Making*, p.151; and for other cases of what Wilkins calls 'breach of chronology', ibid., p.188 n.1; cf. G. Contini, *Saggio*, pp.40-2.

50. See G. Contini, *Letteratura*, pp.588-93; Carducci-Ferrari, *F.P. Le Rime*, pp.83-4.

51. U. Dotti, *P. e la scoperta della coscienza moderna* (Milan, 1978),

pp.15-125; and the same scholar's ed. of the 'Sine Nomine' letters (Bari 1974), pp. cii-xlvi. On P.'s efforts to get the papacy back to Rome, see E. H. Wilkins, *P.'s Later Years* (1959), pp.93-106, 133-5. See too the anti-Gallic invective of 1373, *Prose*, pp.768-806.

52. *Disp. Tusc.* I, 45, 109; cf. *Secretum* III, *Prose*, p.204.

53. See below, ch. III, sections 1 and 4.

54. See G. Billanovich, who thinks *Rerum memorandarum libri* is meant, in the introduction to his critical ed. of this work (Florence 1941), pp.cxii-xiii.

55. cf. P. Trovato, *Dante in Petrarca* (Florence 1979), p.6 n.9.

56. See F. Rico in *IMU*, 17 (1974), pp.315ss.

57. And cf. the exactly corresponding sestina-stanza of 237, presumably written much later.

58. *Petrarca* (Bari, 2nd ed. 1961), 'Premessa'.

59. G. Billanovich dates it as late as 1352-3; see *IMU* 9 (1966), pp.389ss.; cf. H. Baron, *From P. to Leonardo Bruni* (Chicago London 1968), pp.17-20.

60. Especially in the light of such texts as *Fam.* X, 3 (*Prose*, pp.916-938), sent to Gherardo, by now of course a monk, in 1348-9, and the eclogue 'Parthenias', *Bucol. Carmen* I, sent a little later.

61. art. cit., pp.389-401.

62. See below section 3, pp.94-104.

63. Enough here to cite H. Baron, *From P. to...Bruni*, p.20; and the stiffest critic, in this respect, of Billanovich, E. H. Wilkins: *The Making*, p.317, n.1; *Studies in the Life and Works of P.* (1955), p.166.

64. *Confessions* II, 1; Ovid, *Amores* III, 11, 35.

65. P. de Nolhac, *P. et l'humanisme*, II, pp.283-92, Excursus VI, 'Les memoriaux intimes de P.'.

66. *Confessions* II, 1 at l.6, IV, 12 at l.5, VIII, 12 at l.7; *Inf.* I, 1-3 at ll.6 and 10.

67. E. H. Wilkins, *The Life*, p.18.

68. See R. Amaturo, *Petrarca* (Bari 1971), pp.299-300.

69. I say 'in her lifetime' because we do not know when most of the 18 sonnets, 246-63, were composed. On internal evidence 259 would seem to have been written in 1342-3, but we have no firm evidence that any of the other 17 were written before 1348, whereas it is certain that none of the 18 was copied into the final draft of the *Canzoniere* (V.L. 3195, see below, section 3, pp.94-5) before 1373-4 (E. H. Wilkins, *The Making*, pp.184-6). It is probable that of the sonnets expressing a 'presentiment' of Laura's death, 246-54, some at least were written after her death, and this is almost certainly true of the last four poems of Part I, 260-3, which are indeed serenely untroubled 'praise-poems' (see *Opere di F.P.*, ed. E. Bigi, p.1091; R. Amaturo, *Petrarca*, p.319; F. Rico, *Vida u Obra*, pp.284-5).

70. *Petrarca*, pp.299, 318.

71. *V.N.* XVIII, 4-9. See the relevant notes in D. De Robertis's ed. (Milan-Naples 1980).

72. cf. 'miracolo in line 9 of 160 with Dante's use of the term in *V.N.* XXI and XXVI.

73. 1 John, 1.5.

74. cf. Dante, *Paradiso* XXX, 19-36.

75. St Augustine, *De doctrina christiana* I, 7-10.

76. cf. 207.82-3, where this traditional symbol of malign enchantment is explicitly moralised in this sense; cf. Dante, *Purg.* XIX, 1-60, XXXI, 43-5. In *Tr. Mortis* II, 28-9 there is a word-play on *serena*, 'clear,

serene', and *serena*, 'Siren' (on this spelling of 'sirena' see the Petrocchi Edizione Nazionale of the *Purgatorio* (1967), p.315).

77. cf. Dante, *Inf.* IX, 52-7.

78. But see A. Noferi, *L'esperienza*, pp.271-3 and B. Martinelli, *P. e il Ventoso*, pp.236-7.

79. In passing, two linguistic points in 152: at line 4 the rare metaphorical use (not in Dante) of 'rotare', 'to wheel', in the sense of to send spinning hither and thither; and at lines 4-5 the rare compound primatives 'inforsa' and 'smorsa', respectively 'puts in doubt' and 'lets go with her teeth' (or possibly 'takes the bit from my mouth'). The former of these is in Dante, the latter not (P. Trovato has traced it to Cecco Angiolieri, *Dante in P.* (1979), p.13). Petrarch will repeat it in 195, along with no less than four other such verbs: 'sbranco', 'disosso', 'snervo', 'spolpo' (for a like insistence on privatives, see stanza 2 of 125). With 152 and 195 – their stress falling, respectively, on the pain and the perpetuity of the poet's desire – we may link 212, where the accent is on its futility, but which is especially noteworthy for its verbal dependence on Arnaut Daniel and Dante: on Arnaut at lines 3 and 8 (cf. *En cest sonet*, 43-5; and see also *Canzoniere* 239.36-7) and on Dante at lines 9-10, if, as I think, the image here of 'blindly groping' is a reworking of *Inferno* XXXIII, 73-4. Incidentally, this sonnet is self-dated, 1347.

80. See Carducci's perceptive note in the Carducci-Ferrari edition, p.377.

81. This is R. M. Durling's rendering and it seems to me the best possible without the use of a paraphrase to bring out the specially reminiscent

tone of 'casi' (*P.'s Lyric Poems* (Harvard University Press 1976), p.464).

82. For a still more horrifying association of death and eyes, see 300.12-14.

83. *Studi sul linguaggio del P.* (Florence 1971).

84. *Petrarca*, p.336.

85. N. Iliescu, *Il Canzoniere petrarchesco e Sant'Agostino* (Rome 1962), pp.90-1. Iliescu – whose little book is most valuable as regards P.'s Augustinianism – certainly exaggerated the contrast between Laura and the Blessed Virgin. On this point, and in general on the relation of Laura to Mary, see the very pertinent remarks of B. Martinelli, *P. e il Ventoso*, (1977), pp.225-39.

86. cf. E. Gilson, *L'École des Muses* (Paris 1951), p.52, apropos of 'Augustinus'' knock-out blow in the *Secretum*, 'iunge igitur tempora', 'compare the dates!' (*Prose*, p.152): 'les maîtresses dont il eut ensuite deux enfants… donnent un sens précis à cette parole'.

87. *Convivio* III, iii, 12-15; iv passim.

88. cf. *Paradiso* XXIII, 64-6, itself derived from Horace, *Ars Poetica*, 38-40; and cf. *DVE* II, iv, 20.

89. Dante, *Rime* LXXXII, 101-3; *Convivio* IV, xix, 3-7.

90. For the text of V.L. 3196 see A. Romanò, *Il codice degli abbozzi …di F.P.* (Rome 1955). An account of other relevant bibliographical material, with valuable comments, is given by G. Contini on pp.xxxv-xxxviii of his critical edition of the *Canzoniere* – minus, however, the critical apparatus, but with exegetical notes by D. Ponchiroli (Turin 1964).

91. And cf. *Tr. Temporis*, 61; *Canz.* 54.10; 302.8; *Epist. Fam.* XXIV, 1,

29; *Seniles* I, 3, p.737 in F.P. *Opera quae extant omnia* (Basel 1581). In view of these texts, especially of that in *Secretum* III, I think it much more likely than not that Petrarch chose the number 366 deliberately, as a symbol. Contini is of the same opinion, *La Letteratura*, p.576.

92. '"Rime Sparse", "Rerum Vulgarium Fragmenta": para el titulo y el primer soneto del "Canzoniere",' *Medioevo Romanzo* III (1976) i, pp.101-38.

93. *The Life of P.* (1961), p.47. The date of the *Secretum* will be discussed in ch. III, section 4.

94. F. Rico, art. cit., espec. pp.110-116.

95. Carducci-Ferrari, op. cit., p.364.

96. See Contini, *Saggio*, p.37.

97. I discuss this change in some detail in ch. III.

98. cf. H. Lausberg, *Handbuch der lit. Rhetorik* (Munich 1960), 272, 311.1, 347.

99. A. Romanò, *Il Codice*, p.220.

100. E. H. Wilkins, *P.'s Correspondence* (Padua 1960), p.49; *Studies in the Life and Work of P.* (Cambridge, Mass. 1955), pp.228-234; *The Life of P.*, pp.87-93.

101. Texts in Rico, art. cit., pp.108-110.

102. '...those vernacular songs of my youth, of which today I am ashamed and repent, but which are, as we have seen, most acceptable to those affected by the same disease.' I use the translation, slightly altered, of A. S. Bernardo, *Rerum familiarium libri* I-VIII (Albany, New York 1975), p.399.

103. *DVE* II, xiii, 2.

104. Petrarch has one 'double sestina', i.e. of $6 \times 6 \times 2 + 3 = 75$ lines (*Canz.* 332).

105. W. Th. Elwert, *Versificazione italiana dalle origini ai giorni nostri*, Florence, 1973, cites *Canz.* 242.3; cf. 32.11. For examples of Dante's much larger use of 'dialefe' see ibid., pp.24-6.

106. See Elwert, op. cit., p.12.

107. See *DVE* II, xii, 8.

108. In fact *Canz.* 29 is written in what the Provencal poets called *coblas unissonans*, i.e. in stanzas which preserve throughout the poem not only the rhyme-*scheme* of the first stanza but the rhyme-*sounds* as well. In *this* respect, as we shall see, the sestina form is made of *coblas unissonans*. See K. Foster and P. Boyde, *Dante's Lyric Poetry*, Oxford, 1967, vol. I, p.xlvii, II, p.265.

109. P. Boyde, *Dante's Style in his Lyric Poetry* (Cambridge 1971), p.219.

110. cf. e.g. *Canz.* 365, 6 and 7: 'Re del cíelo invisíbile immortále' (no caesura), / 'soccórri a l'álma disvïáta et frále' (caesura after 'l'alma').

111. See K. Foster and P. Boyde, *Dante's Lyric Poetry*, p.lii; W. Th. Elwert, *Versificazione*, pp.52-8.

112. See K. Foster and P. Boyde, *Dante's Lyric Poetry*, pp.265-6.

113. cf. R. M. Durling, *Modern Language Notes* 86 (1971), pp.37-69. Further comments on *Canz.* 30 in G. Contini, *Letteratura*, pp.586-7.

114. *DVE* II, xii, 3-6, cf. v, 5.

115. Further exploration of the 'asprezze' in P., and in general of his 'relative violence', is badly needed. In this I am wholly with F. Suitner, for whom the 'genteel moderation', as it might be called, of P.'s verse has become an insufferable cliché: *P. e la tradizione stilnovistica*, Florence, Olschki, 1979, pp.96-7. In particular I am with Suitner when he says that the idea that P.'s rhyme-words are

for the most part meaningless and banal is 'completely false' (ibid., p.97).

116. On this, and for the preceding remarks on *Canz.* 1, see E. Bigi, 'La rima del Petrarca', in *La cultura del Poliziano e altri studi umanistici* (Pisa 1967).

117. See E. Bigi, *La cultura*, p.39.

118. *Letteratura*, p.579.

119. Thus the last two books treating of P. in relation to his predecessors touch only marginally on his style: F. Suitner, *P. e la tradizione stilnovistica* (Florence 1977) and P. Trovato, *Dante in P.* (Florence 1979).

120. See A. Noferi, *L'esperienza poetica*, pp.113-27; M. Fubini, *Metrica e poesia*, pp.236-61.

121. See M. P. Simonelli, 'Strutture foniche', etc. in *F.P. Six Centuries Later*, ed. A. Scaglione (Chicago 1975), pp.66-104.

122. See Fubini, *Metrica*, pp.328-46.

123. *Prose e Rime*, ed. C. Dionisotti, p.75.

124. 'Strutture foniche' etc., p.100.

125. My rendering of lines 13-14 is in line with those of Leopardi (implicitly), Carducci, Bezzola and Ponchiroli. Alternatively, one might translate (with G. Ponte and R. Durling): '...men struggle for things of uncertain profit and [therefore] often sigh in vain'.

126. See W. Th. Elwert, *Versificazione*, pp.52-7.

127. Wilkins dates both poems 1326-36 (*The Making*, p.350). No.34 is in v.l. 3196, but not 32.

128. On Petrarch's discreet use of rare words see Contini, *Preliminari*, pp.xxv-xxviii.

129. cf. *Paradiso* III, 85, X, 129, XXX, 102, XXXI, 111.

130. Contini, *Preliminari*, p.xx.

131. Contini, *Preliminari*, pp.xxii, xvii. G. M. Hopkins, *Journals and*

Papers, ed. H. House and G. Storey, p.289.

132. M. P. Simonelli, 'Strutture foniche', p.77.

133. *Dante's Lyric Poetry*, pp.259-60.

134. For Contini 'one of the summits of the *Canzoniere*', *Varianti e altra linguistica* (Turin 1970), p.19. cf. M. Fubini, *Metrica*, pp.245-7.

135. Most commentators render 'seconde' (6) as 'favouring, propitious to', which *ceteris paribus* would indeed be the obvious rendering. But here it would clash with 'vento...*sforza*' (8) if this implies, as it surely does, that the 'aure', 'breezes' were from the west – *against* the movement of P.'s spirit. 'Yield' gets support from Dante, *Purg.* I, 105; and Carducci-Ferrari (p.266) seem implicitly to allow it.

136. As Fubini points out, *Metrica*, p.246, line 2 also is virtually without a caesura owing to the proximity of 'rápide' to the dominant stress on 'possénti'.

137. cf. R. Amaturo, *Petrarca*, p.282.

138. The relevance of such cross-references to *Secretum* has been demonstrated by A. Noferi in *Esperienza*, pp.265-71 (a study in semantics, not stylistics) with particular reference to the present canzone, to 189.1, and, through the *Secretum*, to the *De vera religione* of St Augustine.

139. cf. R. Amaturo, *Petrarca*, p.307.

140. Cassell's *Encyclopedia of World Literature*, vol.1, p.432.

141. See W. Binni, *I classici italiani nella storia della critica* (Florence 1954), vol. 1, pp.124-38.

142. Taking as guide through the tangled history of the matter Contini's indispensable 'Presentazione' to the 1957 reprint of the Carducci-Ferrari edition.

143. The reader should consult the
index to F. Flora's ed. of the
Zibaldone, vol. III-IV of Leopardi's
collected works. See too G. Singh,
Leopardi and the Theory of Poetry
(University of Kentucky Press,
1964).

CHAPTER THREE

1. Psalm 90.10, cf. Isaiah 38.10.
2. Compare the cry to God in the
passage cited above from *Canz.*
214: 'But you, O Lord,...' with
the prayer to Jesus in *Secretum* II,
Prose, p.58, and both texts with
Inferno I, 65. It is of interest that
whereas in this last text Dante
adapts the Psalmist's appeal to God
(Ps. 51.1) to *his* appeal to Virgil,
Petrarch, in the *Secretum*, makes a
Virgilian text (*Aeneid* VI, 365-71)
express *his* appeal to Christ – a
thing he was in the habit of doing,
and with *these* lines of Virgil, as
we know e.g. from *Fam.* XXIII,
12, 20, *De otio religioso*, ed.
Rotondi, p.67, *Sen.* VIII, 1 (*Opera*,
Basel 1554, p.915).
3. cf. E. Fenzi in *Il P. ad Arquà*
(Padua 1975), pp.61-115.
4. The letter in question is the
important *Seniles* II, 1, sent to
Boccaccio from Venice in 1363;
see *Prose*, pp.1030-66.
5. *Secretum* III, *Prose*, p.152; cf.
Tr. Pudicitiae, 10-12, 154-9, *Seniles*
IV, 5 (in *Opera*, 1554, pp.871-2).
On Homer and Virgil as
authorities on human nature, see
also *Prose*, p.664.
6. *Prose*, pp.558 and 664; *Bucol.
Carmen* I, 'Parthenias', lines 75-90,
and III, lines 113-20. See G.
Ronconi, *Le origini delle dispute
umanistiche sulla poesia: Mussato e P.*
(Rome 1976), espec. pp.86-92,
145-6.
7. cf. J. Cremona, 'Dante's Views on
Language', *The Mind of Dante*,
ed. U. Limentani (C.U.P. 1965),

pp.138-62.
8. *Fam.* XII, 10. 'David' is of course
the Psalmist.
9. e.g. *Prose*, pp.962-6 (1352), 670
(1353), 1134-58 (1373), and the
two wonderful pages to
Boccaccio in 1366 on the formation
of a personal poetic style through
'imitation' of classical models,
ibid., pp.1018-20 (*Fam.* XXIII, 19).
10. See E. Fenzi, 'Dall "Africa" al
"Secretum"', in *Il P. ad Arquà*,
pp.61-115.
11. *De Oratore* 3, 35.
12. The bulk of the text in *Prose*,
pp.710-66.
13. In P.'s first letter to Cicero,
Fam. XXIV, 3 (1345), *Prose*,
pp.1022-4.
14. *Prose*, pp.730, 736-42, 754-6;
cf. *Rerum memor. libri* I, 25 and 31.
Veneration for Plato was of course
traditional, but in Petrarch it had
two distinctive features, both
illustrated in the texts here referred
to. For, on the one hand Plato had
been the philosopher most
esteemed by St Augustine (*Confessions* VII, 13ss. *De vera religione*
III, 3-IV, 7, *De Civitate Dei* VIII,
4-12), on the other hand Aristotle,
Plato's great critic, was the idol of
P.'s detested 'scholastics'. On the
former aspect of P.'s Augustinianism, see the fundamental study by
F. Rico, 'P. y el De vera religione',
IMU, 17 (1974), pp.313ss.
15. cf. *De doctrina christiana* II, ch.
40; a text known to Petrarch, see
Rerum memor. libri I, 25.
16. P.'s anti-scholasticism runs like a
fiery thread through his prose,
from its first emergence in *Rerum
memorandum* I, 25-6, II, 31 (1343-4)
to the *De Ignorantia* and such
letters of his old age as *Seniles* V, 2
(1364), XII, 6 (1368-70) and XV, 6
(1373). Scholars are divided as to
how to define it – as to what

precisely P. hated in the 'crazy and clamorous scholastic rabble' (*Prose*, p.750). Was it, in the last resort, Ockhamist or 'terminist' logic? Or the cult of science as opposed to the 'humanities'? The former view has been that of E. Garin, the latter of P. O. Kristeller. A third and, I think, a deeper, more comprehensive interpretation is that suggested by U. Dotti in *P. e la scoperta della coscienza moderna* (Milan 1978), pp.175-86. For Dotti the basic motive of P.'s attack was religious – hatred of a truncated and ultimately atheistic conception of the human mind and its capacities. This is more or less my own view of the matter.

17. Cicero, *De Oratore* I, 8, 32.

18. *Metalogicus* I, 7.

19. *Secretum* I, *Prose*, p.52, and *De Ignorantia*, ibid., pp.734-6.

20. *Saint Thomas, Petrarch and the Renascence*, Aquinas Papers no. 12, Blackfriars (Oxford 1949), pp.9-10.

21. And cf. *Rerum memor. libri* II, 31.

22. *Prose*, p.292 – cf. *De Remediis* I, 46; *Prose*, pp.524-6; ibid., p.678; ibid., p.736, cf. 42. *Fam.* I, 8 and 9, cf. *Prose*, pp.22-6, 42, 212.

23. e.g. in the important *Sen.* v, 2, in *Opera Omnia*, pp.880ss, see below p.160, n.36. cf. Piur's edition of the *S.N.* letters, pp.53-6; U. Dotti, *P. e la scoperta* (Milan, 1978), pp.180-2.

24. See section 4 below, pp.167-9.

25. cf. *Africa* IX, 89-107.

26. On this work see G. Martellotti's Introduction to *Prose*, pp.xvi-xviii, and ibid. pp.1064-6, and his later reflections in *Il P. ad Arquà*, pp.171-3; also E. H. Wilkins, *The Life*, p.248, and *P.'s Later Years*, pp.287-92.

27. I omit the *Secretum*, so as not to prejudge the question of its date, to which I shall turn in section 4.

28. As defined by Cicero in *De inventione* (*Rerum mem.* II, 1).

29. *Rerum memor. libri* III, 31, 1; I, 25, 16-17. With this last text P., discussing Plato, excuses himself for a digression on the agreement between Platonism and Catholic dogma; his authority here being of course Augustine. Then at section 25 he returns within his self-imposed 'secular' limits; cf. also IV, 14.

30. See F. Rico, *P. Obras I. Prosa* (Madrid, Edic. Alfaguara 1978), Introduction, passim.

31. Petrarch had possessed a copy of *De Civitate Dei* since 1325 (having in the same year acquired St Paul's epistles); of the *Confessions* since about 1333; of *Soliloquia* and *De vera religione* since before 1335; of *Enarrationes in Psalmos* since 1337 (G. Billanovich in *Il P. ad Arquà*, pp.15, 17-18, *IMU*, 3 (1960), pp.6-7; E. H. Wilkins, *The Life*, p.10; B. L. Ullman, *Studies in the Italian Renaissance* (1973), p.118; F. Rico in *IMU*, 17 (1974), pp.313ss).

32. See ch. II, section 1 above, p.35; cf. pp.15-16.

33. It is possible, however, that Petrarch had already been supplied with 'some foretaste of the Ciceronian MS' by his humanist friends in Verona; cf. H. Baron *From P. to Leonardo Bruni* (Chicago-London 1968), p.56.

34. I take this term from F. Rico, *Vida u Obra de P.*, p.484; cf. also Rico's Introduction to *P. Obras I. Prosa*, pp.xv, xxvss; G. Martellotti in *Prose*, p.xiii.

35. cf. G. Martellotti in *Prose*, p.xiii.

36. *Prose*, pp.726, 730-2, 760; 'Sine Nomine' letters 17 and 18; *Contra Medicum*, ed. Ricci, pp.52-3; *Seniles* v, 2 (The first half of this long and important letter to

Boccaccio, written at Venice in Aug. 1364, was discussed above in ch. II, section 1 (pp.29-31) apropos of P.'s vernacular verse. The latter part of it, as E. H. Wilkins says, is 'a diatribe against the literary and philosophical-religious heresies of the time'; and ends with 'a report of a conversation, in P.'s library, with a visitor who after speaking scornfully of the church Fathers and St Paul went on to say: 'I wish you could bear with Averroes; you would see how much greater he is than those windbags of yours'; to which P. replied, 'Get out, you and your heresy, and never come back'; and then 'took him roughly by the mantle and pushed him out of the house' (*P.'s Later Years* (1959), pp.76-7; cf. M. Bishop, *Letters from P.* (Indiana Univ. Press 1969), pp.239-48)).

37. cf. *Rerum memor. libri* I, 25, 11-12.

38. *Tuscul. disput.* II, iv, 12.

39. *De Civitate Dei* VIII, 1.

40. *De Civitate Dei* XIV, 28; *Confessions* V, 2.

41. *Soliloquia* II, 1.

42. *Confessions* V, 3.

43. *Ab exterioribus ad interiora, ab inferioribus ad superiora. Enarr. in Psalmos* CXLV, 5; cf. Ep. 55.

44. *De moribus ecclesiae* I, 27.52.

45. *De dostr. christiana* I, 59-60.

46. Texts in E. Gilson, *Introduction a l'étude de S. Aug.*, pp.155-76.

47. J. M. Rist, *Stoic Philosophy* (Cambridge 1969), p.37.

48. III, xxvii; IV, xxxvii-viii.

49. The *De vera religione* was very important in this respect; see the fundamental study by F. Rico in *IMU*, 17 (1974), pp.313ss.

50. *Vida u Obra de P., I Lectura del 'Secretum'; Ente Naz. F.P., Studi sul P.*, 4 (Padua 1974) passim.

51. See J. M. Rist, *Stoic Philosophy*,

pp.1-21, 118-22.

52. *Fam.* XXIII, 12 (1359-60).

53. *From P. to Leonardo Bruni* (Chicago-London 1968), p.46; cf. F. Rico, *Vida u Obra*, pp.50-9.

54. See above, pp.18-19, 155. For the date of *De Remediis*, see E. H. Wilkins, *P.'s Eight Years in Milan*, pp.66 and 235.

55. Pages 104, 124, 150, with reference, respectively, to *Aeneid* II, 361-9, I, 52-7, VI, 540-3.

56. *Prose*, p.760, cf. p.746 and *Confessions* III, 4, VIII, 7.

57. See G. Hagendahl, *Latin Fathers and the Classics* (Göteborg 1958), pp.341-5; E. Gilson, *Introduction... S. Augustin* (Paris, 1943) pp.167-8.

58. E. H. Wilkins, *The Life*, p.6.

59. Cicero, *Tuscul. Disp.* III, xxvii, 80; IV, xxxviii, 82-3.

60. In such poems as *Canz.* 1, 62, 70 (st. 5), 80-1, 189, 264, 355, 360 (st. 1-5), 363-6.

61. *Italian Studies presented to E. R. Vincent* (Cambridge 1962), p.48.

62. cf. E. Gilson, *Introduction.* The text of Augustine I cited here is from *De Civ. Dei* VIII, 1.

63. F. Rico, *Vida u Obra*, pp.340-9.

64. E. H. Wilkins, *The Life of P.*, pp.122-7.

65. F. Rico, *Vida u Obra*, p.375.

66. cf. Aquinas, *Summa theol.*, 2a2ae, 27, 4 and 5.

67. An overstatement. A rereading of F. Rico (*Vida u Obra*, pp.413-17) has opened, or reopened, my eyes to the strong vein of Augustinian theology in the crucial passage (pp.204-6) where 'Augustinus' brings his admonitions into sharpest focus. Does 'Franciscus' seek glory? Very well; but the only true glory is that consequent on God-given virtue, not on the 'human curiosity' that literary men play upon. Rico relates this contrast between *vera virtus* and *curiositas* to key texts in

St Augustine; cf. also Aquinas, *Summa theol.* 2a2ae. 167.

68. I take it that the 'maiora' referred to by 'Franciscus' on p.206 are the same as those referred to near the end of the Proem, on p.26. And that both, as tasks (not mere thoughts or intentions) and truly virtuous tasks, are such as to merit the 'true glory' of which 'Augustinus' speaks on p.206 (3 lines from the end).

69. F. Rico, *Vida u Obra*, pp.417-18.

70. E. H. Wilkins, *The Life*, p.39.

71. *Metr.* III, 27; cf. Wilkins, *The Life*, p.46; F. Rico, *Vida u Obra*, p.343.

72. *Bucol. Carmen* VIII, 40-60, 72-7, 94-111. For the circumstances of this eclogue, see T. Mattucci's edition of the *B.C.*, pp.245-61.

73. cf. E. H. Wilkins, *P.'s Eight Years in Milan*, pp.5-6.

74. See F. Rico, *Vida u Obra*, pp.344-7. Rico shows that the 'correspondence' extends at times even to the choice of words, especially as regards *Fam.* XV, 8 and XVI, 10. cf. also the 'Salute to Italy', *Metr.* III, 24, line 11 (in *Rime*, ed. F. Neri *et al.*, p.804). The best account of P.'s life in Provence 1351-3 is in E. H. Wilkins, *Studies in the Life and Works of P.*, pp.81-181.

75. G. Martellotti, 'Critical Note', *Prose*, pp.1163-4; E. H. Wilkins, *Petrarch's Later Years*, ch. 39.

76. *Fam.* XI, 12 (July 1351), as interpreted by Wilkins, *Studies in the Life*, pp.84-5.

77. See note 75.

78. E. H. Wilkins, *Life*, pp.39-47, 66. *Metr.* II, 16 (Nov.-Dec. 1343), II, 18 (1344); *Epist. Variae*, 38.

79. *Fam.* VIII, 3, of May 1349 (transl. by A. S. Bernardo, *F.P., Rer. Famil.*, I-VIII, 1975, p.399). *Fam.* XII, 7 (Feb. 1352), XIII, 12

(autumn 1352), XIII, 7 (Nov. 1352). *Invect. contra medicum* (1352-3), ed. Ricci, p.54, and in *Prose*, p.678.

80. F. Rico, *Vida e Obra*, pp.422-3.

81. G. Martellotti, in *Prose*, pp.1163-1164.

82. *Fam.* XI, 12; see E. H. Wilkins, *Studies in the Life and Works of P.*, pp.84-5.

83. G. Martellotti, in *Prose*, p.1164.

84. E. H. Wilkins, *P.'s Later Years*, p.284.

85. ibid., p.285: the allusions are in *Fam.* IX, 15 and XIX, 3.

86. G. Martellotti, in *Prose*, pp.1164-1165; E. H. Wilkins, *P.'s Later Years*, pp.286-7; *The Life of P.*, pp.218-19.

87. *Fam.* IX, 15 – to a friend, asking for a book P. needed for work on *De viris*; see Wilkins, *P.'s Later Years*, p.285.

88. G. Martellotti, in *Prose*, p.1164; Wilkins, *P.'s Later Years*, pp.285-6.

89. F. Rico, *Vida u Obra*, pp.386-8 (note 478).

90. For 1341-2, see espec. *Prose*, p.16, cf. *Metr.* II, 16. On leaving Naples in Dec. 1343, P., still confident that he would soon finish the *Africa*, left part of Bk VI with Barbato da Sulmona. For 1344, see *Metr.* II, 18, 13-15; for 1347, *Ep. Variae* 38 (to Cola); cf. *Bucol. Carmen*, I, 110-23.

91. *Fam.* VIII, 3; cf. Rico, *Vida u Obra*, p.421.

92. *Fam.* XI, 12; cf. E. H. Wilkins, *Studies in the Life*, pp.84-5.

93. *The Life of P.*, p.119; cf. *Studies*, p.96.

94. *Invectivae c. medicum*, ed. Ricci (1978), pp.73-5; and *Prose*, pp.678-680.

95. cf. E. H. Wilkins, *Studies in the Life and Works of P.*, p.114.

96. cf. *Invective contra medicum*, ed. Ricci, pp.74-5; (*Prose*, pp.678-680); F. Rico, *Vida u Obra*, p.436;

391, n.485.

97. *MLR* 73 (1978), p.443.

98. Especially in regard to Pliny's 'Natural History', Cicero's letters, Quintilian.

99. *Vida u Obra*, pp.9-16.

100. Review cit., p.444.

101. See *Prose*, p.680.

Indexes

INDIVIDUAL POEMS FROM THE *CANZONIERE*
Main references are shown by **bold type**.